THE
Adopted Nurse

A MEMOIR OF COURAGE, COMPASSION, AND HOPE

LISA ASTALOS CHISM DNP, RN

First paperback edition September 2024

Book Cover Design by Isabel Chism
Photography by Mia Hutchinson

ISBN: 979-8-89316-534-0 - eBook
ISBN: 979-8-89316-535-7 - Paperback
ISBN: 979-8-89316-536-4 - Hardcase

Author Contact Information
Email:
theadoptednurse@gmail.com
Instagram:
@drmommypoppins
@theadoptednurse
Facebook:
Lisa Astalos Chism
The Adopted Nurse

dedication

This book is dedicated to anyone who has experienced trauma from abuse, loss, grief, and/or medical issues. May you rise from the ashes like the Phoenix to become the warrior inside you.

Contents

Once Upon a Time...

This memoir is a window into my life and contains my interpretation of events and circumstances in my life. You are about to learn very personal details about me. Some names, identifying characteristics, and circumstances have been changed to protect myself and others. My journey includes emotional, sexual, and verbal abuse that may be hard to process. I also describe medical trauma that has impacted my journey. I ask for your grace as you read my story. And in the words of Cinderella, I hope that my journey will inspire you to "have courage and be kind" (Branagh, 2015). Especially to yourself.

A Note From Anne

In *The Adopted Nurse,* Lisa Astalos Chism writes, "Trauma is trauma. And healing is healing. This journey has changed me. I am different. I found my strength. I know myself better."

That is how I feel after reading her book. I found strength in her stories; and I know not only myself better, but humanity as a whole.

"You are not alone" this book tells you over and over again. And you will be okay—better than okay—if you keep showing up as our most authentic self.

~ Anne Heffron

part one

Grateful and Perfect

My Spark

I am grateful and perfect
It's who I turned out to be
Bought and paid for and loved
But I wonder where's me?
I know I am lucky, I hear them say
But I wonder if things were different
Would I have turned out this way?
I kept my head down
And turned off the noise
Until through the haze
I found my voice
Once the fog cleared
I could see in the dark
That's when I saw my gift
My gift is my spark

chapter 1

Unpacking

December 2023, my daughter Izzy and I were on our way to see the Trans-Siberian Orchestra in downtown Detroit. Hours before, I had received a Christmas gift from my birth father and his wife postmarked "Overnight Delivery". They had received a Christmas gift from me exactly 48 hours ago. I am certain we were not on their Christmas gift list. Rather, their gift was sent solely in response to our gift. I needed to thank them but I was unsure if a phone call would be answered or if I would be blocked again.

The complexity of these relationships will unfold as I share with you how courage, compassion, and hope have intersected throughout my life. My journey began with loving, adoptive parents and later, the discovery of my birth mother's family. In my fifties, I was unexpectedly found by my birth father, which led to a deeper understanding of myself—as a daughter, as an adoptee, and as a person.

Whether you are a member of the adoption triad (adoptee, birth parent, or adoptive parent) or a survivor in any way, thank you for being with me as I tell you a story that has been filled with love, loss, pain, rejection, abandonment, self-awareness, courage, compassion, and finally, hope.

As our Uber driver, Andrew, drove Izzy and I down the freeway toward the concert, I decided this was the right time to make this call and at least leave a message. Izzy was sitting next to me, holding a mirror, applying her lipstick.

"I am calling now. I have to call now. I can't call tomorrow" I said as I watched her.

"No, you can't call tomorrow. Tomorrow is Christmas Eve," Izzy replied as she rolled her eyes.

I was still not certain, four years after he found me, that my birth father would even call me on Christmas Day. I did not want to deal with possible rejection on the *actual* holiday.

The phone rang. "Well, I am not blocked this time," I sighed.

I could sense Andrew's interest as he watched me in the rearview mirror.

It went to voicemail. "Hi there," I said. "Thanks so much for the package. We really appreciate it. I hope you both have a wonderful Christmas. Talk to you soon."

I did not expect I would "talk to them soon." In fact, I knew it was possible I would not talk to them at all.

Immediately after I left the message, as Izzy held her lipstick mid-lip, she said, "That was good."

"Yea, that was good," Andrew chimed in smiling. "What's going on there? Seems like a lot!"

"Oh Andrew, we need a longer Uber ride to unpack this shit!" Izzy added.

Andrew never heard the whole story, but here, you can. Come with me, my friend, as we unpack...

chapter 2

Growing up Chosen

I don't remember ever not knowing that I was adopted. I do, however, remember that one day. I was standing in front of a small closet in the spare bedroom, that was at one time a playroom of my childhood home. My mom, Judy, stood across from me with a small shoebox in her hands. From out of this box, she pulled a few papers and handed them to me one by one. I do not remember how old I was. But I do remember what she said; "Your birth mother was raped but she knew the guy."

I looked up at her as this sunk in.

"She loved you so much she gave you up so you could have a good life, the kind of life she could not give you,"

Nancy Verrier discussed this notion in her book *The Primal Wound*. She cautions that this thread of thinking causes love to be equivalent to abandonment (Verrier, 1993). I will admit that at times, it's hard to think of love and being given up in the same context.

I asked for more information. The shoebox was so small, and there was so little information about my birth mother. Inside it was the only evidence of my beginning.

My mom added that there were no major health issues in my birth mother's family; and there was no identifying information about my birth mother. I looked inside the box thoroughly, as if I would find a secret compartment with more; something, anything. Many times in my childhood, I snuck into that closet when Mom wasn't looking and found that box, opened it, and leafed through the papers. It was all I had of my birth mom.

When I did start to understand the part about her being raped by a man she knew, I understood that it meant I started out in this world as a result of a violent act. At the very least, I started out as a mistake.

I was not planned. I was not wished for. Therefore, I was not wanted.

Despite not feeling wanted by my birth mom, there was always one day a year when I allowed myself to fantasize that she indeed was remembering me: my birthday. Every year, I would think to myself, *today, of all days, she must be thinking of me. Today she must remember that she had a child, a baby girl, who was out there, somewhere.* Every single birthday growing up, I sent her a silent prayer or wish that she would somehow remember me. It was the one time I had any kind of certainty that she must remember that I exist. It was the one day I allowed myself the hope that she wondered about and thought of me too.

The word "chosen" became part of the narrative describing my beginning somewhere around the time I understood what it really meant to be adopted. With the notion of being *chosen*, came the implication that I was different. Different is a label that growing up meant something other than what it means now. Now I accept it; then I felt I was always separate from everyone else. Family gatherings, friend groups, school; I stood out—and not in a good way. At least I felt like I did.

I helped others help me stand out by announcing "I'm adopted" any chance I could. If I was going to be "different", then maybe this would explain why. This acted like a lightning rod and frequently prompted the response I was looking for: questions and sometimes a fascination with me that would last a bit.

Feeling I was different was something I felt just under the surface at extended family gatherings as well. Most of my cousins had siblings, and I did not—this accentuated the feelings of being different.

My extended family never intentionally made me feel different, it was more how I felt all on my own. Except for my cousin Jennifer. Today, she is one of my closest friends. But back then, ironically, Jennifer was the one family member who actually looked right at me one day while we were playing and said, "You can't play with us, you're not really family, you're adopted."

To this day, Jen and I laugh about this as we turned out to be so close.

Aside from some awkward extended family gatherings, my memories of childhood are intertwined with knowing my parents loved me and wanted me. My mom could not have children *on her own*. She had endometriosis, and ended up having surgery that left her infertile. She often expressed what it was like to try for years to have a child of her own. Eventually, my parents made the decision to adopt.

My mom teased me when she described what it was like the first time she saw me. She told me that she and my dad were waiting and waiting for a baby. They had requested an infant girl. My mom told me about the interview with the social worker and how nervous she was. Then the day finally came when she got the call; "We have a baby girl for you."

Soon, my mom and dad would see me for the first time.

She smiled as she told this part of the story. "The first time I laid eyes on you, I thought to myself she is really ugly."

We would giggle over this.

My mom and dad would talk over the next weeks before they were picking me up and taking me "home."

"Are you sure you want to do this Judy? You have been awfully quiet since we went to see her," my dad had asked her.

"Yes, I do," she replied. "We never know how long we will have to wait for another baby. It's just that she's so ugly."

My mom would then get to the next part of this story, the day she actually took me home. "About a month later, the day we picked you up, I gazed down at you and you were the most beautiful baby I had ever seen."

My mom would often tear up when she told this part of the story. In my heart, I knew how much they wanted me and I knew they loved me so much. I look at pictures of them holding me in the days after I came home and the love in their eyes is palpable. I wonder how I, as an infant, felt in their arms. Did I know? Did they feel like strangers?

Nancy Verrier (1993) described in her book *The Primal Wound* how infants know they are stripped from their mother's arms. When I think about the day my mother first told me I was adopted, I remember having an inkling of understanding of why I always felt "off", yet loved.

As a little girl, I hated being alone. I wanted a sibling so much. I would ask my mom why I didn't have any brothers or sisters.

"Mommy can't have children," she would explain.

I was likely too young at that time to understand how she had me. If I had to guess, my mom started telling me I was adopted long before I actually remember that day standing in front of that closet. After all, I can't ever remember thinking I was anything but.

My fear of being alone is something my mom tried to compensate for. She would tell me stories about how, when I was a toddler, she would try to leave me outside on the patio with all of my toys. She would then go back inside to try to get something done while watching me the whole time outside a kitchen sink window. The minute I realized she was gone, I would start to cry. She would then come outside, play with me for a bit and try yet again to go back inside. Eventually she gave up and stayed playing with me. It was the beginning of my mom being my first, and eventually, best friend.

I had every toy you could want, books in a bookshelf, and clothes my mom made me. I felt so cared for. Her love, in part, inspired my life's purpose to care for others. So much so, that I remember feeling guilty that my parents did so much for me. I wonder if children being raised by birth parents feel guilty about how much their parents do for them. When I asked my twenty-something year old daughter this question, she responded, "Only now that I am older do I realize what you do for me." For me, this knowledge didn't come in my twenties, but very early in life.

One of my most vivid memories is a dream I had as a very young girl when I was sick. I had a flu of some sort with a high fever. I lay in my canopy bed, surrounded by a purple frilly bedspread and girly, white antiqued, ornate furniture, and dreamed that my mom was moving these heavy pieces of furniture and some kind of equipment all over my room. She was doing this to accommodate me for something that had to do with me being sick. This dream was so vivid it stuck with me growing up, and as a woman in her 50s, I can still see her moving this furniture around *for me.*

Even in those early years, I began to understand the immense sacrifice I felt that my parents had made to adopt me, raise me, and take care of me. It was the beginning of me feeling like I had to be overly grateful, like I had to work hard to deserve things like love and care. I developed a need to be perfect in order to feel worthy of all they had done for me.

Nancy Verrier relates in her book *The Primal Wound* that adoptees either rebel and exhibit behaviors that sabotage their situation or conversely, adopt the persona of being forever grateful. Early in my life, I began to embody the grateful perfectionist. Being "grateful and perfect" became the lens through which I viewed the world. It is only now, as an adult, that I realize I felt I had to be grateful and perfect to ensure that I was never *given up again*—by anyone.

Even as early as preschool, I understood that my mom and dad were providing the best education they could afford. My mom and dad sent me to a private, Catholic school through high school. In the beginning of elementary school, my mom was a lunch mom. She told me later it was just so that she could come and see me during my day.

I was social and yet somewhat shy as a child. I made friends but my mom facilitated as much social engagement and activities she thought I could handle. I danced, ice-skated, did gymnastics, swam and rode horses.

As I mentioned, I often felt different than everyone else and felt compelled to share that I was an only child and adopted. This was how I learned kids can be mean, like a snake hovering and striking. One day at St. Joseph's elementary school stands out—I remember the eighth grade girls chanting at me, "Spoiled adopted brat! Spoiled adopted brat!" They chanted this over and over until I started to cry.

One of my favorite movies is "Practical Magic" with Sandra Bullock and Nicole Kidman based on the book by Alice Hoffman (Hoffman 1995). Gilliam and Sally were sisters and orphaned when both of their parents died. One day, the young girls were walking along the fence of their yard and their class walked by, chanting, "Witch, witch, you're a witch!"

Their sweet aunts consoled them and said, "They don't hate you, they don't understand us because we're different."

When I saw this movie, I remember thinking, "I get it, it's okay to be different," But as an elementary school child, it was easier said than done. Being different didn't feel okay; it felt isolating and scary. Once again, I figured even if I was different, I could still be good, or better yet, perfect. After all, I had been given so much. I should do something to *deserve* it.

My concept of being good was tested as a young girl when my mom and dad hired a babysitter to watch me intermittently over the summer, after my mom went back to work. Her name was Darcy. The details are sketchy, but what I do remember is one day, she took off her clothes, and mine. She then positioned me on top of her and moved me over the top of her body back and forth. I had no idea what was happening. I can still see her afterwards standing in the bathroom brushing her long, brown hair as it flowed down her back. I sat in the hallway watching as she said, "You can never tell anyone about this or you will go to hell."

Being raised Catholic, this meant I absolutely could not say a word. This happened over and over that summer. I remember thinking something about this was not right. Why would she not want me to tell anyone? But also, I wanted her to like me. I wanted to be good. I couldn't question what she was doing or she might not want to babysit me anymore. She might give me up.

It wasn't what she did to me that I was worried about; it was her potential rejection—and even worse, the rejection of my parents. If they found out I kept a secret, would my parents give me back? Would I be proven not worthy of this life with them?

It was a year later when I could not keep this secret any longer. I finally told my mom. My mom's reaction was not what I expected. I had kept a secret and thought that no matter the reason, it must be my fault. I expected her to be mad at me, and she did seem furious—but not, surprisingly, at me. Her face was red and through her tears she yelled, "*I'll kill her!*"

She then ran across the street to confront the neighbor that referred Darcy to her. The police were soon at our house and I remember a flurry of activity. The police tried to find Darcy but she was long gone. It sunk in that what had happened was, in fact, not okay.

My mom sat me down and explained why what Darcy had done to me was wrong. That day, I learned about sex long before my innocent brain should have had to try to understand. It was a loss of innocence that made me feel more vulnerable. I had trusted this babysitter so much that I kept her secret of what she was doing to me. I was confused and from then on, I felt even more different than other kids my age.

Through the span of elementary school, most of my memories include my mom being an ever-present force making sure life for me was as good as she could possibly make it. She was a Girl Scout leader, went to summer camp with me, helped me with science projects, and fought the bullies along the way. We truly enjoyed each others' company and could sit up all night laughing and talking around the kitchen table. My mom's laugh was infectious. She could be laughing at something and I would be giggling breathlessly, just at the sound of her laugh.

My mom shared my love of all things mystical, as well. The Catholic religion does not approve of any practice that may be viewed as the occult. Despite this, my mom and I played with a Ouija board when I was in high school. We eventually stopped because, well honestly, that shit scared me!

My mom was solidified as my best friend and my champion; my dad, Paul, was a quiet figure in the background. He was a great provider and a man of few words. It didn't seem to matter to him whether he was included; it was enough for him that my mom and I were happy. He was rarely upset with me unless my mouth got ahead of me. My mom always said, "Lisa-Kay, the only thing that gets you in trouble is your mouth!"

My mom used my full name, Lisa-Kay, when she wanted to make sure I was paying attention. Even now, if my family calls me by my full name, it makes me smile thinking of my mom.

Early on, I had come to understand that no matter how many sports I tried (including softball and the line drive to center field that broke my nose), I was not coordinated in any of them. Riding, however, was another story. Horses feel you and become your best friend and your partner; I loved it. Riding became something I came back to later as an adult. But as far as sports, clubs, and other hobbies, nothing much stuck with me.

Until my first year of high school, when I followed my mom's advice.

I was complaining that I did not play sports, I did not have any particular hobbies, and had no idea how to make friends. Mom casually said, "You know, the cool kids are always on the student council."

I looked up at my mom and said, "I don't think I am the *student council* type".

My mom let it go. But the message had been received. And that was how I began high school as a member of my school's student council—as always, striving to follow her advice and always be the *perfect* daughter.

chapter 3

First Love, Crowns, and Going Away

Somewhere during my freshman year, I met my soulmate. Or at least it felt that way at the time. His name was Bobby. He was short, sweet, and adorable. He was popular in an "everyone loves Bob" kind of way. I was in love. He was perfect for me. And to make it even better, he liked me, too. We dated off and on all through high school and were together still when we went on to separate colleges. Bobby and I had break ups, usually instigated by me. I was a sucker for someone else giving me attention, making me feel wanted. But I always went back to this comfortable, best friend, first love kind of love.

Around the time I met Bobby, I also met Jill, my first friend in high school. I will never forget how I felt, as a freshman who knew next to no one, when this shapely, sophisticated girl looked over at me from her locker and asked, "Hey, do you play racquetball?"

Her burgundy pencil skirt twisted as she put her books in her locker. I thought, *Is she talking to me?*

I looked at her and said, "No, why?"

Jill smiled and said, "Me neither but I thought it would be fun. Want to go this weekend?" I smiled. I could not believe the woman-like girl was actually asking me to play racquetball. What had I done to deserve this kind of attention from someone like her?

"Sure, sounds good," I said, looking down with a shy smile on my lips.

Jill and I went that weekend to a racquetball court, then had lunch after. We talked and laughed all afternoon. Our friendship was solidified that day and remains just as solid now. My mom was so happy. She always said, "Girl friends are so important and they come before everything, even boys."

As the months passed, I settled into a friend group of girls who were not like me, as no one ever felt like they were. They were cheerleaders or on the Pom Pom squad. I was famously uncoordinated and a bit awkward. I rarely drank or tried drugs in high school. That did not fit in with my grateful and perfect nature.

At parties, I was the designated driver, although I was relentlessly teased for being terrible at it. This became part of my identity, "Lisa has a car but she's a terrible driver". My dad had bought me a lime green Pinto that I decorated with fuzzy dice and stuffed unicorns lined across the back window. This *fit* my personality and everyone knew it. My friends and I made so many memories driving around in that Pinto. One night we drove to one of my guy friend's house to prank him. We inconspicuously draped toilet paper on his trees and all over his front yard. We then climbed in my Pinto and were almost free and clear—only for my horn to get stuck and announce to his parents we were there. We drove away screaming as the horn continued to blare. Needless to say, we were busted and the following night my house was the next to be draped in toilet paper.

I have always loved Halloween. In my junior year, my friends and I went to a costume party at one of the upperclassmen's house. I was getting ready, dressed as raggedy Ann, and my mom was helping me braid my hair into two pigtails. My costume was a full skirt that twirled when I spun. She handed me a bottle of Boon's Farm strawberry wine and said, "Here, put this under your skirt and no one will see it. Try to have some fun!"

This was so typical of my mom. She always walked that line between best friend and mom. I always knew that if I was lucky enough to have children, I would raise them the same way.

I took the bottle but barely drank it. That was one of many parties where I took care of everyone who drank too much, including Bobby. We were *on a break* and he had started dating someone else. I was heartbroken. But here he was, at this party, drunk. I heard he and his new girlfriend had just broken up. I went for a walk outside to get some air and walked up on Bobby, vomiting all over the brick wall.

"Go away. I don't want to see you," he yelled, as he spit on the ground.

"Let me help you," I insisted, "Wait, why are you crying?"

"Because, I still love you," he slurred.

Bobby and I were back together the next day.

I had settled into a productive, safe high school experience. It was my senior year, and I ran for and won Correspondence Coordinator, on the Executive Board of the Student Council. I had no idea what that meant or what my duties were (I still don't), but I was certain it would earn me a spot on the homecoming court. I had no illusions or desire to be the homecoming queen. I would just be happy to be part of the court. That, I knew, would really make my parents proud (and glad they adopted me).

It was the week prior to the announcement of the members of the homecoming court when my dad became dizzy at work and was rushed to the hospital. He was diagnosed with a stroke. Fortunately, he suffered no serious deficits from the stroke at the time, but he was admitted and stayed in the hospital for ten days.

As the names for homecoming court were being announced, I sat in my homeroom classroom saying a silent prayer. I was not concerned about popularity, I just wanted to make my mom and dad proud. And especially now, with my dad in the hospital, it meant even more to me to make it onto the homecoming court. One by one, names were called off. Then finally I heard, "Lisa Astalos".

The members of the homecoming court were called down to the school office, and received our sashes. I told my mom later and made her promise not to tell my dad. She told me that my dad had called her and said, "Lisa didn't call me, she must not have made it."

My mom kept my secret and later that night, wearing my homecoming sash across me, I walked into my dad's hospital room.

"I made it, dad!" I said smiling, as I snuck into the room from behind the hospital curtain. In truth, my dad only cared because he knew I cared. But he cared about me so much that, ever so tenderly, he started to cry.

It tugged on my heart to see him like this—and as he cried, pure joy and pride came through on his face. I craved this look. It validated that I was exactly what they wanted when they adopted me.

"I am so proud of you," he said through his tears.

My dad was still in the hospital on the day of the homecoming parade. However, one of his coworkers, at the cable company where he worked, figured out how to tape the parade, and show my dad on a portable recorder at his bedside. My dad watched as I rode around the field on top of a car with Bobby by my side, in his football uniform.

The stroke had left my dad extremely emotional and when he returned home, he suffered from severe depression. My dad had been a caregiver for as long as I can remember. He took care of us, my grandparents, his family; anyone who needed anything could count on my dad. But now, he needed to count on *us* to care for *him*. As he recovered, I helped my mom care for him as much as I could. It was my first experience caring for one of my parents. It felt *right* caring for my dad.

This experience caring for my dad cemented what had been bubbling up inside of me all along. I knew as a young girl that I would choose a career caring for others. I had experienced what it felt like to be so beautifully *cared for*. Caring for others felt natural—like breathing.

The decision, to become a nurse just made it official.

After graduating from high school, I prepared to leave home for the University of Michigan in Ann Arbor. My parents were committed to paying for my tuition, which I knew was a sacrifice for them. My mom encouraged me to go away to school, even if my school was only forty-five minutes from home. She told me over and over, "I want you to have the college experience."

I had no idea what that meant and, honestly, neither did she. My parents hadn't gone to college. They were middle-class, blue-collar people who sacrificed so much to send me to a Catholic school and now, a large university.

Despite my reservations about going away to school, I did not want to disappoint them and in August 1986, I moved into my dorm. My cousin Andrea, one year older than me and also an adopted only child, was my roommate. I imagined that being with family, someone familiar, would ease the homesickness I feared.

It is clear to me now that I went away to school before I was ready. The first night after my mom and dad moved me in, I sobbed all night long. Homesick does not accurately describe how I felt. I was traumatized by being away from my parents. I never put it together at the time that I was afraid to be alone. Maybe even afraid of being abandoned again, but I see it now.

My mom later told me that the day they dropped me off at school was the saddest day of her life. She cried all the way home. I was less than an hour from home, but it felt like the other side of the world. I tried to adjust but I felt suspended in the air.

I almost failed out my first semester. I was home on Christmas break that year waiting for my grades to come in. At that time, nothing was computerized and I learned I was on academic probation through the mail. I ended up getting a tutor the following semester, and barely passed.

That first year was spent trying to get through school Monday through Friday in desperate sadness, only looking forward to the day when my mom and dad would pick me up and take me home for the weekend. My cousin Andrea's presence helped buffer my sadness and sense of overwhelm. She was kind, and despite bickering as children growing up, we were close and shared a similar upbringing.

Sophomore year, Andrea had moved into a house on campus with her friends. I reunited with a friend from high school and we decided over the summer to be roommates. During my sophomore year, my roommate was gone most of the time; she joined a sorority, and did not understand me at all. As I laid on my bed sobbing every single night, she would ask me, as she looked down at me, with what I could not tell was disgust or confusion in her eyes, "What is wrong with you? Is it really that bad?"

I never bothered to answer. She would never understand this kind of loneliness.

At least, I thought, I still had Bobby. We would talk on the phone at night, for hours. He attended Kalamazoo College, a private school with a high success rate for admission to medical school. Bobby shared my love of science, medicine, and taking care of people.

I would take the train from Ann Arbor to Kalamazoo on the rare weekends I wasn't with my parents, to visit him. With Bobby, the homesickness faded. He provided a sense of stability when so much had changed.

Until one day, Bobby told me about a decision he was weighing.

chapter 4

Soulmates and Imposters

I had assumed Bobby and I would get married one day. Despite our on again, off again romance in high school, I felt like we had *stood the test of time*. I was only twenty years old; but I thought he was my soulmate.

Bobby's program at Kalamazoo College included a study abroad option, for three or six months. During our Sophomore year, Bobby broke it to me that he was choosing the six-month option. He would leave that September, the beginning of our third year of college.

I cried and begged him over the phone, "Don't leave me that long, please!" I wailed out loud in my dorm room. I was already miserable and felt so alone. I was struggling in school, I missed my parents, and I had not made a life for myself in college. I could not get past the suspended feelings I felt being away from home.

When Bobby chose to go away for six months, it felt like I wasn't good enough for him to stay. I was *unchosen*. Hot tears spilled down my cheeks when he told me. Why was I not good enough for anyone to *keep* me?

"Come visit me over Christmas. It will go by fast," he tried to reassure me. But something inside me felt broken. I could not believe that the love of my life, my soulmate, would leave me.

We spent that summer working at our summer jobs and spending as much time together as we could. I said goodbye to him that fall. I clung to him the night before he left and told him I would visit him for Christmas.

"I will miss you so much," I said, as I tried to hold back the tears that dripped endlessly down my cheeks. I felt like someone was tearing an appendage off my body.

"I will see you in three and a half months, it will go by fast", Bobby said through his own tears as he held me and stroked my hair.

And with that I had no choice but to pull it together and begin my third semester of nursing school. I could not shake the haunting feeling that Bobby had chosen to go away for so long over me. Was this because I equated his choice with me being abandoned and therefore *unchosen?*

I convinced my parents to let me move home and commute for my last two years of nursing school. My dad's response was to buy me a car to replace my Pinto: a slightly used, sporty black Mustang. From that point on, whether it was because I was finally in actual nursing classes, or because I was back home, my grades went up and I felt some of the emptiness lift.

I settled into a routine commuting to school and reconnected with my friends. Most of my circle had somehow ended back at home as well. I was at my home base again and life felt safe and normal.

One night, my friends and I went on a trip to Windsor, Canada. None of us were twenty-one yet, so going on trips like this to Canada was common among my friends, while we waited to be of age and go to clubs in the states. As I was walking toward the club bathroom, I passed a man, whom I barely noticed, and he made some sort of comment. When I ignored him, he responded, "Oh attitude!" Then he had my attention and I stopped dead in my tracks.

We talked for a bit. His name was Jim. He was older than me by about seven years. I was feeling abandoned by Bobby, vulnerable and looking for attention. Those are my excuses; why I allowed myself to become ensnared in a situation that looking back, must have looked like I had lost my mind.

Jim and I started dating. Bobby and I were in touch but had agreed that I could date other people as long as I didn't get *serious*. In retrospect, I had no excuses for getting involved with someone. Suffice to say, I was wounded and, at the time, I felt justified. And I was twenty years old.

Jim seemed worldly and experienced. He swept me off my feet. He was a mechanical engineer and had a master's degree from University of Michigan. He came from a big family and lived a few cities away. He was employed by an automotive company and the pieces seemed to fit. He showered me with attention. And I fell for it all.

In the meantime, I planned to meet Bobby in Spain and spend my first Christmas away from home. I did not tell Bobby about Jim, and I honestly wasn't sure what I was doing. I went to Spain and spent three weeks with Bobby touring Europe. Eventually, I told him about Jim and that I was torn. By the end of the trip, however, I assured Bobby I was ending things with Jim and would wait for him.

But when Bobby came home, I broke his heart and chose Jim instead. I'm not sure what kind of spell I was under, but I could not seem to get myself out of the relationship with Jim. I justified this with "You left me, after all," but I felt terrible. This isn't my proudest moment.

As the months passed, what I saw as Jim's "charms" were having an opposite effect on everyone else. No one liked Jim. In fact, they were planning interventions behind my back designed to get me to break up with him. My dad grew quieter and quieter when he was around. My mom, sensing I was isolated from everyone who didn't like him, did the opposite. She forced a friendship between herself and Jim. She rarely criticized him. Despite that, I felt like I was in a corner. I had met this worldly, educated, experienced man who swept me off my feet and made me feel special. How could I not give him a chance? And a second chance. And another chance.

I blocked out much of what happened over the next few years, but I do remember when Jim told me he wanted to marry me, all the wounds of Bobby leaving me seemed to have a Band-Aid on them. I was once again swept up in the idea of someone *choosing* to keep me. I agreed to marry him. My ring was a ring he supposedly had originally bought for someone else but saved for "the one." I did not like that, but I did not want to appear ungrateful. I was happy someone wanted me, wanted to marry me, and wasn't leaving me. Looking back it is pitiful to realize how low my expectations actually were.

chapter 5

Accidents Vs. Mistakes

J im and I continued dating throughout the rest of nursing school. Graduation and our wedding were fast approaching. I was daydreaming about both of these events as I was driving home from my last day of nursing school and I flew through a red light. I was in shock as a car on each side hit me. My car spun around, in slow motion, and came to a stop. I was shaking, thinking *what just happened?* I sat halfway outside the car and someone asked if I was alright. The realization of what had happened started to sink in; and I started sobbing.

"I'm so sorry!" Through my tears I said, "I just finished nursing school. I am supposed to help people, not hurt them."

I was inconsolable. What kind of nurse was I going to be?

The news came that, while my car was totaled, by some sheer miracle, no one was hurt. Still, someone easily could have been. Later, I sat on the couch in my living room, staring down at the ground, feeling shame wash over me. *How could I do this? How could I hurt other people and let my parents down like this?* What burned most in my memory was what my mom said when she arrived home.

"What happened Lisa-Kay? Did you do something silly?"

I had run a red light. I could have hurt people and myself. I had totaled my car. And all my mom said was "did I do something silly." Tears slowly crawled down my face.

"Yes. I am so sorry, Mom".

My mom hugged me and said, "That's why they call them accidents, Lisa-Kay."

It was moments like this that I wondered what I ever did to deserve my mom and dad's unconditional love.

As my graduation from nursing school approached, I slowly recovered from the shock of the accident. My parents barely mentioned it, I am sure, to not overshadow my accomplishment. This allowed their love and pride to shine brighter than my shame, but my grateful and perfectionist nature was still lurking in the shadow of their love. I leased a new car: a convertible, to symbolize the growth and independence I was striving for.

A few weeks later, as I walked down the aisle of the auditorium at the University of Michigan to pomp and circumstance, instead of embracing my accomplishment and my parents' pride, my gratitude and perfectionism seeped through. I knew I was not satisfied earning my Bachelor's of Science in Nursing (BSN) degree. Graduate school was in my future.

A few months after graduation, September 1990, Jim and I were married in the Catholic church I grew up in. By this time, I was working as a nurse in the cardiac ICU of a local hospital. Jim was late for the ceremony, and as we waited in the vestibule of the church, my dad took my hand, and said the most he ever did when it came to my relationship with Jim:

"You know, we can turn around and leave. It's not too late. I don't care about the money." As he looked into my eyes, I felt the rush of pure love he had for me.

I looked down the aisle and there was Jim standing with his brother, his best man. I looked up at my dad,

"No, it's okay, Dad, it will be okay."

Later, I saw pictures of Jim and I kneeling at the altar during mass. On the back of Jim's soles was written in white the words "Help Me". So much for feeling wanted. I asked him about this later.

He laughed and said, "Oh it was just a joke! Everyone thought it was funny."

Not me. I thought it was crappy.

Somewhere around the second year of my marriage to Jim, the unraveling became so obvious, even I could not deny it. Jim had started visiting his friend in Canada, who worked at a gentlemen's club. Jim would "tuck me in" at night (his words, not mine) and then leave around 11:00 pm. He would come home around dawn. I, of course, did not question this. I was working contingent as an ICU nurse at a local hospital at this time and was enrolled in graduate school at University of Michigan earning a Master's degree as a gerontological nurse practitioner. I barely had the energy to question this weird ritual, never mind tackle it. Plus, I was taught by him not to.

I had fortunately convinced Jim to live close to my parents—literally around the block. My mom came over frequently and continued her *friendship* with Jim. Meanwhile, my relationship with Jim was becoming contentious and I was feeling more and more beat down. I was a graduate student, tired, and scared; working when I was not in school. Jim was becoming more confrontational about every little thing. Once, I was putting on mascara right before he pulled me to him to hug me. As I looked up and blinked to dry my mascara, he grabbed my arms so firmly it hurt and said with a sneer, "Are you rolling your eyes at me?"

I had become so used to watching every move I made that I was afraid to sit down the wrong way. I was often accused of looking at other men out my passenger window as we stopped at a light. "Who the fuck are you looking at?" he would bellow at me. Later, it took months for me to feel safe looking out a car window. I once confronted Jim about some of these controlling behaviors. He agreed we should "talk about it," but only if we went into the basement and sat down with me on his lap while we talked. No windows. No doors. This was Jim's way of controlling the situation in an environment I was basically trapped in. If I was on his lap, like a child, he was controlling me by holding me there. If there were no doors or windows, then no one could hear or see me.

One day, while telling Jim about my Master's thesis, I asked him about his. I watched him stammer about what he did for his thesis and all of a sudden, my intuition took over. I am certain this part of me had been in self-preservation mode. Because once I awoke, it was like I came out of a trance.

As a graduate student who switched programs a few times, I became accustomed to requesting my transcripts. I knew how to prove whether or not Jim had actually earned the degrees he was claiming to have earned. I sent letters to every school Jim said he had attended, and forged his signature asking for verification of dates attended. And one by one, I received back the responses: "I am sorry, we have no record of you attending this school." I did not tell him what I was doing. I was afraid of him and I was waiting for the right time to confront him.

Jim lavished me with jewelry every holiday. Some pieces were so ridiculous it was hard to believe he would spend that much. I had been wearing a diamond tennis bracelet he had bought me; and with it came an elaborate story about how much it cost and how hard it was to get. Around the same time the letters were being delivered back to me in the mail verifying his lack of attendance, I looked down at this particular bracelet and once again, the realization set in. The bracelet was dark and dingy; and no matter what I did, I could not get it clean.

And then it hit me: the bracelet was fake, he was fake. I had married a liar, a cheat, and a manipulative, abusive con man.

Within a week after looking down at my bracelet, as I received letters verifying Jim had not earned the degrees he claimed, I was driving down the road in my hometown with my mom. I had been married close to three years at this time.

I looked over at my mom and said, "This bracelet isn't real, but I need proof."

I pulled into the closest jewelry store I could find; and asked simply, "Can you please tell me what this is?"

The jeweler smiled, "the metal or the stones?"

"Both, please." I waited and thought, *I can't believe I did this to my parents.*

The jeweler came back and could hardly meet my eyes. Looking carefully at me she said, "I am sorry, this is stainless steel and the stones are glass."

I am sure she was shocked when I smiled and said, "Great, thanks so much," bouncing out of the store.

Looking back, pure adrenaline was fueling me. I got back in the car and said to my mom, "I am leaving him. My marriage is over."

"Over a fake bracelet?" My mom said shocked.

"No Mom, over a fake person" I said, shaking my head at myself.

My mom was not shocked Jim was a fake and abusive—she had suspected all along. She was shocked at my sudden decisiveness more than the decision itself. I had woken up. And I could not forget or unsee what I now understood.

In the midst of me realizing who I was married to, my mom, my rock, was preparing to have knee replacement surgery. I needed to put my mess of a marriage aside and be there for her the way she was always there for me. My mom understood and agreed to keep my secret to confront Jim. I focused on her upcoming surgery, and tried to stay calm. I was determined to be the daughter, and nurse, she deserved. Only after she was cared for, would I confront him.

chapter 6

Losing a Part of You

"You will be okay, Mom, you got this," I said to my mom as she walked away to the pre-op area the day of her surgery. She looked back at me with worry etched all over her face—her eyes wary, her brow furrowed, and no smile on her lips.

"I hope so," she sighed as she walked away.

She was 56 years old at the time and suffered from severe osteoarthritis of both knees. She had finally made the decision to have her worse knee replaced. It was close to Christmas; and I had wrapped tiny gifts for her to unwrap each day she was recovering, twelve gifts in all for the twelve days of Christmas. It was something my mom would have done for me to cheer me up and encourage me as I healed. I was so excited to surprise her with the little Dollar Store tchotchkes.

Once surgery was over, the nurses led my dad and I back to see my mom in recovery. She was expectedly groggy and in pain. Once settled in her hospital bed I checked on her again. The impression of seeing my mom weak and in pain was unfamiliar. She was my rock, my champion. She took care of me. It was strange to see her in such a state, but now it was my turn to be her champion.

Right away, I knew something wasn't right about my mom's level of pain. She was tough and had a high pain tolerance, yet, she was writhing in pain. I went to find her nurse, but I was dismissed, and told she had just given my mom something for the pain and would check on her later. I left that night unsettled. The next morning I would understand why.

As I was getting ready to go to the hospital the next morning, my mom called me. I could hear the fear in her voice. She was still in pain. She said sometime in the morning the orthopedic resident had been in. He had asked his attending orthopedic surgeon to check on my mom and when he did, he found she had no pedal or popliteal pulse. This meant that the blood flow to my mom's leg below the knee was interrupted. She was not getting circulation to her lower leg. My mom was calling me to tell me they were doing a stat arterial Doppler test to assess the blood flow in her leg. This test would show the blood flow, or lack thereof, in her leg.

I was frantic. What I thought would be a quiet day sitting with my mom turned into a nightmare that would last several months. My mom was diagnosed with a blood clot in the popliteal artery that went undetected after surgery. The nurse and the resident that had been taking care of her never checked the pulses in her leg. My mom was taken to surgery later that day for a procedure called a femoral popliteal bypass graft, which would revascularize the leg.

When I arrived, my poor dad looked shell shocked. I felt so incredibly guilty that I had not done more the night before. I felt like I had failed my mom by not standing up to the dismissive nurse.

The surgery was successful, but the veins that the vascular surgeon had sewn around the blood clot in my mom's leg broke open two days later. My mom was getting sicker as the tissues in her leg began to die from lack of blood flow. She was trying to be strong and optimistic, but this was the worst case scenario.

I'll never forget the ominous way she looked back at me as she walked to the pre-op room just a few days before. What I did not know was that was the last time I would watch my mom walk on her own two legs.

My mom was becoming sicker and sicker as the tissues in her leg died. She was going into kidney failure and was moved to the ICU. The orthopedic surgeon and vascular surgeon sat down with my dad and I; and explained my mom was going to have to make a decision. If she did not have an amputation, she was going to die.

My sweet, gentle dad could not handle telling my mom. I said I would, but I wondered how I was going to find the courage. My dad and I stood on either side of her bed with hospital curtains pulled all around us, a cocoon of impending doom.

"Mom, I am so sorry, but they are going to have to amputate your leg. If they don't, you are going to keep getting sicker and sicker."

My mom's eyes were closed and she nodded.

I reminded her that our next door neighbor had lost her leg and had a prosthesis and was able to walk and carry on with life. It seemed cruel to try to use this comparison to reassure her about losing her limb, but it was all I could think of to ease her pain. I already felt I had failed her. What kind of nurse, a graduate student nurse, was I when I let this happen to her? I should have pushed more when I saw how much pain she was in the night after her surgery. I knew something was wrong. I should have demanded that someone pay more attention to her pain. I should have checked her pulses. *I was a nurse!* But I trusted the people caring for her. I felt I had blown my chance to care for her properly, to really show her how grateful I was for all she had done for me. And now it felt like because of me, she was losing her leg.

My mom lost her leg below the knee——yet, the whole time, she remained as optimistic as she could be. She was a warrior even more now in my eyes. The orthopedic surgeon assured us that keeping "his knee" (this is how he referred to her artificial knee) intact would give my mom the best possible outcome when it came to being fitted for a prosthesis, but in the following days, it became apparent that was not the best choice. The tissue around the knee had lost too much blood flow and was dying, causing an infection.

The orthopedic surgeon's solution was to remove the tissue and allow the rest to heal. The problem was that he decided to do this at the bedside, with no anesthetic. He would come see my mom every few days, ask us to leave the room, then cut the dead tissue away. This went on until I listened to my mom, from the hallway, scream out loud as he cut the dead tissue away, and something inside me snapped.

I allowed myself to feel responsible for not doing more the night after her surgery. As a nurse, and a daughter, I blamed myself for not being her advocate; but I was not allowing this madness to happen any longer. Courage, fueled by anger, surged through me. I barged in on him cutting on her knee and said with as much authority a twenty-something year old daughter and nurse could muster, "Get away from my mother. You are fired!"

He looked up shocked, I am sure, that someone would talk to him that way. He tried to explain his lack of anesthesia with, "The tissue is dead."

"Do my mother's screams sound like the tissue is dead to you?" I said back through gritted teeth. "Do not touch my mother again."

With my mother's permission, my next move was a phone call to the vascular surgeon. I told him to please amputate the rest of the limb that included the dead tissue and remove the knee. This way my mom would finally heal and begin the arduous process of rehabilitation and fitting for a prosthesis. It was time to move on to healing.

I never saw the orthopedic surgeon again. The vascular surgeon had to do a "guillotine" cut that left my mom's tissues and nerves exposed in order for the infection to clear. Later, they could eventually close the incision and she could move on to rehabilitation. In the meantime, my mom had to be lifted and immersed in whirlpool baths to increase blood flow and help the tissue heal. Watching the technicians lower my mom, using a lift, into a whirlpool bath as the tissue of her limbs were exposed to the water made me feel nauseous. The memory alone still makes me nauseated, particularly the sound of her screams as she was lowered in the water.

The day finally came when my mom's wound was closed and she was transferred, close to home, to rehab at the same hospital where I worked as a nurse. I tried to reassure myself that I had stepped in and was back to being the grateful, perfect daughter who woke up and took charge of my mom's care.

Her spirits were good. My mom was a warrior. She began the long journey to being fitted with a prosthesis and learning to walk again.

chapter 7

You Have My Permission To Leave

A few months after my mom came home from inpatient rehabilitation, I began facing the realization that I needed to finally move on from my abusive relationship with Jim. Perhaps watching my mom's battle back to mobility inspired me. I began participating in a therapy group for women in abusive relationships through United Way. The program was called *Learning to Leave*. As the therapist presented what she called the *Cycle of Abuse Wheel*, I saw my relationship and my sense of self presented before me. It felt surreal and validating to see what I was experiencing was not in my head, or my fault.

The Cycle of Abuse Wheel was first introduced in 1979 by Lenore Walker in *The Battered Woman*. Various Cycle of Abuse Wheels have been adapted over time; the model used in my program was The Duluth Model Cycle of Abuse (2024). This wheel has been found to more accurately describe the complexities of emotional abuse. It spoke to me when it explained how emotional abuse included making someone feel like they are crazy, afraid, intimidated, bad about themself, or guilty without a real cause (Duluth, 2024).

My time in this group helped me garner the strength to leave Jim. I planned to leave while he was away on business. I secured an attorney, called my friends—all of whom were collectively celebrating my decision to leave Jim, and picked the date I would move out.

The night of the move, he called. I tried to stay calm and chat away like nothing was going on. But my voice was shaking and I was trying desperately to get off the phone.

Jim must have caught on that something was indeed up. Because before I knew it he yelled, "Lisa! What is going on? I can tell something is going on there! You sound off!"

He had finally broken down my attempt to stay calm and I screamed into the phone, "I am leaving you tonight and you cannot stop me! Not anymore!"

"Fine!" he sneered through the phone, his voice icey, "you have my permission to leave."

Through angry tears I screamed, "I don't need your permission to leave!"

The following night, as I lay in my childhood room back with my parents, Jim came to the back door. I answered and looked through the screen at him. A crazed, far away look was in his dark, narrowed eyes.

"Give me back the ring or I will take you and your whole fucking family out." He looked so sinister as I handed him the ring and shut the door. That ring, to my knowledge, was likely the only piece of jewelry he ever gave me that was not fake. Later, when the court ordered that he return my wedding ring to me, I took it to the jewelry store to learn the diamond was apparently replaced with a piece of glass.

The divorce was quick. Jim had bought a Corvette and mortgaged the house we owned to buy it. He tried to claim it was his dad's car, but I found the canceled check and was able to prove it was his. I walked away with some cash and health insurance so I could finish graduate school. It was all I wanted—along with my safety and my freedom.

I once again felt I had let my parents down. They had paid for the wedding despite having their concerns. I had not listened to anyone who tried to warn me.

I asked my mom, "How do you feel, since you and Jim had a relationship?"

She looked at me and said, "Lisa-Kay, I only stayed close to him to stay close to you." I believed her. She would do anything for me.

I remember someone telling me, "You are so young. This is a spot in your life, a dot." They were right. I was twenty-five years old, and already married and divorced. My mom had lost her leg, and I still struggled with blaming myself for that. I was not enough for Bobby to not abandon me, and I ran to someone who used and abused me. Is that what I thought I deserved? I had wanted to be married, have a family, and give my parents grandchildren. Was it too late? Now what do I do?

Looking back, I realize I did what I have done all my life: I took what I perceived as failures and, as if to punish myself, I worked harder and pushed myself more. I felt I had to prove I was worthy of love, and worthy of being kept.

chapter 8

The Young Single Accountant

A month before my divorce was final, my mom and her golf buddies fixed me up on a blind date. My mom instigated it by asking her friend Carol, "Hey, are there any young single accountants at the firm you work at?"

My mom told me later, "I am picking the next husband."

Her pick, Bruce, called me at home soon after Carol told him about me. I had no idea he didn't know my divorce was not yet final.

"Hi, this is Bruce," he said.

We talked for an hour—about what, I have no idea. His tone was even, and a friendly confidence came through the line as we talked. I laid on my childhood bed with my feet crossed behind me. It was as if I had never left, or gone through some of the most traumatic events I had experienced so far in my young life.

We both agreed to meet for a drink. Dinner was too daunting. I was still cautious, and not quite sure I should even be dating. I was, after all, a "tainted woman" and not even officially divorced. My court date was coming up, but on paper, I was married.

I walked into the local pub we had agreed to meet at, looking around, I saw no one who looked like an accountant. But then again, I had no idea what an accountant was supposed to look like. Finally, I noticed one guy, sitting with his back to the door of the pub. *Who meets a blind date and sits with his back to the door?* But he was the only guy sitting alone. He was not wearing horn-rimmed glasses or wearing a suit with a pocket protector. He was tall, with broad shoulders, brown hair with just the right amount of curl, and the unarrogant, quiet confidence I had sensed over the phone. *What the hell?* I thought. *Maybe I will get lucky and this guy will be Bruce.*

"Bruce?" I said, hoping my voice didn't give away my nerves. This broad-shouldered, casual guy turned around; revealing a blue open-collared shirt, with a hint of chest hair peeking through. His bright blue eyes met mine.

"Lisa?"

I was shocked and shy all at once. I felt myself blush as I smiled at him. I did not expect to feel this instant connection just meeting his gaze. The way he looked at me made me feel as if I was the only woman in the room. I immediately relaxed, as if my heart already knew I could be comfortable with this man.

We sat and talked for four hours. First, it was just easy, small talk. Where did we grow up? What made you become a nurse? What made you become an accountant? Then we started telling more stories about our lives. The conversation was easy and flowed without any awkward silence.

I, of course, weaved into the conversation, "I am super close to my parents—I am adopted."

"Oh wow, that's interesting! I am so glad you are close to your parents. I am really close to my dad, but I lost my mom when I was eighteen," Bruce said as he looked down for a minute. I instantly felt empathy for him when I saw the look on his face. This man understood loss and how important parents are.

As the evening went on, we moved closer and closer together sitting at that bar. He was too good to be true, and I was getting worried. I was *not* too good to be true. After all, I was not even divorced yet and I felt like a failure. I was young and already had one failed marriage under my belt. Was this really what I should be doing, getting this nice man tied up in all my issues? Finally, as the bar was closing, Bruce paid the bill and walked me out to my car.

As we approached my car—at that time, I drove a Fleetwood Brougham white Cadillac with blue velour interior—Bruce's mouth dropped open. He was practically giddy.

"This is your car?" He said in amazement.

"Yes", I said looking down.

I was so embarrassed. I hated this car. Jim had bought it *for me*. It was not my style, and I felt ridiculous in it. As soon as the divorce was final, I planned to lease something that actually was *me*.

"I love it! My grandma had one of these. It's classic," Bruce said.

And with that he pulled me close to him, leaned over and kissed me. I was shocked, with no time to react, and went with it. Until he slipped his tongue in my mouth. I pushed him away,

"Wow, I was not ready for that."

I was reeling. Who did he think he was kissing me like that? Immediately my mind was fixated that Bruce thought I was easy prey. I was divorced, therefore I am desperate.

He must not have seen all that written on my face, as he simply smiled, "Can I call you?"

I said sure, but inside I was feeling unsteady. I liked him, but was confused. Did he only want one thing from me? Plus, my divorce not being final loomed over me.

The next few days, Bruce called me everyday. I never took his call. The more I thought about it, the more angry I was that he kissed me like that on a first date. On the fourth day, my mom told me, "Lisa-Kay, you have to talk to him."

"Mom, he doesn't even know I am not divorced yet!"

"So, tell him. It's only a matter of days."

I finally took his call, and as nicely as I could, I explained that I was a graduate student, I was not yet divorced, and had finals coming up. I was simply too busy. He asked when I would be less busy.

It was November. My court date was that December. I was working off shifts at a local hospital and going to graduate school full-time. I calculated the months ahead and told him I would maybe call him in April.

"Well, it took a lot of character for you to tell me this, thank you," he replied. And we were off the phone.

I liked Bruce. But I was so overwhelmed with graduate school and my pending divorce that I had no idea if I would ever actually talk to him again.

Regardless, I was trying to be kind when I said I would call him in April. Leaving Jim left me feeling so insecure and unsure of my own choices. I knew I needed some time before I headed back into another relationship. Or whatever Bruce was looking for.

My divorce was final on December 10, 1993. I felt a mix of relief and sadness; it may sound cold, but I had no remorse for Jim. He had lied to me and abused me.

I was proud of myself that I had gotten out of a bad situation. But I was also trying to piece together my self-esteem. The whole marriage felt like my own personal failure. I tried to look ahead and have hope for the future.

With my divorce sorted out, I focused all my energy on graduate school and tried to settle into a routine living back home. I worked all the time, studied, and spent time with my mom, dad, and friends. Then the holidays came. I worked every off shift on the cardiac care unit, including Christmas Eve afternoon, and came back to cover Christmas Day. I justified my choice to work the holidays because I needed the money for school and I wanted to give my colleagues time with their families. I listened while other nurses called their families during our shifts to wish them a merry Christmas.

"I'll be home soon, we will open gifts" or "Have a cocktail ready for me when I get home."

It struck me that I still wanted this. I wanted a family of my own to open gifts with or to wait for me until my shift was done.

That was the moment I thought to myself, did I miss out not giving Bruce a chance? He was sweet, handsome, and really seemed interested. Had I dismissed him just because I assumed he thought I was easy?

I came home Christmas Day and told my mom, "I think I messed up. Maybe I should give Bruce another chance."

The day after Christmas, my mom called her buddy Carol, the matchmaker, and asked, "Is Bruce seeing anyone?"

Carol nonchalantly walked down the hall at the accounting firm she worked at with Bruce, walked in his office and asked, "Are you dating anyone? If not, Lisa is going to call you."

Later, as I sat on my mom's bed next to her, I called Bruce. He answered and I announced, "Hi, it's Lisa. I just wanted to wish you a Merry Christmas,"

"Oh hi, how are you? Merry Christmas."

Bruce's tone was casual and nonchalant, as if he expected my call.

I thought, *huh, he isn't as excited as I had hoped.*

Regardless, the phone call led to a dinner invitation. I was anxious. I was still not sure I was ready. Something about Bruce told me he was a one-woman-kind of guy, and wouldn't want something casual, but I was not sure I was ready for a serious, new relationship so soon. I was not sure I *deserved* someone caring about me deeply. I still felt like I was wearing a scarlet letter on my chest that showed the world I made terrible choices that affected other people, especially my parents.

My mom and her friends were famous for their crafts. The latest obsession was porcelain doll-making. Before our date, I asked my mom and her friends what they thought I should do as they sat around the table painting the faces of the porcelain dolls they made.

Shirley, a pragmatist, carefully added eyelashes to her doll's eyes. "Don't worry," she said, "it will be easier to break up with him the second time."

A few weeks later, at the end of our second date, Bruce took my hand as we drove down the freeway and asked, "Are you all good now, is your stuff all straight?" I knew when he asked me what he meant. He meant he was indeed a one-woman guy, and we were now exclusive.

I also knew I was falling in love with the man who thought I was worth waiting for.

I took a breath, knowing that my answer would lead to a relationship, and responded, "Yes, I am all good now."

And I was.

Life felt lighter. I was in a new relationship. Graduate school was going well. My mom's mobility was improving. Things seem to have settled down.

Until I came home one night and my mom told me she had not heard from my grandma in over twenty-four hours.

chapter 9

One Day You will Understand

I was still living at home—my parents had strong feelings about living with someone before you were married. Mind you, I had already *been* married, divorced, and moved back home. But I respected them, and I also was never a fan of living with someone before marriage. My mom always used that expression, "Why should a man buy the cow when he can get the milk for free."

I was in love with Bruce and wanted a future with him. We had not yet discussed marriage, and I was afraid my mom may be right. No matter how many times he asked, I was not moving in with him until he put a ring on it!

Bruce and I were out late one night. When I arrived home about midnight that night, my mom met me at the door with wide and intense eyes. I knew something was wrong.

My grandma Thelma, my mom's mom, could be harsh with my mom, constantly critiquing her. I remember asking my mom, "Why do you let Grandma be so mean to you?"

My mom responded, "One day, you will understand."

And this day, I did.

"I haven't heard from your grandma all day. Can you go with dad to check on her?" she said, her voice cracking, with tears about to spill out of the corners of her eyes. Something was wrong. She talked to my Grandma Thelma everyday.

I sensed from her clenched jaw and the worry laced on her face that my mom was afraid to go check on my grandma herself. She was afraid of what she might find. Plus, living as an amputee came with challenges. My mom had already taken her prosthesis off for the night and was in her pajamas.

As my dad and I drove down the empty streets with the streetlights casting an eerie glow, I thought, *what if something is wrong? What if she is gone?* My dad and I chatted all the way, each of us not mentioning what we both feared.

The house sounded hollow as we called out her name only to find her in her bed lifeless. The first thing I did was wonder how I would tell my mom that she was gone.

After we called the police and the coroner came, we headed home in disbelief. Dad did not want to call Mom and tell her over the phone. When we arrived back home, my mom was waiting for us at the door.

"I know, she's gone." She looked at me, and added, "This is why I overlooked how she treated me, Lisa-Kay. Now she's gone, but I know I cared for her the best I could."

These words stayed with me and even now, have influenced how I react in certain circumstances. You do not always get do-overs and how you treat those you love matters. It was yet another lesson in compassion and love that I learned from my parents.

chapter 10

Letting Go

B ruce and I helped my parents with my grandma's final arrangements. My mom was grieving, but I could tell she was at peace that my grandma had passed in her sleep. My mom also seemed to demonstrate *healthy grief,* or grief without guilt.

I grieved my grandma but I grieved more for my mom's loss. When I was a little girl, my grandma babysat me and made me cry so many times, my mom promised me one day I would never have to go to her house alone again. As I got older, I was often angry at how my grandma treated my mom.

One good memory I have of my grandma is how much she loved her poodle BJ. I inherited BJ when she died. He was just one in a long line of poodles that have been in my life.

My parents indulged my love of all creatures, furry or scaly. Dogs, guinea pigs, hamsters, and various creatures were allowed in our home. Today, Tiffany, my Devon Rex shares my home with my poodle, Chloe. Chloe is a white toy poodle who looks like BJ, which makes me smile. My grandma loved that little dog so much.

Life continued moving along as I finished up graduate school, and prepared to walk down the aisle again to pomp and circumstance, this time at

University of Michigan after earning a Master's degree as a gerontological nurse practitioner. I arrived home after one of my last weeks of school to find a handwritten note from my mom.

It said, "The director of your program called and you are their first choice to represent your class at convocation. I am so so proud of you!"

Even now, I still have this note in my jewelry box. It is worn, dog eared, and tear stained. When I read it, I remember how thrilled I was at the chance to represent my class. But I was even more moved by how proud my mom was. It was more reassurance that I indeed was a daughter they could be proud of. If they were proud of me, they would be glad they adopted me.

Soon after graduation, I was hired at my first position as a nurse practitioner in an internal medicine clinic. I was expected to see patients for any and all acute or chronic illnesses. My clinical rotations in graduate school had not adequately prepared me for this type of practice.

My training was focused on health promotion and risk reduction of health conditions. I immediately knew I was in over my head. I was staying up late at night reviewing diagnoses and treatments of acute and chronic illnesses. I had ideas for developing a program for the clinic that was focused on screening, counseling, and risk reduction modalities.

I did not get the chance to share my ideas. During my sixth week of employment, I was unceremoniously "offered a transfer."

I pulled up in my driveway, with my lab coat in hand, a few hours after I had left for work. My mom greeted me at the door.

"What happened honey?" she asked, her eyes pleading for me to not break down. She later told me she saw me carrying my lab coat as I walked up the driveway and knew something was up.

Hot tears mixed with shame and embarrassment flowed down my cheeks.

"I was offered a transfer to another position," I said looking down in disappointment. I understood that the transfer was to soften being told I was not good enough to practice in my current role. Instead of being offered additional training or counseled on how to improve my skills, the message I received was that I was simply not worth the effort. Pride stopped me from actually accepting the transfer, and I resigned.

The reality was that I was not perfect, and it felt as if I was given up on. I slumped down on the couch, "I honestly did not know what I was doing, Mom."

"Its okay Lisa-Kay, screw them! They don't know what they are missing!"

I have since told this story to anyone who has ever lost a job. Especially their first job. It's a great story to illustrate that losing a job is sometimes a part of life and leads us to where we need to be. But as an adoptee, getting fired, or offered a transfer, reinforces what happens when you are not good enough to be kept.

The next position I took allowed me to immerse myself in caring for geriatric patients in the nursing home setting. This was rewarding and filled my heart. Importantly, I received the mentoring I needed to transition from an RN role to that of a nurse practitioner. I had underestimated this transition and appreciated an atmosphere that fostered learning and fulfilled my need to care for others who are vulnerable.

The elderly are special. Caring for them over time allowed me to bond with them, as well as their families. Much of what I did during this time involved working with families and helping with advanced directives. Advanced directives allowed the patients' wishes to be carried out as their health declined. This type of practice also helped families feel more comfortable letting go of their loved ones when it was time. I was able to impact my patients' quality of life, and it helped prepare me for later in life, when I was the one who had to help my own family members transition, when it was their time.

Despite how rewarding my practice was, caring for women fulfilled my heart in a different way. The reality is, women are sometimes forgotten, or worse dismissed, in healthcare. The changes women experience in their lifetime from adolescence, to childbirth, to menopause only add to the complex layers of emotions, body changes, and health concerns women face. I had always envisioned myself in a clinic setting taking care of women exclusively. So much so that I went back to University of Michigan for a fellowship in women's health one year after graduating with my Master's degree. I wasn't sure how this would meld into my current practice, but my intuition told me someday this specialized training would be valuable.

chapter 11

The Proposal

M y relationship with Bruce was exciting and stable all at the same time. He was so different from my ex-husband. He was close to his dad, a respected professional, spiritual, fun, and most importantly, kind. I was certain he was the man I wanted to spend my life with.

We had been dating for two years, which I thought was an acceptable time to get engaged. I wanted a family and I was in my late twenties. It was time. I dropped all the appropriate hints, but Bruce did not seem to be getting them. My mom and I ring shopped. I had in mind what I wanted. I would find a way to casually let him know I had found what I wanted at a local jeweler. But as the weeks went on, it became more obvious, Bruce didn't seem to have a clue.

Finally enough was enough—at dinner one night, I came out and said it: "I want to get married and I want you to marry me."

I couldn't gauge what he thought, but his eyes were wide. "Well, I had never thought about getting married."

Ok, I thought, that seems fair. So I waited.

Three weeks later, after multiple conversations with my mom and my girlfriends analyzing how he could not know it was time to move on from being boyfriend and girlfriend, and several meltdowns, I couldn't hold it in any longer.

That night, I had been quiet all day and Bruce asked me, "What's wrong?"

We were in his bedroom, sitting on his bed. I said, "I want a family, I want to marry you. But if you don't want to marry me, I am moving on."

I had given him the ultimate ultimatum. It was risky and I knew it. I held my breath, tears slowly making their way down my face, trying to be brave. This could go either way.

Finally, when I figured he wasn't going to say anything, I got up to leave.

Then he said, "Wait, don't move." He ran into the kitchen as I waited on his bed.

I tried to calm down and figure out, as I had been for three weeks, why doesn't he want me? Why wasn't I good enough?

He came back with a bag tie in his hand. "Yes, I will marry you" he said softly and put the bag tie around my ring finger.

Almost 30 years later, I still have the bag tie in my jewelry box.

Two weeks later, the bag tie was replaced by the ring I had picked out with my mom. It took me an entire day of *fake* ring-shopping before I finally fessed up and told Bruce, "I already found my ring."

"Oh my God, why didn't you tell me? Let's go get it!" Twenty minutes later, the ring was on my finger, size guard and all.

I filed for an annulment because of my parents. They felt strongly about it and if it was important to them; how could I not? I wanted to correct this imperfect blemish on their perfect daughter's record. To this day, I do not understand how five men in a room have the authority to debate the information I provided and deem the end of my marriage *not my fault*. But I went through the motions, and the annulment was granted.

Bruce and I had put a deposit down on a home to be built near both our hometowns. Neither of us ever fathomed leaving our parents. One of the reasons I fell in love with Bruce was his deep connection to his parents. His mom had passed away when he was eighteen from ovarian cancer; and his dad had remarried a woman that wanted nothing to do with Bruce. But he and his dad remained close.

Three days before the wedding and signing for our house, Bruce said to me, "I changed my mind, let's not do it."

I looked at him and without blinking said, "The wedding or the house because either way I'm going to kill you!"

With a laugh he said, "The house, I'm just nervous. It's hard for me to spend money."

"That's just the accountant in you!" I laughed back, "We will be fine, it's a perfect house."

We signed on the house and were married May 17, 1997 at Our Lady of the Woods Catholic Church. My mom and dad both walked me down the aisle this time. My mom had worked so hard learning how to walk with an above the knee prosthesis. It meant everything to me that she was by my side. After all, she handpicked this husband!

chapter 12

Isabel

ruce and I knew we wanted a family and after two years of marriage, we started trying to conceive. It is no secret that being adopted, I had waited all my life to look at someone who might look like me, have some features I had, and carry my genetic traits. In my current practice, I frequently meet women who are adopted and pregnant. I will often say, "Isn't it amazing that you will finally look in the eyes of someone who carries your genetic traits for the first time?" They meet my eyes and nod in agreement, knowing I understand that this indeed is an inexplicable feeling.

A year into nothing happening and being 31 years old, I started to panic. Bruce and I saw a fertility specialist; Bruce checked out fine, so I thought it must be me. While driving home from working in the nursing home, I would look up at night to the stars through my windshield and say outloud to the angels, "I am ready, send her down, any time now." I did this ritual every night for a year while I was waiting.

As part of my evaluation, I underwent a hysterosalpingogram (a test where air is injected into the fallopian tubes to check for blockages). A few weeks later, Bruce had been out of town and when he came home, I figured I had missed my window, based on my calculations of my cycle.

One month later, I was late for my period by one day and called my specialist. I had blood drawn that morning at the clinic. The results would be back by the end of the day. This was before cell phones; as I walked down the nursing home hall that afternoon, I heard the overhead operator say, "Lisa Astalos, outside call line 1".

I sat down and answered, "This is Lisa Astalos."

"Hi Lisa, is this a good time?" the voice on the other end asked. Is this a good time? *When is a good time to hear if your dream of carrying your own child is coming true?*

"Yes, this is a good time."

And then I heard news that would change my life forever: "You are pregnant!"

I could not feel the ground as I walked. When I arrived home, I walked into Bruce's office (he had started his own accounting business and was working from home) and said, "Guess what? I'm pregnant, it's a girl, and her name is Isabel."

Bruce looked up at me with a blank stare as he blinked. "How did this happen?"

"Are you really asking me this?" I could not tell if he was serious. It was actually kind of innocent and sweet. I think he was in shock.

His next question was, "How do you know it's a girl? and why Isabel? Don't I get a say?"

My response was simple; "I just know, and no, her name is Isabel. The angels named her."

The name Isabel had come to me one day as I was driving home. One night, as I prayed out loud to the angels, the name Isabel popped into my head.

Bruce shrugged his shoulders, "Well, okay then. We are having a baby!"

Bruce was generally much more introspective and took his time mulling things over—remember his response to my marriage proposal? And our home? However, he was also used to my decisiveness. He knew that once I really made my mind up, it was not worth the debate.

Reality seemed to finally sink in; Bruce suddenly jumped up from behind his desk and grabbed me, pulling me into a hug that lifted me off the ground.

"Oh my God! We really are having a baby!"

I called my mom first and made her promise not to tell my dad. I wanted to tell him in person, which I did with Bruce later that night. My dad's response was predictable—all he cared about was that I was happy.

"If this is what makes you happy, then I am happy," my dad said as he smiled at me.

My mom and dad went with Bruce and I to our first ultrasound appointment around the twentieth week of my pregnancy to find out officially if I was having a boy or girl. I already knew. But this would make it official. My dad, being the gentle, old-fashioned soul that he was, stayed in the waiting room. I remember wondering what he thought was going to happen since at this time, the ultrasound was only over the outside of my abdomen.

We waited as the ultrasound technician rolled the jelly over my lower stomach and asked, "Do we want to know what we are having?"

"Yes!" I gushed.

"It's a girl," she smiled.

This only solidified what I knew. Bruce did not trust my intuition as much as I did and looked up at the monitor that was displayed on the corner of the wall, "Are you sure that is not a penis?"

The ultrasound technician laughed and rolled her eyes, "No, that is an arm."

My mom started to cry when the announcement "It's a girl" came and reached her arm over my stomach and hugged it. "I am so happy for you," she said through her tears.

Looking back, I realize her tears of joy were because she knew someday she would not be here. She was hoping that my daughter would take over as my protector and my best friend. She had no idea I'm sure how true this would turn out to be. Or maybe she did.

I talked to my daughter all the time and nicknamed her "Izzy" while she was still in my belly. I felt that if she heard my voice, she would know me when she was born. My mom would also sing to her and touch my belly all the time. One of my favorite photographs of my mom is one where she is leaning over from her wheelchair and hugging my belly. She was singing "Izzybelly, Izzybelly, my busy Izzybelly".

My pregnancy was typical. I was sick for about five months with nausea, but I coped. I never lost the sense of pure joy that I was blessed to actually carry a child that would have my genetics.

But my position caring for patients in the nursing home was taking its toll on me. After working long hours for a physician, who owned both a nursing home practice and a family practice, I felt I needed a change. I also yearned to care for women across the lifespan and utilize the skills I had learned during my fellowship.

After careful consideration, I approached the owner of these practices, Dr. Taylor, with an ultimatum; create a position for me in the family practice—which I had no experience in at the time—or I was accepting another position I had been offered. About three weeks later, Dr. Taylor made me an offer.

By the way, there was no other position. I have no idea where I got the courage to take this risk, but it paid off.

I would later understand that I would need to reach deep inside myself for this same courage, as I was about to experience one of the most painful losses of my life.

chapter 13

No Words

A s my pregnancy progressed, my mom's health worsened. It was a vague, insidious decline. Nothing specifically was wrong, yet she was getting weaker and weaker. She needed more and more help transferring between her wheelchair to the toilet. Her prosthesis needed more and more adjustments. My dad and I knew something wasn't right.

My baby shower was an event that should have been remembered with fondness and excitement. But the morning of my baby shower was so painful for my mom and I, that even as I write this, my eyes fill with tears. She was in the midst of her leg swelling intermittently and we had no idea why. Looking back, it should have been obvious to me that something serious was causing the swelling, but at the time, my dad and I were in the eye of the tornado and not sure what was happening. This particular morning, my mom's leg was so swollen she could not get the prosthesis on. She sat on her bedside with me next to her and wept. "I don't know what to do, I can't get it on, and I can't miss your shower," she said as tears flowed down her cheeks.

Eventually, she was able to barely get her prosthesis on and made it to the car. When I helped my mom into the car, I had to bend and lift her prosthetic leg into the car. She was so worried about me doing this; I was seven months pregnant. As I drove us down the road to my shower, my mom and I held hands silently. We both knew we were lucky she made it to the car; and we both knew something was not right.

During my shower, my best friends huddled around and took pictures of all of us. In these pictures, Mom does not look *right*. The days that followed were a blur of not understanding why things did not seem right, despite any clear cause. Maybe it was my intuition, but something was changing, and not in a good way.

During the first years after my mom lost her leg, we vacationed and went on "mother-daughter" trips. We took cruises and went to Disney World. She drove a scooter because distances walking with a prosthesis were getting harder. But at this point, our outings consisted solely of doctor's appointments.

Three weeks after my baby shower, I drove to my mom and dad's house to take her to her eye doctor. She was struggling again that day with her prosthesis. She finally made it out to the car. I had to help her more than I had to in the past. As I settled back into the driver's seat, my mom looked ahead, and exclaimed, "I'm dizzy, I'm dizzy, I gotta get out, I gotta get out!"

My mom seemed frantic and opened her car door as we were still in her garage, and twisted herself around so her legs were leaning out of the car. I jumped out as fast as I could and ran around to the passenger side. My mom then lowered herself out of the car and slumped down to the ground. I sat across from her on the garage floor and looked into her eyes.

"Mom, did you eat, how was your blood sugar?" I said with strained calmness.

In the meantime, I yelled for my dad, who looked at us from the doorway as I said, "call Bruce to come help Mom get up!"

My dad disappeared back in the house to call Bruce. These next few moments are burned in my memory: my mom looked at me, first in my eyes, and then past me. She then slid sideways and down and stopped breathing.

I yelled again for my dad, "Dad! Call 911!"

My dad came running, looked down and cried "Oh my God, Judy, oh my God!" He then ran in the house and called 911. I gave my mom a precordial thump in the center of her chest as hard as I could (a hard punch in the center of the chest that may restart someone's heart). I then started CPR, and kept at it for a few minutes. And then, a voice inside me said, "no, stop, it's not what she wants."

My mom had an advanced directive and I was her Power of Attorney. This is documentation that allowed me to make health-related decisions for her if she could not. My mom had told me years before that if her heart stopped, she did not want to be brought back to life or placed on a ventilator.

"If I am gone, I am gone, Lisa-Kay. Do not bring me back. I do not want to be kept alive."

At the time, I had looked at her and said "I know, Mom, I would not do that to you."

Well, that's what was happening. Her heart had stopped; if I was going to carry out her wishes, I had to stop trying to make it start again.

Stopping CPR was one of the hardest things I have ever had to do. The daughter part of me was screaming, "My God no, don't leave me!" But the nurse part of me knew that my mom had already been without oxygen too long. Even if she did come back, she would have brain damage from the lack of oxygen. I stopped CPR and stood, looking at her, as I carried my daughter inside me, my daughter who would never meet her grandma. It nearly broke me. But it was the greatest gift I could ever give my mom.

I loved her so much that I let her go. It was what was best for her. I wonder now, as I think about this moment, was that the love my birth mother felt for me? She loved me so much she let me go, because she felt it was what was best for me? By stopping CPR, I had honored her wishes. It was the final act of love I ever did for my mom.

The ambulance and Bruce arrived at the same time. My dad came out of the house and I looked at him and said, "I had to stop Dad, it was not what she wanted."

My dad stared at my mom's lifeless body and nodded; he was in shock. Bruce stood by, staring, not sure what to do or say. The paramedics came up to me in the garage, looked down at my mom and asked me what happened. They explained they had to start CPR until we produced the documents needed to prove she was a DNR (do not resuscitate).

As they did a "slow code" (CPR that is slow intentionally), my dad and I frantically looked in the basement where he kept important documents. We pulled folders out of the old freezer he used to lock up valuables and finally out came the papers we needed. I ran up the stairs and out to the garage and screamed, "Stop! I have the DNR."

And at that moment, they stopped CPR.

I covered my mom up with a blanket and put a pillow under her head. I think I forgot I was pregnant until I felt the cramps. I grabbed my stomach and made a noise that snapped Bruce out of shock as he stood staring. "Oh my God, my wife's pregnant!"

The paramedics then turned their attention to me and took my blood pressure. I brushed them off and sat on the couch with my dad, both of us quiet as we waited for the medical examiner.

Later, after the medical examiner quickly determined my mom died on her garage floor of natural causes, my dad called the funeral home. They came to get my mom and my dad told them we would be in the next day for the arrangements.

I went home after and looked out into my backyard. The shock of what had just happened made me numb. I saw my next door neighbor, Angie, in her yard and although we had not talked much in the past, something made me approach her. As I walked up, she saw the look on my face and immediately asked me what was wrong. Despite not really knowing each other, I looked at her and said with an eerie calm, "My mom just died."

Angie immediately grabbed me and started to cry. 'Oh my gosh—I am so sorry!" That day marked the beginning of a friendship that has endured the years and saved me in countless ways.

That night the "cramping" was worsening. I finally agreed to get checked out and went to the emergency room of the hospital. I was numb and Bruce took over, explaining to the nurse what happened that day. As I laid in the emergency room I said a silent prayer for the cramping to stop. I could not have this baby right now.

I whispered to Izzy, "Please wait, baby girl, just give me this week."

I knew I had to help my dad bury my mom. I could not leave him to do this alone. I received IV fluids and eventually the cramping stopped. My dad was, of course, there in the waiting room. Where else would he be?

The next day, my dad and I went to the funeral home and took care of the arrangements. My mom would be laid out one day and the next day we would bury her.

Izzy's crib was built, but little else was ready. I had planned to keep working right up until I had her but now I called Dr. Taylor (my boss) and told him I would be off until after my maternity leave. He expressed his condolences and I was officially off work for the next four months.

I went shopping the day before my mom was laid out. It was the first time in years I had been in a mall without her. My friend Tonya went with me (one of my high school besties and Izzy's godmother) and I bought a new maternity outfit. Thinking back, I wonder why I did that when I was eight months pregnant.

The day my mom was laid out I was on my feet the entire day. I remember standing up at the front and looking over at my girlfriends. They were pointing at me giggling.

"What are you bitches laughing at?" I whispered as I walked over to them.

Jill smiled, "That anklet on your swollen ankle is crying help me, help me!"

That's my friends for you. On one of the worst days of my life they are making fun of me and making me laugh.

We buried my mom the next day. After a Catholic service and a wake, it was over. My dad, Bruce, and I drove out to the cemetery later to check on her grave. As I stood by her gravesite, I had to keep shifting my weight. I was so uncomfortable and I did not know why. I felt I had to urinate constantly but hardly anything came out. We went to dinner and I gorged myself on pizza. Later that night, as I laid on the couch, popping one chocolate-covered graham cracker in my mouth after another, as if they were grapes and I was a Botticelli painting, I felt a trickle of fluid come out of me. I then stood up and water gushed out from inside me.

"Bruce!" I screamed. Bruce rushed downstairs and looked at the carpet. "Oh my God, I can't have this baby right now! I am exhausted! I am not ready!"

As I sobbed and denied what was happening, Bruce calmly said, "Yes, you are having this baby, let's go."

My poor dad, who was also exhausted, made his way back to my house after he had left only an hour before. Izzy had waited just as I had asked her five days earlier. She decided she was ready and came at 6:30 in the morning the day after I buried my mom. I know in my heart my mom gave her a hug on her way down to me and told her "Take care of your mom for me."

When Izzy was born, May 28, 2000, she came out of me with her arms wide, eyes open, looking around. The nurses immediately took her off to the side to be assessed. As Bruce walked over to her, I asked him,"Is she okay?"

I must have talked to Izzy enough while I was pregnant because at that moment, I watched my daughter's head immediately turn to my voice. She heard me and she recognized me. Looking back on that moment, I realize I must have known my birth mother's voice too, and I must have known we were separated. That moment impacted me as an adoptee and verified the trauma my birth mother and I both experienced.

That night, I did something that I will always deeply regret. I asked the nurses to take Izzy to the nursery so I could get some sleep. Now that I understand the impact of separation, I wish I never sent her away. I wish I could have that time back. Nancy Verrier (2003) discussed in her book *Coming Home to Self* the impact of separating a baby from their birth mother, even overnight. She related that separating mother and baby can be traumatic for both and have implications throughout a child's life.

But at the time, I was whirling. I was exhausted. And I was lost. I had just buried my best friend, my protector, and my champion the day before I gave birth to my child—the first family member whose eyes I would meet that carried my genetics. My heart tore in ways for which I have no words.

I tried to nurse Izzy, but I never made any milk. I gave up trying and accepted I would not experience nursing. I was seeing a perinatal therapist that my obstetrician had recommended who thought it was due to the trauma of losing my mom.

My dad came over every day, all day. He went grocery shopping and brought us anything we needed. He knew what stores had all the good deals. I would be greeted by diapers on my front porch or food in my fridge everyday.

The summer after Izzy was born is what I have come to remember as the *dark summer*. I don't think I grieved my mom at all. Who has time to grieve when you have a new baby to take care of? Thinking about it now, it is much like how I never fully grieved being given up as an adoptee. I buried it all, and it festered inside me.

Over the next ten years, my relationship with my dad changed. We grew closer. I knew we were all he had and all he cared about. The relationship I had with my mom used to take up the whole room. There was never space for my dad and I to get close, not until she was gone. My dad never begrudged this fact. If I was happy, he was happy. But now, we grew closer.

Life fell into a comfortable routine. Izzy was growing, my dad was ever-present and part of our family, and I was working part-time in Dr. Taylor's office. With life feeling somewhat settled, the gentle whisper in the back of my mind that I had heard all my life went from a quiet whisper to louder questions. Now that I had a daughter, did I owe it to Izzy to know my family medical history? Where did I come from? Who was my birth mom? Why did she give me up?

chapter 14

Down the Rabbit Hole

Everyday in my practice, I ask women that I am taking care of, "Is there any family history of breast cancer?"

Often enough, they answer with concern laced across their face, "I don't know, I'm adopted."

When this happens, I sit stunned for a minute. It's as if we are sisters and part of the same club—the "I don't know about my family history, I am adopted" club.

I had been a nurse practitioner for several years and learning more and more about the importance of family medical history. Family history would come to mean even more as I became immersed in helping women understand their risk for breast cancer. Current literature reflects that in order to assess risk for breast cancer, family history should be assessed. Breast cancer screening is now based on overall risk for breast cancer (Gregios, Peterson, & Fowler, 2023).

When my mom was alive, she used to say to me, "If you want to look for your birth mom, I will help you." It was a closed adoption through Catholic Charities at the time, now called Catholic Social Services. I always got the feeling my mom was quite confident there was no way to find my birth mom, but I believed she would have helped me. I just never felt I could ask her. My eyes would tear up as I thought about explaining that although I loved her so much, I still wanted to know. Besides, my mom loved me with such a fierce, protective, consuming love that there was no room for anyone else to be in the *mother* category.

I don't remember why after she died, I suddenly started daydreaming about searching for my birth family. It was as if I had always known that I would someday, but each time I allowed the thought to surface, I pushed it down. I think in my heart, I knew that when my mom was gone someday, the thought may bubble up again. When it did bubble up, the feeling of instant defeat also crept into my mind and the possible disappointment of sealed records was overwhelming. I am not sure what the final catalyst was, but one day I decided I would do more than just think about it.

But first, I had to tell my dad.

My dad was a tender soul, whose existence at this time consisted of what he could do to make mine and my daughter's life perfect. I decided I would tell him what I was telling myself; I am only doing this to get my family medical history. I don't need to know anything else. I have a daughter, and it is important that she and I know. It was not just about me. It was about her, too. I was not betraying his love or the amazing life he and my mom had given me. This was just about the medical facts.

My dad looked a bit uncomfortable and wary, but as always, he was supportive of whatever made me happy.

I made the first phone call to Catholic Social Services. I had no idea who I was talking to. I just gave her my information and held my breath. It was the beginning of many surreal moments to come. I was told that the ethnic information would be released first, but any other information would depend on what my birth family had done on their end. I had no idea what that meant. But my heart was thudding so loud I could feel my pulse in my temple, and I could barely hear what the woman on the other end of the phone was saying.

A few weeks later, the ethnicity paperwork came in the mail. This was more detailed information about my heritage along with some medical history. I sat and read it as if it was the details of a winning lottery ticket. It kind of was. Aside from the shoebox I was obsessed with after my mom told me I was adopted, it was the most information about my beginning I had ever seen.

I learned my birth mom was Polish with some English descent. Medical information included a history of blood cancer in the family. No other cancer history was mentioned. There was no cardiovascular disease or psychiatric disorders in her family. There was no identifying information, and it still seemed limited. But actually reading about my ethnic descent and birth mom's family health history was surreal.

About a week or so later, while at my job in the family practice, I saw I had a voicemail on my cell phone. I stepped away and listened to it. It was the social worker from Catholic Social Services. She had left a message saying she had more information for me.

Fantasies about my birth mom washed over me. I could not keep a single thought from leading to the next. Did she remember me on my birthday? Did she want to know who I turned out to be? Would she want me?

I went into my office during my lunch, for some privacy. I did not spend much time in this office, I was always with patients. My desk was simple and industrial, the room smelled antiseptic, and the chair at my desk was uncomfortable. It was in this unassuming room that I would learn more about my birth mother. I took a breath, then called CSS back.

"Hi, this is Lisa Astalos," I said. "There was a message left for me."

"Yes, Lisa! Well, we discovered that your birth grandmother and birth aunt had registered with the central adoption registry in 1995."

My head was spinning. 1995? I would have been twenty-seven years old, almost ten years ago.

"Ok, wow, so what does this mean?"

"This means I have the name of your birth mother and grandmother, and I have your grandmother's address." She said casually.

I could not breathe or feel the ground under my feet. It was as if my life before this moment rushed by in 30 seconds just to get me to this point.

"And my mother's address?" I asked, breathless.

And then she said the words that even now catch in my throat whenever I tell my story.

"So, your birth mom died May 28th, 1973. She was twenty-six."

My mind filled with despair, my head slumped onto my desk, and I began sobbing. Loud, guttural sobbing, that came from somewhere deep inside.

The woman I had been daydreaming about my whole life was already gone, long before I understood what my beginning was. The one person who could fill in all the gaps was gone. The person I had sent a silent wish to every birthday, for as long as I could remember, was gone. Each birthday since I can remember I had thought to myself, she must be thinking of me today. She was, in fact, not. She was gone. I had finally gotten up the nerve to make this call only to learn she was gone.

The reality also set in that my birth mom had died on the exact month and day my daughter had been born, May 28th, 27 years later.

The social worker started to say how sorry she was. But that empathy was not the message she conveyed. The way she told me my birth mother had died felt more like, "Oh, yeah, the wish you were wishing for most of your life, not gonna happen." She seemed to have no idea the devastation that her message triggered.

When I tell my patients life altering, difficult news, I sit across from them and softly speak, preparing them for the news as sensitively as I can. The SPIKES model, adopted from the Oncology Nursing Society (ONS), gives evidence-based guidance on how setting and sensitivity can impact how someone hears difficult news (Kaplan, 2010). SPIKES is an acronym for Setting, Perception, Invitation, Knowledge, Emotion, and Summarize. This model helps healthcare providers understand the intricacies of giving difficult news. This social worker had apparently never heard of the SPIKES Model. I wondered, later, if she was new at this kind of stuff.

When I had finally composed myself enough, she proceeded to tell me who my birth grandmother was and her last known address. And that's where the rabbit hole began to get really crazy.

My birth grandmother's name was Sally Thomas. My birth mom's name was Judi Black (Judi with an "I", my mom was Judy with a "Y"). I had two uncles and two twin aunts. The family had lived in Wyandotte, Michigan which is a few towns away from where I grew up and now live. My adoptive mom and dad also grew up in Wyandotte. Later when I looked up the address, I learned that my birth mom and my adoptive mom grew up only blocks apart. This was a richly Polish, Catholic community. My mom, Judy, had converted to Catholicism to marry my dad.

When I got home that night, I told the story. Instantly, Bruce said, "Let's go!"

"Now? Are you sure?" I asked.

"Yes, you have waited this long; let's go get some more family!"

And down the rabbit hole we went.

We drove to Wyandotte after a quick stop at McDonald's. Izzy was young and hungry. As we pulled up, the neighborhood looked so familiar. It looked like every other Wyandotte neighborhood. The houses were older, traditional bungalows and ranches. This house was a two-story, red brick bungalow, with white trim; and a small porch in front of the house with two outdoor chairs. The whole day was already Alice in Wonderland-ish. *Why not just walk on up*, I thought. So, with Bruce and Izzy waiting in the car, I got out, walked up, and knocked on the door.

The young man who answered the door was clearly not the right age to be my grandparent. My heart sank for the second time that day.

"Hi, my name is Lisa. My grandmother was Sally Thomas. I am looking for her."

The young man, about 30s smiled, "Oh, I'm sorry, the Thomases don't live here anymore. But the neighbor next door has been here for years. She probably can help you get in touch with them."

Ok then, I thought. *The day could not get any stranger, why not knock on that door?* So off I went, and I knocked on the neighbor's door.

I wish I would have had cameras for the next scene as the neighbor's front door opened.

"Lisa?" The woman asked.

"Denise?" I responded.

Both of us were shocked. Standing before me was the nurse who had mentored me as a brand-new RN at the local hospital. I had not seen her since I had earned my Master's degree and moved on to a position as a nurse practitioner.

"What can I do for you?" She asked.

"I am looking for Sally Thomas, she is my grandmother."

Her eyes widened and her mouth dropped open. "Oh my God, you are Judi's daughter." We stood staring at each other. As these minutes passed, I felt like I was in a movie, as if any moment someone would yell, "Cut!"

Nothing felt real. Not only was my birth family so close all along, they were connected to someone I knew, and who impacted my early career as a nurse. I was flushed, felt dizzy and the ground felt tilted. Denise looked just as amazed as she stared at me, as if it was the first time she ever saw me. Neither of us could tear our eyes away from the other.

After what felt like too many minutes, Denise broke the spell. "Oh my goodness, please come inside."

I waved to the car and within moments, Izzy, Bruce and I spilled into Denise's living room and sat down. Denise continued to stare at me and was the first person, besides the not-so-sensitive social worker, to fill in some of the blanks.

We were seated in Denise's living room and she sat close to me, leaning in, touching my hand. The next thing she told me was the second blow I would receive that day: Sally, my birth grandmother, had dementia and had lived in a home-like facility nearby, but had died just weeks before. Denise truly seemed sorry to tell me that I had missed meeting Sally. I had, in fact, just missed meeting her. She died on the exact day that I made the first call to Catholic Social Services. You can't make this stuff up.

Denise quickly followed this news with "You have two uncles and two aunts."

I knew this already from the social worker, but Denise knew far more than they did—including names and phone numbers. She made the executive decision, right then, to call my birth aunt, Janice. Janice and Fred lived up north in the upper peninsula of Michigan and Jeanne, her twin, lived in New Mexico. I was reeling trying to digest that my grandmother was also gone, and that any moment I may talk to a birth family member for the first time. Janice was not home, but Denise left her a message that she had "news" and to call her.

Yes, this was *news* alright.

Denise proceeded to tell me all she could about Judi. Judi had died of leukemia not long after her diagnosis at twenty-six years old. She had been married for the second time, but was headed for divorce number two. Denise told me that Judi would come over and talk to her about being pregnant when she'd gotten pregnant with me. She had asked Denise what to do. Apparently Sally was not happy. Judi's pregnancy was a mark on the family and in the Polish, Catholic community. Denise shared that abortion had been mentioned. I learned later that my uncle J.T. had told Judi not to do it. It was not legal at the time, and she might *get hurt*.

The choice to have an abortion had been on my birth mom's mind. The choice that would lead to whether or not I would exist in this world. As an adoptee who understands that this choice literally translates to my life or death, how else could I feel other than to fight for my life? It is a very suspended feeling to think about not existing; how close I had come to never being born. But, to be fair, anyone in her situation may consider their options. Especially when I found out later the hell she would go through as she carried me.

"Your grandfather died of prostate cancer several years ago," Denise reached out again to touch my hand and softly said, "I am so sorry, did you know he had passed too?"

I could sense Denise knew I was reeling with information overload. She continued to sit close and look into my eyes. I could see the concern on her face.

"It's okay, Denise, I appreciate you filling in all the blanks, even if the news about my grandparents is not easy to hear."

Denise then looked at me for about the fifth time that night with amazement on her face and said, "Oh my gosh, your grandfather was a patient in our unit while you were working there!"

Again my friend, you can't make this stuff up.

This sank in slowly. I do not recall him specifically, but I worked on the same unit, same shift as Denise during the times he was admitted. It is very likely I indeed cared for him. I probably held a stethoscope to his chest as he lay in the cardiac ICU, never knowing I was listening to my grandfather's heartbeat. This made me sad to think about. So close, but in the end it was not for me to know at the time.

Denise and I finally said our goodbyes and she promised to call Janice again. And a few days later, after Denise told Janice she talked to *Judi's baby*, I heard my aunt Janice's voice for the first time.

The notion that she sounded familiar sounds made up and cheesy, but she did. I don't know why. It was the most-loving, comfortable conversation I'd ever had with a stranger. She was a gardener and called herself a *dirt lady*. I loved that. I could hardly keep dandelions alive.

"Fred and I will be downstate in the next few weeks. We would love to meet you!"

This stunned me and my heart melted. It felt as if a warm blanket was placed over me. The fact that they wanted to meet me was overwhelming and exciting. I would finally have the chance to look into the eyes of a birth aunt. Someone who could tell me more about my birth mom.

"I would love that!" I was practically squealing over the phone.

"Ok, then we will make it happen. And I will bring pictures of Judi and any keepsakes I can find."

As we talked for the first time, Aunt Janice told me more about what life was like for Judi when she learned she was pregnant.

"When our mom, Sally, learned Judi was pregnant, she sent her away to live in the Mari-Lac home for unwed mothers in Detroit. I think it was because they did not want anyone to know she was pregnant."

The news made my heart sink. To imagine being pregnant and alone, sent away so no one would know.

"My mom also told Judi that if she told her the name of the father of the baby, she could keep you. But Judi would not tell anyone who your father was."

Thinking about this now, my heart breaks for her. She must have had a reason to keep my birth father's name a secret. Despite being given away, I could not help but have compassion for Judi as I heard for the first time what life was like for her being nineteen, pregnant, away from home, scared and alone.

Janice told me what cemetery Judi was buried in. It was the same cemetery my adoptive mom is buried in. Not only had my mom and birth mom grown up streets away, they were laid to rest in the same rolling hills cemetery with a nearby pond and swans lazily floating by.

Later, after learning where she was buried, I would go to this cemetery. It would take me three tries wandering aimlessly to find her. But finally, on my third try, I came up on a worn gravestone, weathered and grown over from lack of care. "Judi Black; daughter and wife" was carved on the gravestone.

No mention of "mother".

Judi had been forced to erase me from her story. In the end, her pain, her loss was erased as well. Nancy Verrier (2003) writes in her book *Coming Home to Self* about the loss a birth mother experiences. She likens the experience to terror as a birth mother's realization sets in that she will never see her child again (Verrier, 2003).

Judi gave me up, knowing she would never see me again. When I think of my daughter, Izzy, and the bond I have with her, my throat feels tight and tears fill my eyes. I cannot begin to imagine the sheer heartbreak that giving up a child must have caused Judi. I would later learn that she left treasures behind, as clues to how much this loss impacted her.

chapter 15

Poems and Other Treasures

T
he first time I met my Aunt Janice and Uncle Fred was on a sunny afternoon at a family restaurant near my home. They happened to be in town and we arranged our first meeting. I was excited to meet anyone who wanted me; happy to be wanted.

As I walked in the restaurant with Bruce and Izzy, I heard my Aunt Janice's voice, "Lisa! Oh my gosh!" She told me I looked like Judi; my hair was highlighted and I wore frosted pink lipstick which was Judi's signature lip shade. What Janice did not know is my friends have nicknamed me "frosty McFrost" because I never wear any lip shade but frost.

Janice embraced me and it felt…awkward. It is the oddest experience to meet perfect strangers and know they are your blood relatives. It is something non-adoptees can't understand. Sure, non-adopted folks may meet distant family members, but when you grow up never looking in the eyes of someone who has your genetics (aside from, in my case, my daughter), the experience of meeting birth relatives is so hard to wrap your head around. Touching strangers in such a familiar way is sometimes awkward, anyway. And I think

Janice could sense this. She was warm, yet tentative. She respected the space I needed to take them all in.

I had waited all my life to look into the eyes of any member of my birth family. I had fantasized about my birth mom; and now here I was with her sister. The ground did not feel steady underneath me. In truth, meeting Janice one-on-one may have both eased the awkwardness and given this moment the attention it deserved. I had brought my family, but part of me wished I could look Janice in the eyes and just breathe without the attentive eyes of family on us.

Uncle Fred was warm, funny, and comfortable. My Aunt Maryfern, my Uncle Jimmy's ex-wife, was also there. I did come to enjoy getting to know them all, and Aunt Maryfern was very attentive to Izzy. I got the feeling that she may have been divorced from my Uncle Jimmy, but not from his family. I could respect that and it gave me hope that these people truly valued family.

I also learned from Janice that Judi had named me while she was pregnant, apparently knowing she was having a girl. She'd named me Michelle Marie. My Aunt Janice had initially called me Michelle the first time we talked on the phone. It made me uncomfortable, and she quickly called me Lisa from that point on.

Judi had written poems in a notebook. She was a writer as well, of sorts. Two of the poems were about me. Janice saved this notebook along with a few precious keepsakes, and when we finally met, she gave me the notebook. What I read broke apart the pieces of my heart that were already so fragile.

My birth mom had indeed thought of me. She, too, felt the loss. And had she been alive, she would have wanted to know me, find me. She would have loved me. She did love me.

The first poem, written while she was in the Mari-Lac home described her pain as her pregnancy progressed. It is entitled "The Babe".

The Babe

As time passes by,
She starts to show.
Hiding pain with a sigh,
The babe is starting to grow.
She's alone with no one to love,
But prays for the answer why.

Always is praying to God above,
For the day she'll hear her baby cry.
This day won't come soon enough,
She'll face each day with a smile.
Although the road is going to be rough,
Soon it will only be a little while.
That day finally came,
Now my life will never be the same.
For born unto me,
Was my beautiful Michelle Marie.

She then dedicated the poem to me and wrote "For my beautiful Michelle Marie Thomas".

Judi was four months pregnant when she wrote the first verses of this poem and wrote in the notebook, "not completed". She later added the last verses. On September 7, 1968, seven months after I was born, at 2:00 am, Judi wrote a second poem about me she left untitled:

Michelle Marie
Was born unto me,
Although I gave her away,
Although through the years,
I'll shed many tears.
I'll never forget the day,
That I gave my baby away.
Sometimes I ask myself why,
That's the only day I heard her cry.
Maybe she knew that day
That I was giving her away.
I just know she could see,
Cause I saw that she smiled at me.
She knew I was her mother,
And I would never forget her.
And I hope and pray someday
She'll come looking for me.
Then together we will always be,
My Michelle Marie and me.

The initial feelings I had reading these poems were overwhelming, especially as I had been given them within months of learning Judi was already gone. To say I felt cheated, in no way measures the depth of how this felt. I felt as if someone had ripped a part of my history, my beginning, out of my life. Like missing pages of a book just when you get close to solving the mystery—the mystery is left unsolved, you are empty and angry that you will go through the rest of your life not experiencing what you knew was missing. Despite learning more about my beginning, the new information led to more gaping holes.

But with the sour, came the sweet. Some people who came into my life at that time were the ones I nicknamed the *icing on the cake*. My Uncle Fred, Janice's husband, a Marine with a gentle soul, was one of those people. My Uncle Fred had survived aplastic anemia, and was a walking, breathing miracle. After that, Janice and Fred moved up to the upper peninsula and had been there for years. Uncle Fred remains someone I would choose as my family if I was not fortunate enough to already call him uncle.

During this dinner, I learned details about my Aunt Jeannie, Janice's twin. Jeannie was also a nurse and a free spirit who married a gentle soul named Monty. She had two children, my cousins, Jennifer and John (BJ, short for baby John). She studied with Indigenous Americans for a bit, and believed in manifesting and meditation. I loved that. While Janice was "mother-earth" and pragmatic, Jeannie believed everything and everyone was connected through spirit. I also learned later that my grandmother Sally read tea leaves. Maybe that is where I get my intuition from. The idea that I got anything from anyone in the same way that non-adoptees feel they get things from their family is still something that causes my breath to catch.

I first talked to Jeannie on the phone within days of talking to Janice for the first time. I could, again, feel the love come through; along with the same surreal disbelief that I was talking to another birth family member, but it also felt natural. And, I suppose it was easier for them—they were not my birth mom, they had not given me up. They had less skin in the game when it came to explaining to me why I was given up.

I learned more over time about Sally and John, my birth grandparents. John seems to have been a quiet, hard-working patriarch of the family of seven. Sally seemed to have ruled over him. My aunts also filled me in on my Uncle J.T. (John Thomas Jr). He was the celebrity of the family—he moved to California after turning eighteen, and never looked back. He set his sights on becoming a racecar driver working his way up from sleeping in garages to becoming best friends with the owner of the LA Times, Otis Chandler. Otis later sponsored J.T., and raced Porsches alongside him. J.T. went on to work with folks in Hollywood even teaching Steve McQueen how to race as he prepared for the movie La Mans. He often talked of teaching Paul Newman how to race. Even so, my uncle was modest about his time in California. He called celebrities "just regular folks."

Over time I met each of my aunts and my Uncle JT. I did not get the chance to meet my Uncle Jimmy. I was disappointed I never met him before he passed away—about a year after I first found my birth family—but the rest of the family weighed in and seemed to have collectively decided it was best I did not meet him. He suffered from multiple medical issues and seemed to live in a downward spiral. I sensed they were protecting me from him. I did meet his son, my cousin, Andy.

I had not grown up with these people, yet they were all willing to call me *family*. And just like my adoptive family, for various reasons, I would end up closer to some than others. Family is still family after all.

I met Jeannie a few months later along with my cousins, Jennifer and BJ. She traveled from New Mexico to meet me. They were warm and accepting. What struck me first about my Aunt Jeannie was how much I could see myself in her features. While my Aunt Janice seemed to favor the Thomas side, my Aunt Jeannie looked like Sally. And Sally looked somewhat like me.

When I first saw pictures of my family, I was in awe of finally looking at people who shared my features. My birth mom had wide, brown eyes like mine. Her smile was similar, with small thin lips. It is hard to describe how surreal it is to finally look at a picture of your birth mother. She looked oddly familiar, as I noticed features that reminded me of myself.

My grandmother, Sally, had the same wide, brown eyes and small smile, and she was slight in build, like me. Jeannie's smile and the shape of her face looked like mine and Sally's.

Jeannie was loving and affectionate when I met her, but again, I struggled with physical contact. She was a stranger and I wanted to get to know her but that overwhelmed feeling crept back in. We spent the weekend in her town so we could visit them all at once. Janice and Fred made the trip to visit, as well. We met at my cousin Jennifer's home (Jeannie's daughter). Jennifer's son, Kyle, was around Izzy's age. Kyle and Izzy were awkward with each other at first, but later swam together in the pool at our hotel.

We sat at Jennifer's home and talked most of the weekend. Being around my new family was surreal. I learned so many missing pieces about my beginning. My world felt unsteady. Sally had come to regret making Judi give me up, and had later taken out newspaper ads looking for me after Judi had died. My aunt Janice actually had the newspaper ads saved and gave them to me. She ran ads that said "looking for Michelle Marie Thomas," not realizing my name would be changed.

One of the most unsettling pieces of information was when Jeannie confirmed that weekend what my adoptive mother told me: Judi was raped.

"I was home that night. She came home with her nylons ripped and sat on the bed and cried," Jeannie announced while sitting in Jennifer's living room with her legs draped over the arm of the chair.

I spent the next few days with the notion that I was not only a mistake, but I was the result of violence—or at the very least, an act my birth mom did not consent to. I don't think the first time I heard this as a child, in front of that closet in my childhood home, I was able to understand it let alone process it. Now, hearing this confirmed to me as an adult, this information had a much greater impact. I was sad for Judi and angry this had happened to her. I more fully understood why she did not want to tell anyone my birth father's name. In the back of my mind, I also questioned if this was not the narrative that Sally wanted; that Judi became pregnant because she was raped, and therefore it was not her fault.

My Uncle J.T. and Aunt Janice tried to downplay what Jeannie had told me. They tempered it with talk about how things were then; it was the late 60s, Judi was a bit of a *wild child*. Their version was that Judi's claim of being raped may have been an attempt to save face. I actually wanted that to be the story of my beginning, but I was not sure. The story of her being raped was so strong—it was the story Judi told the adoption agency so many years ago. *What if it was true? What if she was raped? Who would speak for her?*

I found myself both wanting to defend her and at the same time angry that I had been told. I had buried the "she was raped but she knew the guy" story for years. Now that it resurfaced, I had to figure out what I wanted to believe, as I would likely never really know. I wanted all the information I could get, but I didn't want my story to be that I was the result of a rape. It was a bit of a paradox.

As time went on, the story of my actual conception became a bit more muddied as no one seemed to want to focus on anything negative. Instead, they wanted to celebrate me being in their lives. I wanted to focus on the good as well—who wants that as their story?

I eventually traveled to North Carolina to meet my larger-than-life Uncle J.T. I fell in love. J.T. was the first person with personality traits that made me question the *nurture vs nature* ideas I had growing up. As an adoptee, I did not get to look at my family members and say "I got my wit from my aunt, or I talk with my hands like my mom, or I got my ability to argue from my uncle," as if these traits were passed down through my blood. I instead thought I took on the traits of the family around me, through nurture rather than nature. Or I tried to convince myself I had. I preached the nurture overrides nature narrative all my life.

Then I met J.T. and I finally saw some of myself.

J.T. had come up as he often said "through the school of hard knocks." My uncle had done so many amazing things and met so many impactful people. He himself was a shining star in his world. He was dedicated, hard working, and never, ever quit. He was organized in an obsessive way and never let himself rest until all his *chores* were done.

I, too, make to-do lists and will not rest until I complete my self-imposed tasks. I, too, am organized and believe everything has a place. Sometimes I wonder if this is an attempt to instill some control in my life. Maybe J.T. felt the same way. We were both very goal-oriented, both over-achievers. My uncle used to say "shoot for the stars kid, you will land on the moon."

I had met my *twin*.

J.T. and I joked about how much alike we were. I was proud that I had a birth uncle who respected me and I could really relate to. His wife, Wendi, was a southern belle, another *icing on the cake* person I would choose as my family. She was sweet, warm, and authentic. She welcomed us with open arms each time we traveled to their mountain top home J.T. had built, in North Carolina. They married later in life and Wendi had a son she had adopted. She could truly relate to some of the questions I had and what life was like growing up *chosen*.

J.T. also gave me a gift that I am certain he did not understand the gravity of: a cassette tape of a phone call he had with my birth mom. Judi was in the hospital at the time, battling a new diagnosis of leukemia. She would pass away months later. But this tape recording captured her voice and froze it in time. I listened to this tape and heard my birth mother's voice for the first time.

69

During the phone call, Judi was in the hospital receiving chemotherapy. J.T. had called her from California. Judi's voice was hopeful, as she laughed with J.T. They chatted back and forth, J.T. sharing stories from his experience working with cars. Judi told him she was looking forward to coming to visit him. The call ended when someone came into Judi's room to administer some sort of medical treatment.

As I listened to the phone call, I thought back to when I carried Izzy and talked to her so she would know me. And I remembered how when she was born, she turned her newborn head to my voice. I wish I could say that Judi's voice was familiar, but that was wishful thinking. What I will tell you, my friend, is that it was unreal to hear her, and yearn for that voice to be talking to me. I was grateful for this gift, but the loss continued to layer.

Throughout this time in my life, as I fell down the rabbit hole of meeting my birth family, I had to maneuver bringing my dad into the loop each time I learned more. I had to explain to my dad that finding out my family history was now turning into a full-blown expedition of finding a new family.

We were out to breakfast a few days after I learned about my birth family and visited Denise. "Dad, I have to tell you something."

He immediately looked concerned, as if I was going to tell him Izzy or I had a medical problem. His brow furrowed as he looked down, not wanting to meet my eyes.

"Is something wrong?"

"No, Dad, it's actually good news," I reassured him.

He was clearly worried about me. I was worried about him. I have heard so many adoptees express how much they fear hurting their adoptive parents as they connect with their birth family. I believed in my heart that because it was *just* aunts and uncles, it was something my dad could adjust to; At least that's how it seemed.

"Remember when I contacted Catholic Social Services?"

"Yes," he said with a tentative tone.

"Well, I got some information. I actually learned who my birth family is."

I paused to let this sink in. My dad looked up at me and to my relief, he seemed less worried and was more wide-eyed with a curious look on his face.

I then stammered out the information as quickly as I could. I wanted him to know I had learned about aunts and uncles. Not parents.

My dad seemed happy and relieved, I think. We were a small family and more family for me perhaps reassured my dad that I would have more people around who cared about me.

From then on, I kept my dad informed every step of the way, and he genuinely seemed intrigued with each bit of information about my birth family I learned.

My dad had talked to J.T. on the phone and, honestly, I think after hearing about my uncle's celebrity status in the racing world and in Hollywood, my dad was a little star-struck. But Janice was my only birth family member that actually met my dad face to face.

My Aunt Janice and Uncle Fred were in town again for a visit, and I brought up to them an introduction to my dad. This was my way to include him. My dad had agreed, but he had a shy, tentative look on his face. I believe one of my dad's concerns was me getting hurt. And I understand he may have also had fears that my *new* family would replace my old family. I knew that Janice would know how to show their intentions were good.

As Janice walked up to him in the driveway, she took his hand in hers, looked him in the eyes and said, "Thank you. Thank you for taking such good care of Lisa."

Just like my dad always could, he let his tender heart show through. He was so choked up he could not speak. All I could imagine was what this must be like for him. His daughter that he was so devoted to and her birth aunt standing staring at him and thanking him. It was two separate worlds converging in the most beautiful way.

And instead of fear, I know he felt love.

chapter 16

Me Too

N ot long after my new family folded me into their life, I felt the urge to return to school. I knew I was not done when I graduated with a Master's Degree. It was the same feeling I had when I had earned my BSN. I knew I would earn a doctorate in my field. By this time, my practice had grown and I was feeling more comfortable in my role as a nurse practitioner. Izzy was already in second grade and although she still needed her mom, I felt my family was ready for me to go back to school.

Whether this was me following my grateful and perfectionist state of being or wanting a doctorate for my own professional growth, I am not sure. What I do know is that I have never regretted the decision. Earning a Doctor of Nursing Practice Degree (DNP) changed my life. It lit a fire under me to expand my practice and my scholarship.

Despite feeling more comfortable in my skills as a nurse practitioner, the environment in the family practice clinic had begun deteriorating. The reasons why would make headlines during the "Me Too" movement. Before transitioning from the nursing home practice to his family practice six years prior, Dr. Taylor would pick me up in his red corvette every Thursday afternoon for lunch. We would then round on patients all afternoon. Every single week.

He once looked at me and said "You know, Lisa, everyone thinks we are having an affair."

At the time, I was grateful for this position that allowed me so much autonomy. He complimented my skills regularly, and I wanted to please this professional I looked up to. But I would describe my day to Bruce in the evening and he would look at me sideways. "Lis, I think he has a crush on you."

"No! He is just really nice to me," I replied with my eyes wide.

I am still not quite sure why, but after practicing in this setting for about six years, the atmosphere changed. It may have been because I stopped looking at Dr. Taylor with doe eyes as I became more confident. My practice had grown and my schedule was frequently booked out several weeks. Patients began referring their friends and family to see me. I was the only female healthcare provider in the practice and women especially seemed to appreciate having the option of seeing another woman for their healthcare. It was rewarding to know where I had come from, being offered a transfer in my first job as a nurse practitioner, to having the reputation of being capable, skilled, and caring.

It was Dr. Taylor's birthday and the other physician in the practice hired a "birthday gram" singer to come in at lunch to sing and dance happy birthday. Later that day, in the lunchroom, the entire office staff, who were mostly women, gathered around the lunch table and watched as a woman in lingerie gave my boss a lap dance. I do not fault her, she was making a living. I fault the *professionals* I worked for who hired her. We looked on in shock, not sure what to make of this. Eventually, about ten minutes in, I walked away. I did not hold back and told the office manager how uncomfortable I was that this would happen in our lunchroom. I am sure my words made it back to Dr. Taylor because that same day he looked at me and said in a sarcastic tone, "Don't worry, Lis, I was thinking of you the whole time."

I will never forget the sneer on his face. I felt my cheeks redden. I looked down at the ground, speechless, and sick to my stomach. I had no reply. What does one say when they are made to feel like a piece of meat, instead of a professional, in their own place of work?

Ironically, right around the time this happened, I had begun researching and inquiring about nursing doctorate programs and decided to apply to

Oakland University's Doctor of Nursing Practice (DNP) program. This was an inaugural program and I was the first to apply. During the interview, I met my mentor Dr. Morris Magnan. Morris scared the crap out of me during the interview but later became one of my best friends. I was admitted to the program in Spring 2006 and finished in December 2007. It was the perfect program for a grateful and perfect overachiever. It was also a life-changing experience that I am proud I was a part of.

One of the stipulations of admission to this program was the requirement to finish in eighteen months and attend full-time. I had to reduce my hours. I approached Dr. Taylor, explained my intention to return to graduate school and added I would not be able to work full-time. Initially, he seemed open to a reduction in my hours, but as the atmosphere in the clinic changed between us, he avoided further discussions about my schedule. My intuition told me to have a backup plan, and I applied for another job, closer to home, in an Internal Medicine clinic. I knew he was not thrilled with me those days, especially after my reaction to the incident in the lunchroom, which had been a few weeks prior. I was waiting for him to tell me if I could reduce my hours, as well as waiting to hear about the other position.

Out of the blue, between patients, Dr. Taylor must have been feeling especially nasty as he looked over at me and asked, "Can I talk to you for a minute?"

I said, "Sure, here?"

"No, my office," he replied with a clipped, cold tone.

As he closed the door I thought to myself this cannot be good. And I was no longer comfortable being alone in a room with him. I felt very uneasy as he shut the door to his office, turned to me and said "If you are going to work here, you cannot go to school." I stared at him and I could involuntarily feel my eyes narrow.

"Ok," I said. "Let me think about this."

He looked back, his eyes cold, and said "Ok fine, let me know what you decide."

It was exactly two hours later that I received a phone call regarding the other position I had applied for and was offered the job. This job was closer to home, and part-time was an option. I walked up to Dr. Taylor and asked, "Can I please talk to you for a minute?"

We walked back to his office and he again closed the door. I looked him in the eye and said, "I am giving you my two weeks notice. I am going back to school." I tried to look calm, but my insides were shaking and I was sick to my stomach.

This is when he looked at me and said, "I am not sorry you are leaving. You are a good nurse practitioner, but not a good employee."

My calm facade faded and my insides felt like jelly as my eyes filled with tears. I looked into his eyes. Immediately he looked down, uncomfortable and shuffled his feet. I turned and walked out.

I gave two weeks notice, but I did not think I would last those final two weeks. The environment had turned toxic. My coworkers would hardly talk to me. I also understand that, in some instances, once someone is leaving, in order to protect themselves others feel they can't display any loyalty to the person leaving. But the tension was so thick, and I have no idea why other than Dr. Taylor may have set the tone.

I approached Dr. Taylor in his office about a week after I gave my notice and told him I was leaving sooner than previously indicated. He looked in my eyes and said, "I am sorry for what I said, about you not being a good employee. I saw in your eyes how much I hurt you."

It was the first redeemable thing he had said to me in months. It helped take the sting out of what had happened. But my heart just was not in staying and I left.

This was years ago and I remember it vividly, as if it just happened. On the surface, it could appear that he had grown tired of the ambitious nurse practitioner. Perhaps the notion of my returning to school for a doctorate was too disruptive. Or maybe my obvious distaste for what had happened earlier in our clinic lunchroom got under his skin. Despite the more obvious rationale for how toxic the environment had become, inside my head played the familiar mantra, "*You are not good enough. That's why things have changed. That's why he won't support your goal to return to graduate school.*"

I had worked so hard to increase my skills and build a practice I was proud of yet my confidence had crumbled when I heard Dr. Taylor say "I was not a good employee." It was so easy for me to blame myself, and question my worth.

It was not until I was out of that environment for several months that I was able to put more pieces together and understand what had happened. I started doctoral study and began working in a new practice with colleagues that fostered my growth. The physicians I worked with encouraged me, mentored me, and once again, I began building a practice. My female patients appreciated that I was a woman in an all-male practice. My heart was healing as my practice once again grew. It was validating and rewarding and helped me to understand what had happened to me. I finally was able to change the narrative of not being good enough to keep to the more likely scenario: "After what he said to you, you did not look at Dr. Taylor with a look of admiration anymore; he saw in your eyes what you thought of him, and he gave you that ultimatum to get rid of you."

As with many position changes, by choice or not, we often move to where we are supposed to be at that time in our lives. Hard situations, often, come with rewards if we have the courage to learn from them, be honest with ourselves, and find the strength to work hard and turn difficult situations into better ones. Perhaps through this transition, I was preparing for a time in my life that would require even more courage and compassion from deep within.

chapter 17

Weight and Loss

My new position turned out to be a wonderful, nurturing environment. The two male internal medicine physicians I worked with were both supportive clinically and continued to help me grow my knowledge base caring for an internal medicine population, as well as supportive of my endeavor to return to graduate school. I worked part-time and was able to juggle doctoral study, my practice, and time with family. My practice once again grew.

This practice was close to my home, my dad, and Izzy's school. Izzy was in second grade at the same elementary school I had attended, St. Joseph's. I was able to work part-time as a lunch mother, just like my mom. It gave me precious time with my little girl, and she loved it when I was there. She would run over to me, give me a hug and squeeze me.

"Mommy can you stay longer? I want to go home with you," she would say as she looked up at me with her beautiful hazel-green eyes. I could not get enough time with her. Even at a young age, Izzy was becoming my buddy. The dynamic between us was so similar to the one between my mom and I. I never wanted to put pressure on our relationship to mimic what I had with my mom, but somehow it did, as if by design.

My dad was able to pick Izzy up from school if Bruce and I were working. Bruce had started his own accounting business and was working from home, which allowed for flexibility in his schedule, an advantage to raising a child. But my dad was a traditional guy who thought that men should earn the bulk of the household income and should work outside the home. I would catch him side-eyeing Bruce when my dad suspected he was not working enough or pulling his weight. It was a frequent argument between my dad and I, in private, as I tried to help him understand that things were different when you owned your own business and could work odd hours. Despite my dad's concerns, Bruce's business was growing.

My dad was nonetheless devoted to us and often offered to pick Izzy up and bring her home from school. They would stop for ice cream, the dollar store, or whatever Izzy was up for. She was the light of his life, and it showed. He and Izzy had developed a special bond. One of my most vivid memories is watching them walk away hand-in-hand; my dad's tall, broad shouldered frame contrasted by this little girl walking next to him with her arm stretched up to reach his hand. We were all my dad had, and we saw him every single day. And seeing him every day meant I was less likely to notice his weight loss.

Perhaps that's why I was shocked when he came over one day as he did every day and nonchalantly announced he had been to see his doctor and had lost seventeen pounds. He told me this as if he was announcing milk was on sale. I stopped and looked at him. Then I could see it. I felt the ground shift underneath me and I knew. I was going to lose my dad, too.

I went upstairs to Bruce's office, sat down, and as I let the breath slowly escape my lips, said, "My dad lost seventeen pounds. He has cancer and he is going to die."

"What?" Bruce bellowed, "How can you say that? You don't know that!"

"Yes, I do." I don't know how I knew, but I did. Maybe it was my intuition or maybe it was being a nurse practitioner. But I knew. I just knew.

The next few weeks I accompanied my dad to what I call the "weight loss work up." Finally, right after his upper endoscopy procedure (a scope that goes down the esophagus into the stomach and takes pictures and pieces of tissue), the anesthesiologist looked at me while my dad was still asleep and said, "He's got a mass in there and it's not good."

When I think about this now, and the sensitivity I have when I tell my patients they have a difficult diagnosis, such as breast cancer, I am struck by his callous, casual delivery.

When my dad woke up from the anesthesia after the procedure, his eyes immediately locked on mine. There was no sugar coating or hiding it. I did not then, nor do I now, have a poker face. I tried to stay even and calm when I told my dad he did indeed have a mass (tumor) in his esophagus. His face fell in front of me, but I honestly thought he too knew when he realized he had lost so much weight.

Cancer was later confirmed by a biopsy. My dad was stoic through the whole process from weight loss to diagnosis. I went to every appointment with him and talked to every specialist. I was his daughter, his advocate, and his cheerleader and had to tell him the news each step of the way. Including that he was being diagnosed at stage 4. Stage 4 Cancer means the cancer has spread from the original place it was diagnosed, to other organs in the body, such as the liver.

One of the tests my dad had during his evaluation showed possible tumors in his liver. He was scheduled for a CT (computed tomography) scan at 8:00 pm. That would confirm if this were the case. I drove him to the radiology center near his home. It was just us; me, my dad, and a few staff. The radiologist who read the scan was a colleague I knew from my days at the local hospital cardiac care unit. She began reading the scan on the spot for me.

Then she stopped, zeroed in on a spot, and said what I did not want to hear. "Right there, that small area there," she said, as pointed to show me, "That's cancer in his liver."

My heart dropped in my chest. They were right, and this confirmed it— my dad had stage 4 esophageal cancer; and it had begun to spread to other parts of his body. Everything felt so heavy at that moment.

How was I going to tell him?

The same way I told him he had a tumor on his esophagus. The same way I told my mom she was going to lose her leg. The same way I told my dad I had to stop CPR because it was what my mom had wanted. I had to find the courage.

My dad had gone out to the car and sat in the parking lot, waiting for me to talk with the radiologist. He knew when I got in the car, I would know if the cancer had already spread. I walked out to the car, my heart thumping in my chest, my throat tightening. *Stop*, I told myself. *You have to be strong. You have to have courage. Always.*

I opened the car door and sat next to him in the passenger seat. He looked at me and knew by my face. I then calmly said, "I'm so sorry, Dad, but it is stage 4. It has spread to your liver."

I will never forget what happened next; a single tear slid down his face, and he turned to me asking, "Will I make it to your graduation?" I was in the midst of doctoral study at Oakland University and on track to graduate in a month and a half.

It struck me and broke my heart that after telling him something so traumatic, all he cared about was making it to my graduation. It also made me realize, in that moment, my dad knew he was going to die.

I fought back the tears. I knew I needed to stay strong and calm. But I felt as if I was dying inside. I had already lost my mom. How was I going to lose him, too? I tried to find the words to somehow comfort him. My strong, capable dad. This amazing man who had cared for me and made me his own. I owed him so much.

I stared back into his eyes, eyes that bared the soul of a man who understood what I was telling him. As our eyes met, I took a breath, and said, "Yes, you will definitely be there!"

We sat for a bit in the parking lot of the radiology center. We were both quiet. Neither of us knew how to find the words. I held his hand, as we sat there together, in the night with the glow of the parking lot lights shining down on our car. Sometimes, there just are no words that can comfort you. The presence of someone you love sitting with you, breathing the same air, and feeling the same sense of dread and loss, is all you can do to show how much you care.

My dad drove me home and then went to his home alone. I can't imagine what that was like. He had missed my mom so much in the years since she'd been gone. Now he was facing a terminal illness, without her.

The days that followed included consults and treatment planning all focused on my dad's goal; attending my graduation. The oncologist carefully calculated my dad's chemotherapy not to overwhelm him, so he could attend my graduation. I went with my dad for his infusions and he tolerated chemotherapy well.

In the midst of my dad's treatments and doctors visits, I finished my DNP project with the invaluable mentorship of Morris. My project included developing and testing a middle-range theory about spiritual empathy. Morris and I published our work in the Journal of Nursing Education (Chism &

Magnan, 2009). It was uncanny that my doctoral work included developing the concept of spiritual empathy. Caring for my dad was a very spiritual experience, and as a practicing Catholic, he often mentioned his spirituality as a source of strength.

The day of my graduation from Oakland University came and my dad was indeed there up in the highest part of the auditorium. I walked in with my class to pomp and circumstance for what would be the final time, and looked up to see my dad smiling, waving both arms back and forth so I could find him in the crowd. I will never forget the pride in his eyes as he beamed a smile down to me.

Over the next months, I would consistently take my dad to chemotherapy. He would occasionally stay with me—for multiple days, often ten or more—until he was strong enough to be on his own. I lived ten minutes away from his home, but I was always there if he needed anything.

During one of these stays, my dad started making little side comments about Bruce's work schedule. This happened when either Bruce went fishing with his buddies in the middle of the week, or took a nap in the afternoon. The night before Easter, after my dad had been at my house for eleven days, Bruce had gone up to his office to work, after waking up from a nap. My dad looked at me and said, "It's about time he does something around here. You do everything!"

After that, we exchanged words and I reminded my dad that although he was welcome, this was my house and I did not appreciate his critique of Bruce's work schedule.

"Dad, stop, you know it's different when you own your own business."

"I just don't like it when you do everything. Maybe he needs to get another job, since this one takes so little of his time," he said, sarcasm laced in his tone.

That was it. If my dad was well enough to nitpick Bruce, he was well enough to go home.

"Time to go home, Dad."

And without much resistance, he packed up his overnight bag and went home. Not much more was said between us on the subject. I kept quiet, afraid I would say something I would regret later.

The next day, he sheepishly walked in my back door with a ham for Easter. "Oh, hi Dad, are you coming over later to eat it?"

"If you want me to, I will," he said, eyes down. My dad's sheepish demeanor with shoulders hunched, eyes down, sent the message he was sorry he overstepped.

I acted as if nothing had happened between us. "Of course I do, Dad, why wouldn't I?"

No words about the incident were said. There didn't need to be. He knew I loved him. And I knew his heart was in a good place. He was just looking out for his daughter.

I remembered during these times what my mom had taught me about caring and family. Despite my grandmother being critical, Mom was always there for her. I understood why she'd done this after my grandma was gone. And I understand now. You can't get the time back; and I owed my dad so much. He had taken me as his own and given me a beautiful life. My grateful heart understood how lucky I had been.

chapter 18

Fake It Till You Make It

My dad had completed chemotherapy and the tumors in his esophagus and liver had shrunk. He was officially in remission. Life settled down a bit, and I was wrapping my head around how earning a doctorate in my field impacted my practice. After searching for a resource to help me understand how to incorporate my doctoral education into patient care, I had an idea that appeared in a dream. Two months exactly after completing my DNP degree, in December 2007, I woke my husband up at 2:00 am and told him, "I need to write a book about the DNP degree." Without opening his eyes, he slurred, "ok honey go back to sleep." I did, but when I woke up, the idea was still percolating.

I talked about my idea constantly to anyone who would listen. The DNP degree—a true practice degree for nursing which is now considered the terminal degree for advanced nursing practice—was new at the time. It draws conceptually from the Institute of Medicine's (IOM) "To Err is Human" report (IOM, 1999) and reflects the specific aims thought to improve healthcare and reduce medical errors. When I was admitted to Oakland University, they were funding twenty-two of us, including a stipend, through a large grant they had been given. At that time, there were thirteen DNP programs across the state. For perspective, there are now over 430 programs nationwide. I had a great opportunity, as one of the first DNP graduates, to talk about the degree and maybe shape its path going forward.

My idea to write and publish a book about the DNP degree was perhaps another example of showing that I was overly grateful. I had been given the opportunity to return to graduate school funded by a grant. Being grateful had always felt transactional for me; I felt I did not deserve good things or circumstances unless I gave back in exchange. Now, in my fifties, I try to embrace the true meaning of being grateful. It is still a struggle for me as I have lived my life through the lens of showing I was grateful in this way.

Eventually, I submitted query letters describing my idea for a DNP book to three major publishing companies. Jones and Bartlett responded and within three hours I had a meeting scheduled. Three weeks after that meeting, I submitted a proposal. I had nothing but an outline and an idea. I had not published anything in my life, but before I knew it, I had signed a contract with Jones and Bartlett and six months later, I delivered the manuscript in person.

My book was the first to describe the role development of a nurse with a DNP degree. Included were chapters on role development as a nurse leader, clinician, policy advocate, and educator. I also provided extended content on professional issues, such as how to handle the title "Dr." as a nurse with a doctorate, marketing oneself as a DNP prepared nurse, and educating others about the DNP degree. I concluded with a chapter about the future of the DNP and nursing education. Although the book was evidence-based, it was written in a very conversational, less formal tone.

Bruce and Izzy flew to Boston with me for a long weekend to hand off my jump drive and three hardcopy chapters. While Bruce and Izzy swam in the hotel pool, I sat at a long cherry wood table flanked by members of my publishing team. Prior to this, all meetings had been over the phone. One by one they asked me more details about my now finished manuscript.

Finally a team member from marketing looked at me and said, "So Lisa, what courses do you think your book is appropriate for?"

I looked at her with a blank stare for what felt like too long as the pieces fell into place—they were marketing my book as a *textbook* to be used in universities. I had imagined my book on the shelves of Barnes and Noble, sitting and waiting for a would-be DNP student to wander by and say, "Ah… just what I was looking for!"

I excused myself and went to the restroom. I splashed water on my face and stared at my reflection and said out loud, "Oh my God. Now what are you going to do? Who do you think you are, thinking you could write an actual textbook?" The imposter syndrome was surging through me. I made my way back and did the only thing I could do: I faked it. I described several chapters and suggested courses that matched the concepts I had just written for would-be DNP students.

Later, back at the hotel, Bruce asked, "So how did it go?"

I sat on the bed, staring ahead as I had earlier, and described what happened. Bruce listened and then said through his laugh, "But you didn't write it to be a textbook!"

"No! Stop laughing!" I said as my voice broke, giving way to tears filling my eyes.

"This is perfect. You wrote this book out of pure ambition. You had no idea where it would fit or how it would be used. You just wrote it," he replied and I could see the pride and amazement in his eyes.

I sighed and let the breath slowly out as I spoke, "Well, this will either be okay or be a total fail. There is no going back now."

My textbook, "The Doctor of Nursing Practice: A Guidebook for Role Development and Professional Issues" (Chism, 5th Edition, 2024) was adopted by over 200 universities, and is currently in its fifth edition. My idea to provide a resource to others with a DNP degree, in its conversational style, was adopted as I had written it, despite my having no idea it would be a textbook. Pure ambition, the need to give back, or maybe a combination of both led me to make a contribution to my field that I am proud of, even if the imposter syndrome still surges at times.

Not long after my book was published, I lost yet another job. The internal medicine practice I had been working at during doctoral study was forced to privatize, and my contract was terminated. The physicians I worked with were sorry, but they barely had confidence that they would make it on their own let alone keep me on. It was a blow. I took it personally as any one with my background might. *Why wouldn't they figure it out and keep me?*

I was once again forced to move on and once again it turned out to be life-changing. I looked outside of the safe bubble of the town I lived in, and found a position at a cancer institute in Detroit within a comprehensive breast center. I knew nothing about breast health, breast cancer, or working in a cancer center, but I knew I would finally be caring mostly for women, and it felt right.

I was as green as green could be, but I was able to care for a population of women (and sometimes men) who really needed care. Within six months I was in love, and I stayed at this center for twelve years. During my time there, I was awarded the Compassionate Caregiver Award and a Nightingale Award as a Distinguished Alumni Oakland University. I felt needed, appreciated, celebrated, wanted—it was like a drug. I loved the patients and the people I worked with. I was, and still am, passionate about caring for breast cancer survivors. Part of my work caring for this courageous population involved developing a menopause and sexual health clinic dedicated to caring for breast cancer survivors' menopause and sexual health concerns. I earned certification in both of these areas and this remains a part of my practice today. I am certain my specialty in these areas has made a difference in my patients' lives.

It was also uncanny that my dad had been diagnosed with stage 4 esophageal cancer just a few years before I began working in a cancer center. It seemed my previous training, caring for patients at the end of life in the nursing home, and my current role, in a cancer center, were about to intersect and challenge not only the nurse in me, but also the daughter.

chapter 19

Becoming an Orphan...Again

M y dad remained in remission for about two years. Along the way, he needed radiation for bleeding in his esophagus. In December 2009, almost exactly two years after his diagnosis, my dad realized he was getting weaker and weaker. He had lost his appetite and could not enjoy food like he had used to. He tried chemotherapy again, but it was hard on him, and by the end of January, he was done. He looked at me one day and said, "I don't want to leave you and Izzy, but I don't want to do this anymore."

When he told me this we were laying together in his bed in my childhood home. I had lain in this bed so many times growing up. As a young girl, I came into my mom and dad's room when I was scared and crawled into bed with them. As a teenager, my mom would wake up and knock on the wall three times to see if I was awake. If I was, I would knock back and then climb out of bed and jump in bed with her. We would lay there and talk all morning until my dad came in and asked us if we were ever getting up.

Now, laying with my dad, in this same bed, I could feel my heart break. My eyes filled with tears and I knew. My dad was tired. And I had to love him enough to *let him go*.

I reached over and put my arms around my dad.

"I know, Dad, I get it. I'll be here with you. Every step of the way."

My practice in the nursing home had taught me how to help families accept that their family members were tired and their quality of life was poor. It was surreal to be on the other side of things.

I went with him to the oncologist. He told her he didn't enjoy food anymore, he was tired and he didn't think the treatment was helping. I think she was shocked. Physicians, even oncologists, are trained to save lives. But my dad was making the decision to be done with his.

The oncologist looked at my dad and nodded. I saw the understanding in her eyes. I also saw compassion as she looked at my dad, and then at me.

"We will give you the numbers to some hospice companies. And I will send the referral." She gently reached over and touched my dad's knee. As she did this, I watched as a single tear slid slowly down his cheek.

I couldn't breathe. It felt as if the air had been sucked out of the room.

She had shown such simple compassion in that moment. Her expertise and title were stripped away and she was a human watching another human make the decision to stop treatment for a disease that was killing him.

I often think of this moment when I tell patients difficult news that will change their life. I remember that I am not just a nurse working her job, but a human sitting with another human at a very traumatic time in their life. Trauma-informed care is specifically designed with the goal of not retraumatizing an individual by taking into account the perspective of the individual who has been traumatized (SAMHSA, 2014). Having been told difficult news throughout my life has informed how I deliver difficult news.

We chose a Catholic hospice company and they came to evaluate my dad. They handed me the *Box*, with all the medication that would be necessary to ease my dad's discomfort when the end was near. The box had Ativan for anxiousness or restlessness, liquid oral morphine for trouble breathing, and scopolamine for secretions that can develop when someone is close to death. The medications do not speed up an imminent death, but help ease the discomforts caused by the changes that occur when we die. I remember thinking, *how will I know? How will I know when the time is right?*

I had taken care of many patients and their families during the end of life. I had counseled so many people about quality of life, not quantity. Yet this was my dad. My parent.

It was a heaviness that felt familiar. I had to stop CPR for my mom years before. I knew her wishes at the time and made the decision to respect them. At that moment, I had to love her enough to let her go. It happened so fast, and I slipped into autopilot; and I would do it all over again for her. But asking me to watch and help my dad die was asking me to once again blend being a daughter with being a nurse. I was not sure I had it in me to do this, and lose another parent. They had been my lifeline. If it were not for them, who knows where I would have ended up. I was given up, and they had taken me as their own. Now I was going to be an orphan again.

My dad was stable for a few weeks at home with hospice care, and I checked on him daily on my way home from work. Toward the end of February, my dad was getting weaker and weaker. He did not want a hospital bed but he needed more and more help. Then late one night he called me; he had fallen.

That did it—I made the decision to move in with him. I took an indefinite leave from my practice at the cancer institute. Bruce brought a mattress over and I slept on the floor in the room that had once been my bedroom—my mom had converted it, years later, into her craft room.

My days consisted of sitting with my dad, trying to find things that he felt hungry for, which was not much. One of the last meals he was hungry for was Kentucky Fried Chicken. He loved extra crispy and I accidentally got original recipe. I was so upset. It was the last real food he ever wanted, and I messed it up.

My dad asked everyday, "Are you sure your job is okay?" My dad and his stellar work ethic always shined through.

"Yes, Dad, it's fine, don't worry."

The days progressed and I was exhausted. My dad fell again one night and I had to call 911 to help him get up. He finally gave in and let me order a hospital bed and a bedside commode as his weakness progressed.

Bruce, Izzy, and my friends were amazing and doing all they could. If it were not for them, I never would have made it through this experience. Izzy, who was ten years old at the time, even pitched in emptying his bedside commode and sitting with him. She was on Easter break and off school at the time. She insisted on staying the night with me and we slept on the twin mattress in my childhood bedroom. I was so happy to have her there with me. She was my little buddy. It was around this time that I first realized she would likely go to nursing school.

But despite their help, I was still very alone in this.

It was tax season during this time, and Bruce was working out of our home seven days a week. As my dad grew weaker and weaker, I needed help getting him from his bed to his commode. I would call Bruce, and no matter when it was, he would drop what he was doing, come over in his suit, and lift my dad from the bed to the commode and back into bed.

One time, after Bruce had left and my dad was settled, I sat with him, leaned over and as I kissed his cheek I said, "See, Dad, Bruce is a good guy. You have nothing to worry about. See how he cares for you? He takes good care of me and Izzy, too. And he always will."

My dad smiled and nodded. We both knew what this meant. All of my dad's worries that Bruce did not take care of me and Izzy, or pull his weight, were calmed. Bruce had shown my dad in simple ways that he was there for him, and for Izzy and I. It was a moment of understanding between my dad and me.

As exhausted and alone as I felt caring for my dad, I would not have had it any other way. It was a sacred time. I would sit with him and read or study—at the time I was planning on taking my exam to become certified as a Menopause Practitioner through The Menopause Society.

My dad was declining, becoming even weaker and had woken me up one night every hour to use the bedpan. He was insisting he had to urinate, but never did. I hurt my knee trying to prop him up and pull him. Even with weight loss, my dad was 6'2" and 140 pounds. I could not understand what was going on as I tried over and over to help him onto the bed pan. I laid on that mattress and wept. I was so exhausted. I wanted to go home. But going home meant my dad was gone.

My dad's neighbor, whom I had grown up with, came over one day during this time and told me "This is the most spiritual you will ever feel." She was right, and a dream I had that night proved it. I was in my childhood Catholic Church, sitting in a pew. My mom was next to me and my head was leaning against her shoulder. I could see the sun streaming through the beautiful stained glass windows. I stared into Mom's blue eyes as she said, "Lisa-Kay, this is restlessness."

I had been so afraid of not reading the signs and knowing when to open the "box," but when I woke up, I knew. My mom was telling me it was time to start the hospice medications.

I talked to my dad and told him that Joe, our wonderful hospice nurse, was coming over to insert a Foley catheter so he would not have another night like the last. He was starting to become less coherent. With Joe by my side, I gave my dad his first dose of liquid morphine under his tongue. My dad seemed to relax and closed his eyes. He was semi-conscious the rest of the evening, and would nod to acknowledge that he heard us. That night, everyone who mattered was by his side. We prayed out loud for him. That was the last time my dad was alert. The next day, he became unresponsive.

I was sitting with him when one of my best friends, Suz, who is also a nurse, stopped by and brought me a coffee.

At that moment, my Uncle Jim, my dad's brother, came over to sit with my dad. He was older than my dad, and the last of four brothers.

I sat outside his room and talked with Suz while Jim went to visit with him. Suddenly, my Uncle Jim cried out, "Lisa, he's not breathing!" I ran into the room I had just walked out of—and my dad was gone. He had waited for me to walk away and for my uncle to get there.

The arrangements were exactly as we had done for my mom, just ten years earlier. My dad was laid out one day and we buried him the next day. It was Izzy's first experience losing someone so close to her. She stared at my dad in the casket and tears slowly crawled down her cheeks. She loved her grandpa so much. Even now, as she talks about him wistfully, I see the pain in her eyes.

"Grandpa Paul was a one-of-a-kind, Mom," she said.

"Yes, I know Izzy. He truly was. I was so lucky to have him for a father."

I was numb for days after he passed. At one point, Bruce looked over at me and said, "You look so sad, I am so sorry. Let's go lease you a new car." This was so out of character for Bruce. He was not a spender. I smiled at his efforts as I realized the cloud of sadness around me was palpable.

Bruce reached out to my Uncle J.T. and told him I was not doing well since my dad passed. J.T. and I had grown close by this point and talked all the time on the phone. I was surprised that after wanting to know my birth mom all these years, I felt so bonded with her brother. It was not what I would have expected but then what frame of reference did I have? How could I possibly *expect* anything?

About a week after I buried my dad, I was home and heard my doorbell ring. I answered the door to my aunt and uncle standing on my porch. J.T. had driven from North Carolina just to show that he cared and he was there for me. Tears filled my eyes. It was surreal, a dream come true to have a birth uncle care so much for me that he actually drove through five states to be with me during one of the saddest times of my life. We spent the weekend talking, laughing, and remembering my dad.

The bond between J.T. and I continued on for years to come until he, too, passed away. Izzy and I traveled to California to visit J.T. and Wendi in 2020, but this time it was to say goodbye. My uncle had been diagnosed with myelodysplastic syndrome. Izzy and I gave my Aunt Wendi some much needed reprieve while I saw my uncle one last time. It was a bittersweet visit. He had been in my life for about fifteen years, and I was not ready to let him go. My uncle died about a month after that visit.

I went back to work the following week after my dad died, and I remember driving down the road thinking, *I don't want to be sad. I don't want to grieve for my dad.* So, I didn't. I *chose joy,* or so I told myself. It was one of my many coping mechanisms.

I realize now I knew—from as early as I can remember—how to push away pain. In her book *You Don't Look Adopted,* Anne Heffron (2016) wrote about adoptees burying grief as a way to cope with knowing you were given up. It has worked for me so far, so why not? I bottled up the grief and put it away for another day. What I did not realize at the time is by doing that, I was not taking care of me. I was not showing myself the compassion I needed to allow for grief.

chapter 20

Bruce's Grief

Bruce dealt with grief differently. He stared at it straight on and seemed to feel it deeply. Bruce's mom passed away when he was eighteen years old. I know this was an incredibly traumatic time in his life. He had just graduated from high school. He was close to his dad, Orvil, all his life. Orvil had remarried a woman who caused drama and heartache for both Bruce and his dad, simply because of her insecure jealousy. She demanded all of Orvil's attention. And one day, at eighty-seven years old, Orvil had had enough.

Orvil and Anna, Bruce's mom, had a 125-acre farm in the country. Orvil and Bruce loved this farm with the charming little house and weathered barn on the property. Going to the farmhouse on as many weekends as we could was a part of the package when I married Bruce. Orvil had discussed on many occasions that if anything happened to him, he wanted Bruce, not his current wife Linda, to inherit the farm.

Bruce, Izzy and I were on vacation in Florida when Orvil called Bruce and said, "Son, how solid is that prenup?"

"Your prenup? Pretty solid, Dad."

"Ah…well, that's good."

When our Florida trip was over, Orvil picked us up at the airport and never went home again. Orvil decided to leave Linda and declared he was moving in with us. Bruce put a bed together for him in our guest room that night.

Now before you canonize me for sainthood, my friend, understand that I didn't much care for this at first. Orvil was opinionated—he thought if he heard a conversation, he could insert himself in it—and it took several months for Orvil to find his place in our home. But he eventually did and I know his last few years were the most peaceful he had in decades. He, like I, had *chosen joy*.

About two years after Orvil moved in, his routine blood work came back abnormal. He was eventually diagnosed with myelodysplastic syndrome, a form of pre-leukemia, that caused his bone marrow to stop making blood cells. The treatment was to watch and wait. When he progressed to actual leukemia, Orvil made the decision to die.

Bruce was beside himself when Orvil decided it was his time to leave this earth, and expressed feeling helpless. He was not as accustomed to the dying process as I was. I was a nurse, after all, and I had been here before—in the nursing home caring for patients when it was their time, my mom, and then my dad. We called the same hospice who had cared for my dad.

Izzy was seventeen years old at the time and by this time had decided to become a nurse. She told me she wanted to go to nursing school a few years before, when she was in tenth grade. One day, while I was picking her up from school, she bounced in the car and said, "Mom, I decided what I want to do."

In her first year of high school, Izzy had made friends with some girls who turned out to be bullies. I had been through bullying in school, but these girls were a special kind of mean. One in particular was able to turn Izzy's whole friend group against her. There was nothing harder than sitting back watching the mean girls attack my daughter. To try to buffer what she was experiencing, I encouraged her to recognize what I had learned; the world is so much bigger than some small girls who have to be mean to others in order to feel good about themselves. As a way to see how big the world is, we started planning for college and visiting schools early. Her career choice was still undecided until she announced to me that day the news that melted my heart.

"I want to be a nurse! Remember when Aunt Jill's dad, Mr. Dillaha, was sick in the hospital? I think I knew then."

My best friend Jill's dad was in the hospital when Izzy was fifteen. He was recovering from surgery for oral cancer. He had a tube in his nose that went into his esophagus to feed him as he recovered. The tape securing the tube had come undone and Izzy reached up and secured it with more tape to his cheek. As we were leaving the hospital that day, Izzy looked at me and said, "It felt really good to help Mr. Dillaha."

At that moment, I had to hold myself back from exclaiming, "You should be a nurse!" I wanted Izzy to come to this decision on her own, and now she had.

I tried to act nonchalant and calm when she told me this news, but inside I was bursting. The thought that my little girl would follow in my footsteps filled my heart. Izzy set her sights on and was accepted into the University of Detroit Mercy School of Nursing. I imagine the pride I felt was similar to how my parents felt when they were in these shoes. My goal growing up had always been to make them proud. I could only hope they felt half as proud of me as I felt of Izzy.

When Orvil appeared to become weaker, Izzy seemed compelled to step in and help the same way she had helped Mr. Dillaha and her Grandpa Paul. Orvil could no longer make it up the stairs and we did not have a lower level bedroom. He did not want to move his bed into our living room, so Izzy called a company to set up a stair lift chair in our home. Orvil was so thankful. He rode that chair upstairs until the day before he died.

As he became closer to dying, I once again opened up a hospice box of medications, and gave him some liquid morphine under his tongue to calm him down and help his breathlessness. Bruce was so afraid I would give him too much and hasten the process. It was painful for Bruce to watch his strong, capable father become so weak and breathless. Bruce's face showed the worry and the pain. His jaw was clenched, his brow furrowed. He snapped at me each time I gave him a dose of morphine, "No, don't give him more, you just gave it."

I would reassure him I knew what I was doing and I was helping him. I turned off the daughter-in-law switch and was the nurse again.

On the day he died, Orvil was sitting up, trying to catch his breath. He said to me, "I'm having a hard time dying."

"I know Orvil," I said softly as I stroked his back. I gave him another dose of morphine and Bruce walked away.

"I can't stay here and watch," he said as he turned away, shoulders hunched, stifling a sob. "I'll be downstairs."

I could feel Bruce's pain as I watched him walk away. I knew he was depending on me to help his dad. The only thing that held me together in these moments was going on nurse-autopilot, knowing I was doing the most humane thing I could. I was easing Orvil's symptoms and helping him have a good death. I felt awful for Bruce. Orvil living with us had been a hard adjustment for me, but I was so glad he was with us, especially now. Caring for my parents had felt natural. It was how I was raised and it was a part of who I was. Now caring for Orvil felt natural too—like breathing.

I helped Orvil lay down and on his side. I sat with him as he drew his last breaths. And then it hit me: another parent was gone.

After I was sure he was gone, I went downstairs to tell Bruce and watched my husband crumble. I called the hospice company and the funeral home. Tears streamed down my face as they carried this once strong, stubborn, capable man away. Now, he looked so small and frail.

Orvil's ex-wife, Linda, came to the funeral home and flung herself over the casket sobbing. Bruce and I stood by quietly watching. Bruce eventually laid his hand on her back and said "It's okay, Linda, he knew you loved him." This was so impressive to me and I was glad Izzy was standing there watching her dad take the high road and attempt to comfort Linda even after how awful she treated him.

Linda and Bruce had a tenuous relationship over the years. When Linda and Orvil first married, Bruce shared with me that she was initially kind. But as the years went by, just before I came into Bruce's life, Linda's attitude toward Bruce changed. Orvil and Bruce were close. They often went to the gym together, the family farmhouse, and genuinely enjoyed each other's company. Linda started telling Orvil she did not like that they spent so much time together. It became clear that she did not like Bruce, and she did not hide it.

By the time I came into the picture, there was tension whenever we were all together. We never knew if Linda was going to be nice or nasty. I tried to win her over in the past, especially when she or Orvil had a health concern.

Years before, I had stopped by one afternoon to check on Orvil. He had a cough that was not going away, and Bruce was worried about him. I walked in their home, stethoscope in hand and listened to his chest as he took deep breaths.

Orvil smiled at me, despite not feeling well and said, "Thank you Lisa, I appreciate you checking on me."

"Of course, Orvil." I smiled, then turned to Linda. "I am worried about him, Linda. He has quite a bit of congestion. I think he needs a chest x-ray."

Linda watched the exchange between us and added, "Well, the doctor said he doesn't need one."

"Ok Linda, but if he isn't better by tomorrow, you should probably take him back to get checked."

"Well you're not a real doctor, what do you know?" she said with a sneer on her face.

I was not that shocked. We had become accustomed to her nasty side. I stood up, looked down at Orvil and said, "Orvil, let me know if you need anything."

Orvil looked embarrassed. "Thank you Lisa, I will let you guys know."

During Linda's exaggerated display of grief, sobbing with her arms across Orvil's casket, I held my tongue. I was sure she had enough of her own demons without anyone else adding to the mix. Izzy was watching and I thought about how Bruce had just demonstrated how to treat people even if they treat you poorly. Izzy had also just watched us care for Orvil, much like how we had cared for my dad. I was hoping she was absorbing what it meant to be family and take care of each other.

In the months that passed after, I was also impressed by how well Bruce grieved his dad. He was visibly sad and was not afraid to show it. He eventually turned the corner and now talks about how much he misses Orvil in a wistful, yet fulfilled way.

I envied how he processed his dad's death. Did I not know how to grieve or was I just so damn scared that if I let down my guard and let the pain in, it would never stop? Or was it because I was striving so hard to show how grateful I was, striving so hard to be perfect, that I didn't have space to grieve? When did I learn how to shut out the sadness?

Maybe it was the day I heard, "You are adopted. Your mother was raped, but she knew the guy."

part two
Found

Walking Away

Upside down went my world
I was pulled under the spell
And in the beginning
There was no way to tell
Looking into your eyes
Whose genes I carry
I should have been cautious
It should have been scary
But nothing prepared me
And my love was true
I was busy being grateful
Too busy with you
From the way we both smile
To our silver strands of hair
I believed that you loved me
And would always be there
No one mentioned the pain
It seared through my soul
As you walked away
And forgot I was yours

chapter 21

Spitting in Tubes

The question of whether or not I was conceived in rape is one that hovered over me. I had received some answers, but they were stories filled with truths, half truths, and the parts in between.

My Aunts Janice and Jeannie both recalled one night while Judi was home, pregnant, and not yet banished to the home for unwed mothers. The phone rang; Jeannie answered and the voice on the other side asked for Judi, saying, "I think I am the father of her baby."

The rest gets fuzzy. Jeannie's version is she asked who he was and he hung up the phone. At one time the story included more colorful details in which she screamed, "You bastard!" and then he hung up. Peppered in this story is Jeannie's recount of what happened the night Judi came home late after being out with friends in June 1967. Jeannie recalled that after being out, Judi arrived home during the night. She had been drinking.

According to Jeannie, Judi was crying quietly, sitting on the side of the bed. Her nylons were torn in shreds and and she told Jeannie she had been raped. Jeannie was thirteen at the time. Later, when Sally learned Judi was pregnant, she told her if she could name the father, she could keep the baby.

Judi sobbed and said "I swear I don't know his name."

Whether she ever knew his name or not, Judi took to the grave any accurate information about who my birth father was.

After all these years, I had accepted there would never be any way to know who he was.

Or so I had thought.

For Christmas 2018, Izzy, who was eighteen, bought Bruce and I, along with herself, Ancestry DNA kits. She thought it would be fun to find out what our ethnicity was. Me, being her birth mom and adopted, left her not knowing part of her heritage. She was curious to know more than just Bruce's ethnicity and that I was Polish and English. I was oblivious at this time to what DNA testing could potentially reveal. I had no expectations; and the thought of what may be revealed honestly never crossed my mind.

Mid-January 2019, she and Bruce *spit in the tubes*. The results would take three weeks. I have issues producing saliva and suffer from dry mouth, so I was in no hurry to do the DNA test, and was happy to wait for their results. Besides, at this point in my life, I had found my birth family and was settled with the family I had. I was practicing at a cancer center, caring for women with breast, menopause and sexual health concerns including breast cancer survivors. I was writing the revisions for my textbook. Life was full and busy. I did not give spitting or not spitting in a tube a second thought.

I feel you rolling your eyes at me, my friend, and I don't blame you one bit.

One weekend night about three weeks later, Bruce had gone to bed, and Izzy and I were sitting up talking. Izzy was looking at her phone and suddenly said, "Oh, my DNA results are in."

"Cool, what are you?" Was all I asked, barely looking up from my phone.

Izzy proceeded to run through her results, "Oh my gosh I am….." Then with a curious tone, eyebrows furrowed together, she said, "Wait, who's this guy? It says I have a high match with him. I thought we knew all of your birth mom's side?"

Now she had my attention. I looked at her phone and saw the match she was referring to. There was a picture associated with the name, Nicholas Winters; a man with silver hair, finely-chiseled features, and black reading glasses perched on his nose. He had a serious, pensive look on his face, as if deep in thought. The match was high and we immediately looked up what this meant. The number implied close family, likely grandparent, with a statistically high degree of certainty.

"Grandparent? How can this be your grandparent?" I said, staring at her.

Izzy looked at me with wide eyes. She then slowly said, "Oh—my—God, *it's your birth father!*"

We then raced up the stairs, busted into my bedroom, jumped on my bed and woke up Bruce. "Wake up!" we said in unison.

Startled and annoyed Bruce said, "What's wrong?"

"I found my birth father, he popped up on Izzy's DNA results."

Bruce was half-awake, and showed as much enthusiasm as someone woken up out of a sound sleep could.

The next day, fully caffeinated, he was much more amazed and inquisitive. "I always told you to look for him! Now what are you going to do?"

Google and Facebook searches turned up a little information about this man who had grown up in Warren and was now seventy-four years old, but he was alive.

Finding this man who had or had not raped my birth mom hung over me for the next several days. I took the obvious next step and mustered up the courage (and saliva) to spit in my tube. Within ten days, I had my results. It seemed even more real, at that point. The match with Nicholas Winters showed up for me, too, and the likelihood was high that he was a parent—there was a statistically high degree of certainty.

A few months later, I paid for a thorough background search on Nicholas Winters. My search resulted in more information; he was married to Karen Winters and he had a son, Scott. That meant I had a half-brother! Scott was more than *icing on the cake.* He was my *silver lining.*

Nicholas Winters had been born in Warren in 1945. He had worked for the government services administration and was a freelance pilot. Listed in his occupations was "J.W. Nicholas Law Firm" so I assumed he was an attorney. There were no criminal records. Nothing was in the background report that said *rapist.* He now lived in Missouri, 640 miles away.

He had a wife, a son, and a family. My brother was only fifteen months younger than me. I sat on this information and let it sink in. Whatever the circumstances, I thought to myself, I was not going to disrupt someone's life just to satisfy my need to know if he did or did not rape my birth mom. I was not going to pop up in someone's life and say, "*hey, you're my dad!*" I knew with certainty that I could not interfere with someone's life, or marriage.

My brother was another story. All my life, I had wanted a sibling. He may want to know I exist. *Would he want me in his life?* This felt less risky—but how do I contact my brother without contacting my birth father?

Months went by as I wondered if my birth father saw the match on his end of AncestryDNA. Was he getting notifications that said "You have a new match on Ancestry?"

If so, was he clicking on it to find that it said, "You have a parent/child match with a statistically high degree of certainty?"

Eventually, having been given up already, I began to assume he saw it and was ignoring it.

If so, I told myself, *then why should I care at all?*

It had been ten months since I had spit in the tube and run the background check. I had gone from, "I can't believe he doesn't see the notification he has a match and does not contact me" to "I don't want him to contact me." On my end, I had stayed silent, deciding it was not my place to upend his life.

On December 14th, 2019, I sat wrapped in a blanket on my plush, fuchsia couch sipping on coffee staring at the snow falling out of my family room window.

Bruce looked over and asked, "What are you thinking about?"

"Family. I wish I had more of it" I answered.

Bruce's response was careful, "You have us: me and Izzy."

"Yes, I know. But you know what I mean. I miss my parents. I miss big Christmas gatherings." My birth aunts now both lived in the Upper Peninsula, and although we visited them, they were thirteen hours from me. My uncle, J.T., was even further in North Carolina. It was not realistic that we see them all over the holidays.

When I was a child, holidays used to include extended family, one side for each holiday. But as time went on, and folks passed away, the gatherings became smaller and smaller—a weaning of family over the years.

As I gazed without blinking at the snow, I felt nostalgic and sad, but hopeful. At that time, hope meant something very different to me. Hope was innocence. Hope was full of promise. Hope meant that the unknown was sometimes safer than the known.

I counsel women everyday about the decision to have genetic testing for cancer. I give women permission to consider this decision carefully. I tell them, "Once you know, you can't unknow." At which time, some patients will look at me as if a lightbulb just went on in their head. Some will continue to pursue genetic testing, wanting to know everything, and some will pause and step away, understanding what it means to not be able to *unknow*.

The permission to "not know" is powerful and something many adoptees may agree should be a choice. Adoptees who search, or are found, should make this choice as if there was a box that they could check: "Check here for I'm going for it and understand I can't go back" or "Check here for never mind, I'm good." Being found is different from searching, as I had done years before. When you are found, there is no box to check.

This particular snowy Saturday, Bruce and I had a date night away planned. We were going to dinner and a hotel for the night, a cozy retreat in the midst of the busyness of Christmas. However, this morning came with a surprise, and that surprise arrived without a box to check and without a choice to make. Because once the unattainable answer to a mystery is placed in front of you, no matter what the consequences of knowing the answer may be, how do you not turn the page?

Minutes after Bruce had asked me what I was thinking about, I checked my phone and saw it across the screen:

You have an Ancestry DNA message from Nikwinters.

Time stopped. My whole life of not knowing or having the choice to know, including coming so close only to learn that Judi had died years ago, came down to this moment.

It would seem I had a choice to ignore this message. But did I really? Did I really have a choice to ignore an actual birth parent reaching out to me?

Some may argue I did. Some may understand I did not.

Regardless, for the second time in my life, I looked down the rabbit hole and jumped in.

chapter 22

Perhaps We'll Be Friends

B ruce, who had been a cheerleader when it came to my pursuit of birth family, was almost as dumbfounded as me. "What does the message say?" He asked, eyes wide.

I read the message aloud:

"Hello, It appears we have a close parent/child relationship on Ancestry DNA. Please contact me. If I do not hear from you, I will understand. Nicholas Winters."

Beneath his name was his email and a phone number. I stared at the message. I, then, woke up Izzy.

"No way!" She said, "What are you gonna say?"

I was not sure what to do. The past eight months were a blur behind me. But then, I felt the shift happen. I sent an email to him.

"Hello, yes, it appears you are my birth father. I was adopted. My birth mother, Judi, died when she was twenty-six. I was given up at birth. Yes, I would like to talk to you, Lisa."

His response was quick, a matter of minutes. And, as I sat in my bathrobe trying to get ready for our big date night amidst the chaos of the morning, I read my birth father's first email back to me.

"Hello, I wrote about you in my first novel. My pen name is J. W. Nicholas. How did Judi die? I saw your picture and I knew you were mine; you have an eccentric look about you. When can we speak? Now is a good time, or later today. Nick."

The book he had written three years ago was a novel about a defense attorney named Nicholas whose daughter, that he never knew about, finds him. Once again my friend, more crazy stuff you can't make up. In the book, Nicholas's daughter does a background check and he is alerted that someone has looked into his background. Nicholas meets his daughter, who by the way, has a daughter. That crazy *fiction* was happening right now, in real life.

My birth father had dedicated this book to "all the unclaimed daughters," three years prior to meeting me. At the time when I first read the dedication, it seemed surreal. Did he know about me? Did he know he had a daughter out there? My Aunt Jeannie remembered someone calling the house claiming to be the father of Judi's baby. But even that does not answer whether or not he knew he had a daughter.

I was entranced and felt I had been touched by an angel. As an adoptee in a closed adoption, you never believe you will ever know the name of your birth parent, let alone connect with one.

Within minutes of the very first email, I felt the "*I feel seen*" spell take hold of me. It was in his words and the way he wrote them. I was accustomed to emails that were brief, to the point, and intentional, but his emails told a story—something I learned as time went on that my birth father was a master at.

My response was brief;

"I can't speak today. I am going away for the night. Maybe tomorrow. Judi died of leukemia. Do you know who she was? What do you mean by eccentric? Lisa."

Minutes later, another email.

"Eccentric is special, different; not like everyone else. You stand out, I can see it. I mean no offense. I am eccentric. I see the silver in your hair and I see my own. I barely remember Judi I am afraid. Yes, tomorrow is good. You can call anytime. Please tell me when. Nick."

Casually telling me in one sentence that he "barely remembered Judi" was not really as casual as he made it seem. It was as if she were an afterthought. She was not an afterthought. The lingering *"your birth mom was raped but she knew the guy"* echoed in the back of my mind, as if a warning. I pushed away this flickering warning aside and chose to focus on what was in front of me; my birth father paying attention to me.

Bruce never mentioned the rape story during this time. I later asked him if he was concerned given what I had been told. He thoughtfully replied, "No, I guess I was being selfish. I had lost my father and I missed him. I was just excited to have a new father-in-law in my life. I guess I should have thought about it, but I gave Nick the benefit of the doubt."

Eventually, Bruce and I made it out of the house and began our date-night trip, but the whole night was consumed by my birth father reaching out to me and the exchanges between us. Emails continued throughout the night. Each time he responded, Bruce would ask with a look of wonder and smile, "What did he say?"

I would read each exchange, back and forth to him. Finally, in one of the last emails of the night, my birth father wrote to me something that sent chills through me and brought Bruce to tears:

"Perhaps we'll be friends."

The idea that we would ever know each other let alone become friends was so foreign to me as an adoptee. I was never supposed to know who he was. Even unsealed records did not offer any clues to who my birth father was. It was not until the technology of the times that what was unknown, would become known.

In the back of my mind I remembered; this man had called my birth mother's house and hung up over fifty years ago and along with this came the questions: Did he or didn't he rape my birth mother? How would I feel if I actually talked to him on the phone and had the chance to ask him? Would I have the courage to ask?

chapter 23

The Phone Call

I woke up the next day afraid it had all been a dream. My head was swimming. I could not keep my thoughts together. *Had my birth father actually reached out to me? Does he actually want to talk to me?* I suddenly felt, at fifty-one years old, as giddy as a little girl—but this excitement was quickly followed by, *will he want to get to know me? Will I be good enough for him?*

And in the distance, begging to be asked: *Did he rape my birth mom?*

Despite being a self-proclaimed over-achiever, I still struggle with feelings of insecurity. Compounded with my own insecurity is the notion that I was in contact with a birth parent who I inherently already felt abandoned by. Adoptees, even those raised in healthy, loving environments, may struggle with insecurities about themselves and in relationships. The literature on the subject has noted several themes related to adoptees' insecurities that include adoptees feeling "set up to fail," "fear of rejection," and "fear of abandonment" (Feeney, 2005, p. 46; Verrier, 1993). It has been suggested that adoptees' insecurities and fears of rejection are more pronounced, even if it is only a perceived fear, during times of stress (Feeny, 2004). Years later, I am beginning to understand my own natural fears of rejection. But at the moment, I was in the midst of personal contact with my birth father and my fears of rejection, despite my initial euphoria, were growing.

We set up the phone call for 2:00 PM on a Sunday afternoon. Izzy wanted to be in the room, but Bruce intervened. "No Izzy," he told her.

I added, "This is too private for now. I promise I will see how it goes and maybe you can say hi."

My nineteen-year-old daughter was a bit sullen, but agreed—the first of many hard lessons she would learn on this journey. I am sure it was a hard reality.

I had decided that I would call him Nicholas. It was what he had called himself in his first message to me. It was formal enough to put a boundary in place for me. I felt, at that time, that he could not ever be *dad* or *daddy*.

The hour finally came and I called the number he had given me. There was a certain intonation to his voice that struck me as familiar, or impactful. Maybe even at this early stage, Nicholas had a certain power over me.

We engaged in some meaningless chatter and I honestly don't remember how I got through the first few minutes. The warmth I felt through the phone the first time I talked to my aunts and my uncle was not there. Instead, Nicholas was careful, measured, inquisitive. He asked more about Judi. I filled him in on what I had learned about my birth mom years before. He confessed again that he could not really remember her. This bothered me. In hindsight, I wish I would have held him somehow more accountable to remember her. I chose to once again push his nonchalant *lack of memory of her* aside, letting him off the hook too easily.

Throughout the beginning of the call, I felt uneasy—but also desperate for him to *like* and *want* me. My fear of rejection was real, even early on. And I was shaking inside. I was scared, and I wondered how I sounded to him. I was holding my breath too much and had to remind myself to breathe.

There was one question I had to ask more than anything, and about twenty minutes into the call, I could not hold off any longer.

"I have something I have to ask you, and you are not going to like it."

I should have been more forthright in my question, but nonetheless, the little girl in me wanted him to *like* me, *accept* me, and above all, *not give* me up (again).

His response was an exaggerated and audible deep, sucking breath I could easily hear through the phone. "Ok, go ahead, ask," he said in that careful, measured tone.

My question was really more of a statement:

"My birth mother said she was raped but she knew the guy."

There, I said it. Years after my birth mom had died, years after she came home that night and told my Aunt Jeannie she was raped as she pulled off her torn nylons, I had finally been able to go straight to the source. Judi's claim could finally be said out loud to her accused.

His answer was quick, adamant, and most of all, exactly what an adoptee who had just connected with her birth father was *not* prepared to hear. "No!" he said, defiance in his voice. "Absolutely not! There was no penetration!"

What struck me most was talking to a stranger, a male stranger, my actual birth father, and hearing words like "no penetration." It turned my stomach. I was not prepared for this.

He then added that they were in the backseat of a car. He had not forced himself on her but rather had engaged in "heavy petting." It was then, he told me that he had begun to remember her more, but her face *escaped* him. He remembered that they had another date and she had told him she was pregnant and had been to the doctor and "the hymen was intact." There was so much detail in his description of the few times they had been together. Nicholas related that in that moment when Judi told him she was pregnant his flippant reply was, "Well now at least we don't need to use protection."

I came to be, that night, in the backseat of a car. As he spoke, Nicholas continued to weave the story with more details, adding to the mystique of the *miracle* of my existence.

He continually insisted there was no penetration, but being a nurse, I knew this was nearly impossible. "Heavy petting" was not going to result in a sperm making contact with an egg inside a uterus. But I was so determined to connect with this man that I told myself, it could, hypothetically, happen.

I also learned that Nicholas knew about me for 30 minutes before he sent the first message to me through AncestryDNA. *Thirty minutes.* I had sat on the information about him for eight months. It struck me that I had the insight to understand that attempting to contact him could potentially turn his world upside down. I knew he had a wife and a son. Instead, I sat back and considered how impactful hearing from a daughter, he likely did not know, would be. Yet his reaction to learning about me was to immediately contact me with no consideration for how hearing from my birth father would affect me. I was conflicted by this—a part of me wanted him to reach out, proclaim how happy he was to know I existed, yet another part of me was aware of his lack of consideration for me and how this would impact my life.

When he saw the alert from AncestryDNA, he called his wife Karen to check it out. Nicholas told me repeatedly, "Karen just stared at the computer with a blank look on her face." He appeared annoyed by the fact that she had so little to say.

He told me about her reaction in this way over and over—it seemed to set the tone early on that Karen was less enthusiastic than Nicholas to learn he had a daughter.

Regardless, the fact that he had a family comforted me at the time. I knew how important my family is to me. Even in those months of never hearing from him, I did not want him to be alone. I wanted him to have a life with a family he loved. Despite not knowing if he had raped my birth mother.

After about an hour and a half, which felt like five minutes, I felt him ending the conversation. I knew Izzy had wanted to be a part of the moment I talked to my birth father for the first time. "Wait," I said, "Someone wants to say hi to you." I went to the room Izzy and Bruce were in, and put Nicholas on speaker. "Say hi to your grandfather" I said smiling and handed Izzy the phone.

"Um hi, I guess that's what I am." His voice was tentative and I thought I could pick up a hint of irritation.

"Hi, it's so nice to meet you!" Izzy's voice was warm, excited, and she started chatting away with him. She added she was so happy to have more family and especially another grandfather as she had lost both of her grandfathers and had never known her grandmothers. Izzy was practically giddy while she was on the phone with him, but their exchange was very brief. And after a few minutes he asked to talk to me.

I took him off speaker and when I was back on the phone he said in a voice laced with a subtle sharpness, "Don't ever put me on speaker again, okay?"

Nicholas may have been trying to hide his irritation but I picked up on it, and it set off an uneasiness in me. I was surprised that someone who learned he had a granddaughter would even care that he was on speaker. I simply responded, "Ok, I won't."

It was a red flag that I ignored. I should have been more guarded, more careful. I should have held back and taken my time to get to know him over time. But I was swimming in the euphoria of his attention and feared his rejection all at once.

I had just met and talked to the man who was partially responsible for my existence. I had just met someone whose true identity had almost completely disappeared when Judi died four decades ago. I had just talked to the only living person who contributed to half of my DNA. I finally had the chance to confront the man behind the rumors that Judi had been raped.

For her, I needed to know the truth—and I wasn't sure I knew the truth, yet. For me, growing up *chosen*, a mistake, a possible result of violence, there was no going back to not knowing. There was no careful reflection, no proceeding with caution, no careful guarding. I was all in. And I crawled closer to the spider in the center of the web.

chapter 24

Emails and Other Strands of the Web

O ver the next weeks following that first phone call, my life became consumed with any form of communication with Nicholas. I accepted his shaky explanation of my beginning, as if God had proclaimed that I was indeed a *miracle,* and therefore not a mistake. I know what you are thinking, my friend, but stay with me as I pull you into the complex connection. There were phone calls scattered here and there for the first month. But the invisible threads that began to weave between us were really spun through email.

Prior to meeting Nicholas, emails I exchanged with anyone consisted of terse, brief statements with the intent to convey factual information. A few lines was all I ever wrote to communicate messages in cyberspace. But now I was hungry for any morsel of information that would paint a fuller picture of this man who had just injected himself into my life.

At first, I asked Nicholas a myriad of straightforward questions.

"What are you like when you get angry?"

"I have a temper, but then I get over it quickly."

"What was your relationship with your parents like?"

"I was very close to my mother. We were best friends. My father was strict, more the disciplinarian,"

"Where did you go to school? What college did you go to?"

"I went to Warren High School, then the Marines. My father was in the Air Force, a pilot. I wanted him to be proud of me, so I joined the Marines. He died in my second year of being enlisted so I had a hardship discharge and came home to help my mom." He then added, "My father was hard on me, he made fun of how I ran. He told me I ran like a girl. He was always strict with me, sometimes physical."

"That sounds hard,"

"It was. But I always knew he loved me. My father often told me a biblical story when God asked Moses to kill his son to prove his loyalty. He would look me in the eyes and say to me: Son, I would look God in the eyes and say no! I will not kill my son!"

When I read this, I felt empathy for him. He seemed to understand the importance of family, through the good times and the bad. I sensed his grief for his father, as well as their difficult relationship. When I pushed Nicholas on his relationship with his father, he seemed to push the topic away. So I shifted my questions.

"What happened after your dad died? What did you do for work?"

"After I came home to help my mom, I went to cosmetology school. It was funded through the government because of my service in the Marines. I became a hairdresser. Later, after my mom died, I became involved with Scott's mom, Carol, and we moved to Chicago."

"Whoa, wait a minute! How did your mom die? She must have been young!"

"She was coming home from her honeymoon after marrying some jackass I hated. He was not good enough for her. He didn't treat her right. She told me right before she married him Nicky, I am sorry to leave you. And I know you don't like him, but I need to do this to take care of us. They were driving home and veered off the road into an embankment. The jackass claimed my mom was driving. But he had the imprint of the steering wheel on his chest. I know that son of a bitch killed her! She was my best friend."

"Oh my God, that's awful! I am so sorry. I lost my mom young too. I was thirty-two. She was only sixty-four. It is so hard to lose your mom."

Later, in another email, I shifted the subject again. *"What happened with Scott's mom, why didn't you get married?"*

"I loved her. I wanted to marry her, but she had been married and did not want to marry. She was ten years older than me. We were together fourteen years, off and on. But then we grew apart and I left for the last time."

"So how did you end up married to Karen, what happened in between?"

"I preferred the company of older women. I was with one woman, Zena, for ten years. She was intellectually stimulating, but I could never marry her, that spark just wasn't there. There was another woman, Gretchen, for about five years. She was a psychologist. She was adventurous and daring, but I did not like her son. And I knew I was not interested in her anymore. One day, I remember standing on the steps of my apartment in Philadelphia, telling her it was over. She crumbled into my arms right there on the steps, sobbing. I watched as a woman walked by and gave me a look of utter disdain. I will never forget that. There have been so many women in my life; but no one I felt I could be with forever. And I always seem to leave them and hurt them."

Nicholas had a tendency to tell me things that were hard to process. Like the "no penetration" comment.

Another few emails later, I pushed for more work history. His background check had said something about working for the government and for a law firm. I had commented on this earlier as we were talking about how long I had gone to college to earn a doctorate.

"You are an attorney so you understand how long I had to go to school to earn a doctorate."

Nicholas simply went with it, agreeing.

Then a few emails later, I asked:

"How did you end up practicing law? Where did you go to law school?"

"I later took some college classes just for the sake of learning. I was fascinated with art and history. Then I took a position working for the government, I took courses in contract law. That's how I ended up working with contracts for the government."

This was not sitting with me. He didn't actually go to law school—that was a lie of omission. It reminded me of my ex-husband, Jim, pretending to be a mechanical engineer, but I was caught up in the excitement and once again chose to ignore something right in front of me.

Nicholas added more to his account of his work history and managed to do it in a way to create the image of a carefree, independent, worldly man.

"I quit my job two summers in a row to ride my motorcycle across North America. The government hired me back each time and I would go back to work either in New York or Philadelphia. Picture a man, with silver hair, brightly colored clothing, riding his bicycle through the city streets, carrying an umbrella when it is raining, with a little chihuahua in the basket of the bike. That's your father. I am different."

This struck me. I had always felt *different*. I had attributed it to being adopted and an only child; but also because of my love of all things mystical and unique, like unicorns. Reading about this man who too feels he is *different* was intoxicating. And the notion of whether or not he raped my birth mom was pushed further to the back of my mind. I was full of the dopamine rush of attention.

A few emails later, I continued my questions.

"Ok, but how did you end up in Missouri?"

"I moved for a promotion. I regret it, and I have ever since. I don't belong here. I am urban. I belong in the city, with all the art and the culture. I know I will not stay here forever. I call it Misery, not Missouri."

"So when did you get married, and how did you and Karen meet?"

"It was a dating service I joined as soon as I moved to Missouri. Karen seemed nice. So we went on a few dates, I decided she was not for me, and I was about to break it off with her. When she was diagnosed with a tumor in her abdomen that had to be removed. She told me this just as I was about to break up with her. I decided I could not leave her. I would stay with her while she recuperated then break up. After her surgery, we were walking down the hallway and I was helping her. She was not yet steady on her feet. She looked at me and said, we look like a married couple. And I said, well maybe we should get married. That was it. Twenty years ago. I have regretted it often. I tried to get out of it. Two weeks before the wedding I told her, I can't do this, I can't marry you. It's not right. She looked at me and said, but I have family coming. It's all arranged. You can't back out now. So I backed down and we were married. She's a nice person. But we have nothing in common.

She does not understand me. No one ever does. I am a loner, yet I love to be around people. I love to watch them. Once I talk to them, they often bore me and I make up stories about them in my head. I pretend to listen, nodding here and there. They never know I am a million miles away in my own world."

I was fascinated with the way my birth father answered questions in stories. It was so interesting the way he could create an image and bring me right there into the picture. I gobbled up the emails like someone who had been starved for information for decades. At the same time, I started to question if I would be what he perceived as *boring*. Would he tune me out too and move on? I found myself hoping I would be interesting to him.

We emailed each other constantly, sometimes up to four or five emails a day, back and forth. Seeing his email pop up in my inbox sent anticipation and excitement through me. *This is my actual birth father*, I would think. And he was attentive—he would answer my emails, fill in the blanks, and do it in such a way that left me wanting more information. He was so attentive, in fact, that the attention was quickly becoming addicting. My days were measured by how often I would hear from him. I found myself purposely telling him little secrets or tidbits about myself I did not usually talk about. Some things were mundane, such as how I liked my coffee. Others were deeply personal, like how I cheated on my first love Bobby even though I felt he was my soulmate at the time. Nicholas would respond,

"I understand, my girl, we are the same."

Being "the same as someone" when you are carrying 50 percent of their DNA is something you cannot wrap your head around when you are adopted. People used to comment that I looked like my father (Paul) and I would feel I had to quickly explain, "Oh, I am adopted."

They would then look at me and say, "Wow, that's such a coincidence." It fell flat on me because the sensation of looking at someone and truly seeing myself reflected back never happened until I had my daughter. Now, it was happening again.

As the email frequency intensified, it became obvious a relationship was forming. The awkwardness of the first phone call was fading at warp speed. And something else was happening. Nicholas was waking up someone inside me who felt *seen* for the first time. I understood later that this person he was waking up inside me was the little girl, Michelle. And Michelle had never felt seen before. He expressed over and over "We are blood. You are my blood daughter" as if solidifying the magic that had happened.

My emails to him started to slowly change too. Instead of a few basic sentences, I began mirroring him. I started to tell him stories too. It became a challenge for me, and later I realized I craved his responses to my newly descriptive, storytelling emails. Each email I wrote had a beginning, a middle and an end. I had never considered myself creative, but it was as if Nicholas was drawing this out of me. The game was to write a compelling, impactful story, then anxiously await his likewise response. Within his responses were more affirmations that he, too, wanted to know more about me. I was truthful with him, but I also felt that familiar tendency of showing my gratitude and striving to be perfect. I wanted to portray that I was the *perfect, long-lost daughter* that he had always wanted.

As if on cue, he began telling me over and over, "I always wanted a daughter. I would dance around and tell Karen, if I had a daughter, and she wanted a car, I would say what kind, a Mercedes? If she wanted a planet of her own, which one? Pluto? Mars?" Each time he said something like this, I would sit transfixed, marveling at how lucky I was that he wanted me. My birth father wished for me and he wanted me.

Sometimes the emails contained actual stories he wrote. He was a gifted writer, that was clear. One story he sent in the first few weeks after he contacted me was called *The Silver Dollar*. Nicholas spun a story about how he had gone in the ocean with a brand new silver dollar tucked in a hidden pocket in his bathing suit. He dove down into the deep blue water and found a hidden spot to hide the silver dollar, certain it would never resurface. He returned to the catamaran after his dive and toasted to his secret silver dollar that was now part of the endless, deep, blue ocean. Then, years later, a woman with silver strands in her hair, wearing a white gown, walked up to him—in the palm of her hand was the silver dollar he had buried long ago. I was lost, he buried me, and now, there was no hiding it; I was found and standing before him.

I printed that story off and carried it around in my pocket so I could take it out and read it whenever I wanted. Each time I read this story I could feel the warm rush of being wished for and wanted.

Through emails and some phone calls, it was evident Nicholas was impressed with my accolades. He would go on and on about the fact that I had published a book, that I had earned a Doctorate and won various awards. He also told me I looked exactly like his mother and her side of the family—more word candy for me to gobble up. Some emails included pictures of himself and his mom. I did not see the same resemblance with his mom that he did. But I definitely saw it between him and I. We had the same stature, cheek bones, smile, and set of our eyes. I was certainly a shiny new toy in his life, but I wanted him to see me for who I was inside, the person I am, not just my accolades or my appearance. In time, I told myself, he will see my spirit, my heart. For the moment, I was just grateful he wanted me in his life.

People close to me saw the shift. Nicholas was all I talked about. Bruce was so understanding and was "team Nick" as he called it. Izzy, however, was struggling with my new obsession. For the first time in her young life, she found herself sharing my attention with someone.

Izzy was in her second year of nursing school, and about to start her clinical rotations. She wanted to tell me all about her placement and her anxieties but at the time, I was spacey and distant, only wanting to talk about Nicholas. She called me out one day and as we were driving down the road and said, "You know, I am starting my clinical next week. There are other things going on!"

I lost it. I pulled over immediately and said, "You have no idea how important this is! This is the first time in my life I have met someone this closely related to me. You have no idea what this means to me, and you never will. Now, you need to realize that I have a life outside of you!"

Izzy looked at me and seemed a bit stunned. Her eyes were wide and filled with tears.

"I'm sorry Mom, I just miss you. You seem so far away lately."

She was used to my full attention 24/7. I had been somewhere between a *cool mom* and a *helicopter mom* all her young life. Now for the first time, her best friend, her champion and her mom, was off in Nick-Space and orbiting further away. Now, I feel bad that I was so harsh with her—but in the moment, I felt justified.

As our communication continued at a fevered pace, Nicholas shared more about my brother Scott's mother, Carol. Carol was English and her family was nobility. She was ten years older than Nicholas and left her family to be with him. His relationship with my brother, Scott, was rocky while Scott was a teenager, especially when Carol and Nicholas separated. Nicholas became only a part-time dad. He had had a tenuous relationship with Scott's mother, but talked about her fondly and seemed to have regrets about how he had treated her. She passed away several years ago.

Along with emails, phone calls became more frequent. The first time I asked him if we could talk again was a few days after we first spoke on the phone—and dozens of emails later. He agreed and I sat on my bedroom floor like a teenager nervously chatting away, filling the space as I hoped I was interesting enough for him to stay on the phone. It was this phone call that I asked him, "Do you curse?" and held my breath hoping he was not going to be disappointed with my more than colorful language.

"Fuck yes I curse!" he responded with a laugh. This, of course, sent me into a fit of giggling. He was becoming a confidant, a best friend. And to add to the amazement, my actual birth father.

One night during these formative weeks as this delicate, intense relationship was budding, I heard my phone chirp with a text message. *"Bonne nuit ma Cherie, sleep well"* appeared on my phone. My birth father was wishing me good night in French. It felt paternal and mystical all at the same time, the epitome of being seen and feeling like I was the most special daughter in the whole world. It took my breath away. It became a regular thing for months, a text I waited for every night. And it made me feel closer and closer to him.

Sometime in December, during the first few phone calls, Nicholas mentioned coming to Michigan to meet me in person. He casually said, "Maybe I could come there in April and we could have coffee." I laughed out loud at the time and boldly said, "April! Why are you waiting so long? I have waited years to know you! You should come sooner!"

"Well, okay, maybe I will," he said and I could hear him smiling through the phone.

One night soon afterward, he shocked me with a text that simply said, *"Goodnight my lovely witch."*

All my life I have been drawn to things we do not understand. I have always loved candles, oils, and herbs. Mystical stories have always been my favorite genre to read or watch. I believe in intuition, and in manifesting what you want in your life. I have always been fascinated with Tarot cards and had psychic readings. I found out from my Aunts Janice and Jeannie that my Grandmother Sally, who by the way was also a practicing Catholic, read tea leaves. In fact, years ago, she had worked as a reader at The Boston Tea Room, a tea shop near my hometown. My mom and I had frequently gone to this exact tea shop and had our tea leaves read. Nicholas knew *none* of this yet—it just had not come up. So imagine the shock when I read that text. How had he picked up on my fascination with all things mystical? It became a term of endearment for a while, and I found myself trusting him quicker and more easily than I had ever trusted anyone.

chapter 25

The First Meeting

O nce I told Nicholas I wanted to meet him sooner than April, he took it from there. I did not push for a date. He emailed one day and said,

"January tenth is speaking to me as the day I will meet my daughter."

And so it was set.

On Christmas Day, despite feeling completely satisfied with gifts from my family, I searched on ebay for the perfect black booties to wear the first time I met my birth father. I settled on a pair of pre-owned Christian Louboutins. The red bottoms would make me feel like I owned the room instead of feeling like the world would quickly close in. I *needed* the booties to feel my power.

As the day for the meeting came closer, Nicholas told me over email that he wanted to meet me *alone* for the first time. He told me he hesitated telling me this as he did not want to scare me. Funny thing is I was thinking exactly the same thing. There needed to be no other distractions the moment I first looked into his eyes. I remembered how awkward at first it had been when

I met my aunts so many years ago, and how I had wished I had one-on-one time with each of them for the first meeting.

I responded to Nicholas that I, too, wanted to meet him alone for the first time and then figure out a time we would share time with my family. He was arriving on a Friday and staying until the following Wednesday. He made arrangements to stay with his cousin, Julie, who lived about a forty-five minute drive from me. I had no idea what the weekend would look like, and hesitated to make plans beyond the first meeting.

Anxiety, excitement, and apprehension are words that fall flat. It was as if my existence was being explained, as if my place in the world would be solidified. I would understand why I was here on this earth, at this time. The ghost of feeling like a mistake, a problem to be taken care of, would be put to rest. A birth parent would claim me as his and I would no longer feel *given up*. I would feel worthy of all that life had given me, all that I had worked my butt off for. It felt as if the earth were shifting and the impossible was possible. After all, I was never supposed to know this man's identity let alone meet him face to face.

One day, a few days before the meeting was set to take place, Nicholas called me while he was driving his dogs around in the car. He called his two Papillons *the girls*. I think they filled a void that he and Karen shared, as she had not had children of her own. Scott came into her life when she was in her fifties, and he was already a grown man. Nicholas had told me she had never had pets in her life; while he always had small dogs or cats he cherished. He told me he brought art, color, and the love of a pet into her life.

It seemed that more frequently, Nicholas was calling me while he was away from the house. One day he said something that at the time stirred so many mixed feelings inside me I had no idea how to feel, or how I should feel. As he was driving around he said, "I am calling while I am driving the girls around. Karen gets upset when I talk to you so much. I think she's jealous."

This immediately felt familiar to me. After all, my husband had lived with this experience for decades. Orvil had remarried after Bruce's mom died several years ago; at first, Linda was accepting, but as the years went on, she became more and more possessive of his time. Bruce and Orvil would go to the family farmhouse and she would rant about Orvil being gone for the weekend. I watched from the sidelines as Linda made life miserable for Orvil over her jealousy.

125

Hearing that Karen was showing signs of a potentially similar pattern terrified me. I did not know how to feel about this. On one hand, it made me feel oddly special, like Cinderella. On the other hand, it felt like an omen of complications that would threaten this delicate, new bond I was forming with Nicholas. After all these years, I wanted to freely be able to carve a place in my life for this man and I wanted to be a part of his. Would Karen resist this until the end, as Linda had? Would Nicholas decide this was too much to deal with and abandon me? *Was* I too much to deal with?

On the day Nicholas arrived in Detroit he called and said, "What if we don't like each other?"

This sent my fears into overdrive. I was already worried he would perceive me as boring. I tried to reassure him—and myself. At this point, there had been dozens of emails and phone calls. We had formed a bond that existed across four states through phone lines and cyberspace. How could we not like each other?

Nicholas had already pointed out countless similarities. Physically, our hair had turned gray early (silver, as he called it), we had the same smiles, and we had the same stature. I colored my hair a deep black over my gray except for around my face—I left those pieces naturally gray, as a symbol of feeling *different*. Intellectually, we were both writers and had an expansive vocabulary. We both loved all things mystical and we found the same things funny. At one point, I took a picture of his author picture on the back of one of his novels and my author picture inside my textbook. I put them side by side and sent the picture to him. I titled the picture "Father-Daughter Authors." With all the similarities, the laughter we had already shared, the awe we both felt in being found, what could go wrong?

The actual day of The Meeting finally came. Nervous energy abound, I did what I do when I need to be in control: I cleaned. I had already fully cleaned and organized the house weeks before. Today I set aside the morning to clean and organize my spice rack. Bruce got a kick out of it, and filmed a video of me climbing up on top of my counter and pulling the spices down and replacing them in the order that made sense to me. In the video, he asked, "What are you doing Lisa?" He smiled as he said it and I could feel his teasing. It was so reassuring at the time.

I carefully selected the outfit I would wear to meet my birth father for the first time. A black sweater dress with white sleeves that my daughter had given me for Christmas topped with my new-to-me Louboutin black booties and a black quilted Chanel bag. Izzy, never one to miss documenting the moment with photos, made me pose for pictures once I was ready to go.

"Don't forget! We want pics as soon as you meet him!" Bruce and Izzy shouted in unison as I darted out the door.

Finally, I took an Uber to Detroit. Nicholas had wanted to meet there as he had grown up in the area. It was a neutral, urban setting. Detroit has gentrified over the last ten years and the city has since become a jewel of eclectic restaurants, shopping, events and waterfront activities—all while maintaining a vibe that resonated with those of us who grew up here. I was excited for him to be a part of such a transition. Nicholas had told me he was urban at heart and preferred being around people yet also felt isolated among them as an observer. The restaurant we would meet at was my choice—Izzy helped me pick it out. I chose it for its setting but more for its name, The Apparatus Room. It had a mystical feel.

I listened to Elton John on my earbuds in the back of the Uber to calm my nerves. I could never go back after today. This was it, the defining moment of how I began. It was as if my whole life I had waited for this. I wanted to bottle up all the feelings and thoughts racing through my mind so I could take them out later and feel what I was feeling again, but I could not; and I knew as I approached the restaurant, I would never have these tingling moments of anticipation, excitement, and fear again. At least not like this.

The Uber pulled up. It was raining; I popped up my umbrella and ran inside. I had envisioned that Nicholas would be sitting alone at a table and I would have a moment to collect myself and confidently, in my time, decide that I would walk up, touch his shoulder for him to turn and look at me for the first time, much like when I met Bruce for the first time. It gave me that much needed sense of control to picture that this is how it would play out.

That was, however, not how it happened. As I walked into the vestibule of the restaurant, I scanned the restaurant for a man that looked like the pictures he had sent and I had found on his background search; slight build, about 5' 6", blue eyes and a head of silver hair. Before I could get myself together, it happened—Nicholas came out of nowhere, and was suddenly in front of me. He stared into my eyes with an open gasp and did not say a word. He continued to stare at me until the awkwardness took me over. I took his hands in mine and said, "It's you."

Nicholas made no move to get out of the vestibule—finally I told him we needed to move out of the way. He asked if we could sit and we moved to a pair of chairs in the lobby. He continued to stare at me. In my entire life, I am certain I have never been stared at like that before. It seemed a bit theatrical (even to me), and I wondered about the authenticity of his reaction. Was he staring so dramatically because he thought he should? Or was he genuinely that enthralled?

Finally I told him,"Ok, you are making me uncomfortable." But in truth, that feeling of being *seen* was drawing me in, now with the power of being in-person.

Something else happened in those first few minutes. Nicholas called me "Michelle." I had told him the story of my birth mother, Judi, naming me Michelle while she was pregnant. According to Nicholas, they both suggested names. Michelle, if I was a girl. I cannot recall if Nicholas came up with this later or how he now suddenly remembered this. But I put this in the same category of the fact there was *no penetration*—something a touch too *out there* to be believable. But accepting his *stories* gave my beginning a *better* story.

I sensed that Nicholas felt a sense of resentment in not being part of my beginning, now that he knew I was real. Perhaps consciously calling me "Michelle" gave him a sense of control over my existence—he was naming me, claiming me. From this point on, Nicholas exclusively called me Michelle. When my Aunt Janice called me Michelle, it felt awkward and foreign; but with Nicholas, it felt intimate and special. This is something I cannot explain. What I do know is that I loved when he called me Michelle. It symbolized that I belonged to him. It made me feel special and it recognized who I was before I was given up. I was someone before my name was changed, and Nicholas saw this. He saw the little girl inside me.

Finally we moved into the restaurant to sit. I told him I really needed a drink. Prior to meeting for the first time, Nicholas told me he took a *vacation from* drinking. He told me it had been about eighteen months since his last drink. He said nothing about having a problem with alcohol, and I had no reason to think that it was an issue. That said, he had told me on his own, "When I meet my daughter, I will drink Champagne with her."

As we sat down, Nicholas looked around awkwardly and said, "I don't like these seats." He had told me prior he was *peculiar* in public. I offered to move and once we did, he settled in and we ordered drinks. Somewhere between moving to new seats and halfway through my glass of wine, I started to relax.

The conversation went from awkward to easy. Nicholas had an infectious laugh, like my mom. His laugh alone made me burst into giggles. At times, we did not even know what we were laughing at. Other times, the conversation would turn serious. Nicholas would look in my eyes in that piercing way that made me feel as if there was no one else in the room.

"You know, I flew my plane right over your house and I did not know you were there. I flew from Missouri home to Michigan from time to time," he said as he stared at me.

"You flew over my house? How often?" I was mesmerized at the thought of my birth father flying over me throughout my life. I also wondered why this had never come up in the many emails and phone calls prior to meeting him.

"Yes, I may have told you, my father was a pilot. He flew in the Air Force. I earned my pilot's license years ago and bought a plane. I just sold it recently."

"Oh my gosh, I love that! I can't imagine what it would be like to fly with you."

"Maybe I will buy another plane. Then I could come and see you whenever I wanted."

I felt the rush of warmth fill me at the thought. I never wanted the night to end.

After a bit, I suggested we go to The Whitney, a nostalgic Detroit place for me. Izzy and I had high tea every Christmas in the beautifully decorated dining rooms. The 1880s home was restored to its earlier glory, and was now a restaurant with a bar on the third floor called The Ghost Bar. I wanted to show it to Nicholas, and suggested we get a drink there.

Making our way up the beautiful, artful, deep mahogany staircase, Nicholas stopped a minute telling me his knees had been replaced and he was stiff at times. We stopped at a bathroom and I waited for him. When he came out, he asked me for hairspray. This was a new one for me, a man wanting hairspray. With my spray, he fixed his head of silver hair that was swept up in a pompadour. Later, as we sat in The Ghost Bar, Nicholas looked over at a painting and told me he wanted to go take a closer look. I said, sure and then he did something else I was not prepared for. He held out his hand and said, "Will you join me?"

As we walked over to look closer, the table of ladies having a girls' night out looked up at us walking toward the picture on the wall that was behind their table. They commented on my hair, which Nicholas took as an invitation to chat. We proceeded to share "our story" and I know we both enjoyed their awe at "how long-lost father and daughter had connected against all odds." This only added to the reverie and fascination of the evening.

As we sat and laughed, Nicholas mentioned Karen randomly, saying, "Karen's idea of excitement is wearing beige." I looked at him shocked. I was conflicted because although it was funny, it was also catty. I was also quickly getting the idea that Nicholas was missing excitement in his life. Looking back, I realize I symbolized this for him at the time. He had been going about his life, retired, doing some traveling, writing—but something had been missing. I was not only a *new-found* daughter he always wanted and could be proud of; he was also finding, in me, the spark he once had in his younger life.

The night was getting longer and I could tell he was getting tired. Before leaving The Whitney, I had the idea to return the next day for brunch. It would be the perfect setting for Nicholas to meet Bruce and Izzy. He agreed, and I made a reservation for the next day. As we said goodbye I leaned over and hugged him. The previous stiffness when I had reached for his hands earlier was gone. As I drove home in my Uber, I felt like none of it was real.

The next morning getting ready for brunch the same nerves I had felt the day before were replaced by excitement and anticipation in seeing Nicholas again. Izzy was now the one who was nervous, obsessing over what she would wear. I tried to calm her, and she was snippy. "You already went through this. You don't have to be nervous now."

She was right. As I was putting on my makeup, I had a thought. I did not want the day to be over when brunch was over. He had come too far, and I had waited too long, to not spend time with him. And the thought of it was unsettling. I texted him and asked how he felt about driving me home after brunch and spending some time in my home. He responded quickly, "Sounds perfect."

My family and I sat at The Whitney and waited. Bruce went to the restroom and just as he was coming down the same mahogany staircase, Nicholas walked in. Izzy, in her own funny way of stating the obvious, said, "Oh my God, Mom, they are going to run right into each other! Now that's awkward." Sure enough, close to our table, I watched as Bruce shook hands with my birth father for the first time. Bruce called him Nicholas having heard me describe him for weeks. "Call me Nick," he said to Bruce. This struck me a bit—he hadn't said that to me. Much like I was someone else with him (Michelle), he was someone else (Nicholas) with me.

Izzy's turn was next and she hugged him as she said hello for the first time. I could feel her nerves. The lunch was a bit awkward, as sometimes the conversation lagged. Bless him, Bruce tried to engage Nicholas.

"So how does it feel to be in your hometown again, how long has it been since you were here?"

Nicholas looked at Bruce as if he wished he was somewhere else. He barely looked him in the eyes and said, "It's been too long." He then looked at me and added, "But now I have a reason to come home." As he said this looking directly into my eyes, he smiled and I felt the rush of love again.

Izzy then sparked up and said, "I heard you are coming over to our house! I am so glad we get to spend more time with you. We should pull out mom's old albums and look at pictures."

Nicholas looked distant again, but smiled at her without actually responding.

I was not sure how I felt about this. But I hoped Izzy would let it go. It seemed overwhelming for Nicholas. And me.

After we ordered lunch, Izzy looked at me, her eyes anxious as if asking me to fill the void. The silence was awkward; and Nicholas looked around the room as if he was bored. Bruce seemed comfortable in the silence, but I could tell Izzy was desperate for more easy conversation. I was at a loss how to fill the empty space that seemed to hover over the table.

Finally, the topic of politics—of all things—came up, something I felt should not be discussed in mixed company. But thankfully, it was common ground for Bruce and Nicholas. And eventually, the conversation went from awkward to easy.

When it was time to go, Nicholas laced his fingers through mine, and said, "You are coming with me." My stomach did a flip—I would have gone anywhere with him.

Izzy looked at me wide-eyed. "Mom, what about me? Can I come with you?"

I had planned on showing Nicholas my hometown on the way. I wanted this time to share this with him alone. "Izzy, we will be back home with you and Dad soon. I promise." Izzy looked sad, but kept quiet. Thinking back, I once again feel I could have included her. But I was so hyper-focused on my own emotions I did not want any distractions from showing Nicholas where

I grew up. It felt like that familiar intersection of worlds I felt when my Aunt Janice met my dad, Paul.

On the way home, we stopped for a coffee and as Nicholas ordered, his east-coast accent rang through. I giggled which turned into a laughing fit—once again, more comfort was established between us. As we drove around my neighborhood where I grew up, I showed him my childhood home, the school I went to, and nostalgic parts of town.

At one point he looked over at me and said, "You know I know you don't believe me. But the minute I knew you were mine, I loved you."

At the time, I did find this hard to believe. He had told me in emails that he loved me as a daughter already. But this was up close and personal. I felt awkward again, but thrilled at the notion that my birth father could love me.

Later, in my home, I could tell he was overwhelmed, and I felt for him. He was in his new daughter's home surrounded by an atmosphere that was all *her*. At some point Izzy, again suggested I get out the album of all the pictures and mementos I had collected from finding my aunts and my uncle, including pictures of Judi and the poems she wrote about me. I told Izzy no, but she would not let it go. Finally Nicholas picked up on this not-so-silent exchange between Izzy and I, and asked, "What do you want to show me?" I was touched. This was sure to be painful and awkward for him but he was willing to indulge Izzy.

We looked through the album and mementos. Nicholas looked into my eyes in that piercing way. "You have wanted to know where you came from your whole life, haven't you?"

This man understood what I had so often been afraid to reveal. *Yes*, I had wanted to know my whole life where I came from, who my birth mom was, why I was given up. Over the last few decades, much has been revealed. And now, as my birth father sat in my family room, I had more answers than I had ever dreamed I would have.

I also noticed something else. I had never been around a birth parent, so I had no reference to compare this feeling to, but instead of feeling awkward being touched, I felt like I could not get close enough to him. As he sat across from me, I consciously felt the need to close the space between us. I got up and moved closer to him on the couch. This was something I realized I was doing more and more as time went on. And I wonder, what would it have been like to be around Judi? Would I have felt this same need to touch and be touched? I suspect I would have.

All my life I rejected the notion that there was a bond with birth parents that was different from adoptive parents. I was a firm believer that nurture won over nature. Now, I was questioning all of these beliefs. In my core, I was realizing what I had never been allowed to know. Genetics are strong. The bond between birth parents, if allowed to develop, is real. And it scared the hell out of me. I was experiencing parental love from an actual birth parent whose company I genuinely enjoyed, but I felt so vulnerable. If he decided this relationship wasn't for him, there was no one else who could possibly hurt me so deeply.

As I found myself trusting Nicholas, bonding with him, I was developing a relationship with someone I never allowed myself to dream I would meet… and I was also setting myself up for the ultimate rejection. What if this does not work out? How would it feel to be rejected for what would feel like the second time by a birth parent?

Plus, I had pushed the questions of how I came to be so far off in the distance that I barely gave it another thought. Instead, I grasped the narrative that I was a walking, breathing miracle. It was a better story to explain my beginning than the alternative.

The next day I arranged for Nicholas and I to have dinner. Izzy planned to join us later in the evening, but I would meet him first after work for drinks. As we sat in another restaurant in Detroit, Nicholas recruited our server to walk around and use my phone to take pictures of us without us knowing, as if she were a spy collecting evidence. Nicholas had an eye for all things art and had dabbled in photography. One of his photographs years ago had won an award. He was partial to candids. As we sat and talked over wine, I was transfixed. Later, when I looked at the photos on my phone, I was in awe of what she had captured. There before me were two strangers who looked strikingly alike; silver hair, similar bone structure, hands that mirrored each other. The most intriguing features of the pictures was what was being said by the body language. Nicholas was leaning in, staring with a look that said there was *zero* chance he was bored. I had a sly smile on my face as I talked, as if I were trading classified secrets. Those pictures ended up being some of my favorites; I shared them on social media. There was so much going on in these pictures, a lifelong history being revealed and rewritten all at the same time.

The next day, Izzy and Nicholas made arrangements to meet at the Detroit Institute of Arts. It was Izzy's idea. She has the wonderful ability to pick up on people's interests and loves to plan outings. She listened carefully when I told her the story of Nicholas taking me across The Ghost Bar to admire a piece of art, so she came up with the idea to spend the day with Nicholas at the D.I.A.

I was concerned when Izzy called me in the early afternoon. She was at the D.I.A when they planned to meet, but there was no Nicholas. I started to panic. I thought about worst case scenarios—he was ill, he got in a car accident, he got tired of me and went home. Any and all things that would break the perfect spell of the weekend. Eventually he texted Izzy, said he was sorry and would explain later. He was an hour late meeting her. I was relieved he was fine, but the niggling feeling of doubt and concern was not completely gone. Something was brewing beneath the surface. I could *feel* it.

Later, I heard the details of the day from both he and Izzy. He never told Izzy why he was late but instead rolled his eyes when she asked and told her, "Something came up." Beyond that, their outing at the D.I.A was a success. Nicholas knew art and shared stories with Izzy as they perused the various pieces. Later over snacks, Izzy entertained Nicholas with stories about our family—ironically, describing what it was like when Orvil moved in and, at eighty-seven years old, divorced his wife, Linda.

That night, the last before Nicholas flew back home, we sat tucked away at a pub east of the city sharing a steak. Nicholas finally told me that Karen had been having a hard time the entire visit. Initially, after our first meeting, she had called and asked him, "Well, what did you learn?" I remember thinking it was an odd thing to ask someone who had just met his long-lost daughter. His reply was even more perplexing to me. "She is a handful."

This left me questioning exactly what was a *handful* supposed to mean. I began to feel bad—was I responsible for upending Nicholas's life? I can imagine what you are thinking, my friend—he was the one who had contacted me and upended my life. Regardless, the underlying current of guilt persisted. I didn't want to be a handful. I didn't want to cause him any chaos.

I was not sure how to feel. He was reassuring me everything was okay, yet he was also telling me that Karen had *carried on* and sobbed every day he was gone.

"She does not drink," he said, "but she drank a whole bottle of wine the other night."

I was confused by her reaction. Why was him being here, meeting me, a bad thing? Just under the surface was the real question: Why was *I* a bad thing?

We sat in the booth and I tried to ignore the sense of foreboding that came with his description of Karen's reaction. It was my last night with him, at least for a long time—the knowledge that Karen felt the way she did only added to my uncertainty that I might not see him again.

I found myself successfully changing the subject. I shared with Nicholas more about my own spiritual path, a path Izzy and I, both, seem to share. I described my deep roots in Catholicism and how much I loved the symbolism and miracle of the mass. The Catholic Mass, in itself, is a ritual, one I deeply respect. I was raised and will always identify as Catholic. But I also feel that there is so much more to believing in a higher power that we do not understand. We both share the same love of what we can't explain, like intuition, or praying for/manifesting what you wish for. Spirituality is sometimes complex, but nonetheless there are commonalities. I also explained how I had studied spiritual care and spirituality in my doctoral study. Treating others with kindness and compassion is threaded through many different faiths. And in the end, that is what may hold us all together—no matter how we choose to express our own spirituality.

I then asked him why he started calling me "my lovely witch," and if he believed in things we cannot explain.

He looked a bit surprised I would come right out and confront him with this question. Then, after a few moments, with a serious look in his eyes, he told me a story about a time when he learned his own intuition may have saved his life.

"I was living in Philadelphia on Spring Garden Street. One night, I was out at a bar I loved, The Traffic Stop. I walked out of the bar after more than a few drinks and I had an uneasy feeling. I could not explain it. It was just an overwhelming sense of dread, as if I knew something bad was going to happen. I looked down an alley just outside the bar and something told me to go the other way. I turned and started walking opposite the alley. A few minutes later, another guy walked out of the bar and I heard him start walking down the alley. Then I heard the commotion behind me. I turned and watched in the distance as two other guys jumped out as he was walking by and attacked him. They had a knife, I saw it glimmer in the lowlights of the alley. The guy they attacked fell down to the ground and the other two jumbled through his pockets, took something, and ran further down the alley. I ran home to my apartment and called the police. I have no idea if the guy they robbed was okay. I guess I will never know. But after that, I started to trust my gut. It may have saved my life."

I felt reassured—I was not alone with my deep trust of my own intuition. In fact, intuition seemed to be one of many threads of connection growing between us. Genetics, once again, stared me in the face. Nature was proving to me that I was wrong, all these years, when giving it zero credit. I had been almost pompous in my insistence that nurture would win, but nature was, in fact, stronger than I had ever been allowed to understand.

As the night came to an end, that foreboding of being abandoned crept in again. Nicholas hugged me goodbye and promised me we would stay in touch, but at that moment his phone began to ring and the weariness in his eyes was ominous. Karen was calling again, and it felt like an elephant was sitting on my chest. I held back tears and tried to breathe. As he walked away, he looked as if gravity was pulling him down, shoulders hunched, and with a heavy sigh, he was gone.

I cried all the way home. I should have felt buoyant and exhilarated with the new relationship I had just forged with my actual birth father. But instead, my intuition knew a storm was coming.

chapter 26

The Space In Between

The time between our first meeting and the next time I would see Nicholas was marked with several events that not only upended my world, but the world as a whole. Nicholas assured me he was "working on Karen" so she would eventually be reassured she was not being replaced and would accept me into their lives. This was puzzling to me and upsetting all at the same time. He emailed me one of many emails describing her angst over him visiting me.

"Karen has been a mess since I came back... I hold her, I try to calm her, reassure her she is not being thrown to the trash heap."

I would ask him over and over "

Why is she afraid you are throwing her away?"

"Because she is threatened by you. She told me she was afraid I was leaving her and moving to Michigan to be closer to you."

I sent Karen a card in the mail right after Nicholas left for home in an attempt to reassure her. I wanted her to know I was grateful for meeting Nicholas and wrote I was "looking forward to meeting" her. I never heard back from her that she received the card—later Nicholas told me she said she thought it was *snotty*. I was so confused and torn at this point. I could not understand what the problem was. Nicholas shared that Karen felt left out because she was not there when we first met. We both had agreed the first meeting was to be just the two of us. My family had understood. Why couldn't she?

I was lost. I told Bruce "No way am I going to be responsible for ending a marriage!" Bruce would try to calm me down by rationally explaining that it seemed all too familiar to what he had been through with Linda and his father. He reminded me that I was not causing problems, there were problems in their relationship before. I was the scapegoat.

I wanted to believe him. But all the while, I was being told by Nicholas that his life was now upside down. He would write to me about the miracle of finding me and folding me into his life, and then also write about the hell he was living through to have me in his life. I felt I was spinning in the eye of a hurricane and could not find my way to shelter. I wanted him in my life more than I had ever thought I would.

Once Nicholas returned home from our first meeting, he told me he was ready to finally tell my brother, Scott, about me. He had held off, explaining that he was trying to come to terms with the reality that he had a daughter. He had not been ready to tell Scott. I was patient. I wanted to meet Scott, at least over the phone, but it did not feel my place to initiate contact. Again, I did not want to be the one to disrupt someone's life. Nicholas came to me. I would let him lead me to Scott.

After I told Nicholas I had wanted a sibling my entire life, he told me more about Scott. Scott had struggled after his mom, Carol, died of lung cancer when he was thirty-eight years old. Scott had health issues as well, and was trying to do the best he could taking care of himself.

Nicholas called me the day he told Scott about me. He added that Karen had told him not to tell Scott about me, but he did anyway. I felt immediately wounded by this. Bruce was angry when I relayed this information, and his first question was something I did not allow myself to ask over the next several months: Why was Nicholas telling me these things?

Instead, I asked myself why would Karen not want Scott to know he had a sister? What was wrong with me? What had I done that was so terrible that she would not want Scott to know me? Did she think I was going to fade away, go back to not having anything to do with Nicholas or Scott?

When I asked Nicholas this exact question, he told me, "Yes, that is exactly what she wants. She wants you to go away."

Nicholas often added more colorful descriptions of Karen's *rants*, as he called them. She supposedly wanted me to "drive off a cliff." Her nickname for me was "that fucking bitch." I was confused and scared. More emails from him described Karen's feelings about my presence in Nicholas's life:

"Michelle, There are times when I have clarity, when I feel I have an understanding of the situation, and then it dissipates... I awoke this morning trying to understand what set her off yesterday. I can't put my finger on it, like a vapor: now you see it, then it's gone...Yesterday her narrative changed: she wants me to believe that having you in my life is ruining my health. She is totally blind to her own behavior. While she was going on and on, I was thinking, she doesn't see it; she doesn't see that her behavior is creating this...she doesn't see it".

My fears of being rejected and let go were surging through me. I was angry this was becoming my story. At one point, I boldly declared to him "When you step up and act like a father, you can claim me as your daughter!"

I was so forthright and self-righteous at this point, wrapped up in the fairytale of the miracle we had found each other, the male and female version of the same person. I thought we would live happily ever after as best friends, confidantes, and the ultimate father-daughter team. I also thought Nicholas was strong, independent, and that he truly loved me. I did not understand how complex his life, or at least the beginning of his life, had been. I did not, after all, truly know Nicholas.

Scott and I eventually connected over the phone and we clicked instantly. Scott is sweet, simple yet complex, loving, and has had a challenging life. He does not have a malicious bone in his body. I have since nicknamed him my "silver lining" sibling. Shortly after our initial introduction over the phone, I called Scott to gauge what he thought about Karen's rejection of me. He was immediately comforting and reassuring. He told me not to worry. It did not matter. Nick, as he called his father, would always pick his children over anyone else.

Why, I thought to myself, would anyone be in a position to have to choose between their children and a wife? Then I remembered Orvil and Linda. It seemed a very real idea that Karen, indeed, wanted me out of the picture. And if so, how would Nicholas deal with this? More importantly: Why was I being told every play-by-play exchange?

Karen may not have been thrilled I was now part of their lives, but what was Nicholas telling her that led to so much animosity toward me?

chapter 27

Fights

E
arly on, when most communication consisted of emails, I recall asking Nicholas what he was like when he was angry. Eventually, I found out firsthand. Nicholas liked to hang up on people, and then not answer. I confronted him about this at first. I was stronger and had a sense of self-worth in the beginning of our relationship. My first email calling him out on his anger toward me gave me hope that he understood he was hurting me. But looking back, he also dismissed what he had done. He wrote:

"My daughter wrote that I showed anger at her.

That wasn't anger. Let's call it frustration. So then, what was I frustrated about? Well, her father said, I can't remember, but I'm sure I was in the right. After all, have I ever been wrong? Of course not.

See how differences are so easily settled. On the other hand, your father is sorry he hung up on you, but he doesn't like it when you show him the stubbornness you got from him. Only show him the good things".

Sometimes after a *fight*, days would go by and I would desperately try to reach him, scared that this was it, he was abandoning me and we were done. All of these fights were centered around his reaction to Karen's reaction to me. I was waiting for my birth father to stand for me, fight for me. I imagine I hit the ultimate nerve when I said, "You walked away once before, fifty-two years ago. Don't walk away now."

He told me later several times that it cut him deeply to hear those words. I tried to take it back. I was devastated that I had hurt him so much. It is only now, years later, that I realize that was Lisa, not Michelle, talking. Lisa was stronger and had a sense of her worth, despite her insecurities, even if she was eternally grateful and striving to be perfect. And I wish Lisa had spoken up more, but Michelle was desperate for her birth father to love her, accept her, not leave her. Michelle would have done anything, and often did, to make her birth father happy.

Nicholas was also drinking more and more. Karen had seen one of the pictures that our server in Detroit had taken. In the picture, there was a half-full wine glass on the table between us—Nicholas told me Karen became livid when she saw this.

I was confused by this reaction and I did not understand why she was so upset. He had said he was taking a *vacation* from drinking, but he'd also said one glass wouldn't be a problem, since it was a special occasion. It was much later, as the months went by, that I came to understand why the wine was a problem.

Nicholas had never told me that alcohol had been a serious problem in his life. I did not have anyone close to me with a drinking problem—I didn't see the signs. Nicholas went on to tell me that *I* had been the one to say, "You have to have a drink with me while you are in Detroit. " This not only angered me, it made me question myself. Should I have assumed he had a drinking problem? Should I have figured that out? I have no idea if I said that. What I do know is that I never would request that someone with a *known* drinking problem drink with me. I do remember him saying, "I will toast my daughter, and have Champagne while I am there." Champagne was apparently Nicholas's drink of choice. But so was wine, and sometimes Vodka, before he realized that was not a good idea.

In retrospect, the only hint he had given me, before meeting for the first time, that alcohol was a problem was a story he'd told which happened a few months before he reached out. He said he was finding that each day, when he got up in the morning and sat down to write (he was freshest in the morning—another similarity between us), he started earlier and earlier with a cup of wine on his desk. Then he decided one day, shortly after his knee replacements, to quit.

He never hid it at first, and while he often talked about his grandfather who had a drinking problem, it still did not occur to me that it was really an issue for him. I believed it was an overreaction due to Karen—what was going on in his life at home seemed to intensify the frequency of the drinking. Indeed, I believed it was circumstantial until much later, when I saw who he became when he drank way too much for way too long.

The emails between us continued. Despite the poetic reassurance he gave me over and over, I was fearful he would have enough of the tension at home and walk away from me. The tension, the underlying current he described it as, was nearly all he talked about some days.

When he was not talking about Karen's reaction to me, he wrote me some of the most amazing stories—one of which became a bit of a series that involved a father-daughter crime solving team named Natasha and Charles. Natasha and Charles traveled and went on adventures together, scoping the globe and righting wrongs. Among the stories, Nicholas would weave how he perceived me, or Natasha. One of these stories in particular, *Natasha's Guilt*, showed me he saw my compassion for all living creatures:

The morning sun touched the treeline as a steamy mist rose from the river. Natasha pushed her canoe from the muddy banks, drifted out to deeper water, and paddled against the mild current. She had a .45-caliber handgun holstered to her hip; a camera with multiple lens lay on a burlap bag in the canoe. The canoe had an outrigger on each side to prevent capsizing in turbulent water. As she paddled around the first bend, the current was easier to paddle against.

Farther on, the river narrowed. Natasha passed under the low-hanging branches, around another bend, and was once again in deeper water. Here, the muddy banks were several feet wide and then disappeared in the dense foliage. A crested heron waded in shallow water near the shore. A monkey swung from one branch to another, screeching.

Natasha lay the paddle down and reached for her camera. She adjusted the lens to bring the heron closer. At the moment she clicked the shutter, a crocodile exploded from underwater to take the heron. It was over in seconds. A gray feather floated to the surface.

The commotion brought nearly a dozen crocodiles from the muddy banks into the water. Three of them moved effortlessly toward the canoe. Natasha turned the canoe and headed to deeper water to ride the current back downstream. One of the crocs, the largest one, twice the size of the canoe, followed her. Her instinct was to paddle faster, but she knew she could never outrun the croc, both of them riding the current.

A half-mile ahead of her, the lay of the jungle rose just enough to slow the current. Natasha lost sight of the croc. She looked from side to side and behind her. There was nothing. For a moment relief settled over her, and then, noiselessly, she saw the croc, its nostrils and eyes just above the surface, staring at her. She raised her paddle and brought it down hard on the creature's snout. The croc opened its huge jaws in retaliation and clamped down on the outrigger. The canoe jostled and tipped one way and then another.

Natasha's heart beat rapidly. If she fell into the water the croc would take her to the bottom, dismember and swallow her, a limb at a time. The croc opened its jaws and let go of the outrigger, only to clamp down on it again. If he attempted a third try, he could take the canoe apart with her in it.

Natasha withdrew the .45-caliber from the holster and clicked the safety off. She gripped the pistol with both hands, her arms outstretched. She waited for the right moment, until the sight was centered between the croc's eyes.

Charles had been working in his studio to finish a project they were working on. He knew Natasha was anxious to get home to her husband and daughter. He suddenly heard a commotion on the riverside of the compound. He got up to pour a third cup of coffee. As he turned from the coffee maker, he saw Natasha come across the compound, onto the front porch, open the screen door and enter the house. He watched her a moment longer. She crossed the room and sat down, but said nothing.

"Would you like coffee?" he finally asked, "Or something stronger?"

"Stronger" she repeated, not hearing her own words.

Charles sat down next to her in the oversized armchair. Natasha scooted over to make more room for him. He put his finger under her chin and turned her head to look into her eyes.

"I've seen that look before," he said.

"What look?" she mumbled.
He raised her chin... "Guilt."

(Reprinted with permission from J. W. Nicholas)
I ate these stories up, savoring every morsel, reading them over and over. Every time I tried to mirror these stories with my own creative writing, they seemed to lack the spark and creativity he had written.

Despite the tension and drama that was part of Nicholas's world, my world was met with more support for my newly-found relationship. Bruce was still team Nick, and Izzy and I talked through her initial insecurities about being included.

"Izzy, it is hard for you to understand, because I am your biological mom. But imagine being raised by someone else, and even though you loved them so much, you still yearned to know who you came from. Then you meet them and they seem like a soul mate. Like someone you have always known."

"I know, Mom, I want you to be happy and I want to be supportive. I get it. He is really cool, and really fun. I get what it means for you to spend time with him. Even if I don't want to share you all the time!" She smiled. "I want to spend time with him too and I hope we get to do more together."

Izzy understood how attentive he could be. More importantly, she has a kind, compassionate heart and wanted me to be happy, even if it meant sharing my time.

My friends were curious about Nicholas. They wanted me to be happy, yet also wanted me to be cautious. My Aunt Janice felt the same way: happy, but cautious. I updated her regularly.

"It's uncanny, Aunt Janice! He is a writer, he's funny, and he is so attentive. We have so much in common. I think he really wants me to be in his life."

"Ok, Lisa, just please be cautious. You don't really *know* him," she spoke slowly, in a calm, and measured voice.

"I know, but I already feel like I have known him my whole life. It's so crazy. And I want to believe him—that he did not rape Judi. I really want to believe him."

"I know, I do too. After all, Judi may have just been scared and used that to get my mom to not blame her for getting pregnant. We don't really know the truth. I just want you to be happy. But I don't want you to get hurt."

My Aunt Jeannie was also more supportive of Karen than I expected her to be.

"Well, Lisa, understand that Karen has had Nicholas all to herself all these years. It has to be difficult to open up and let someone else in. Maybe in time she will lighten up and it will be okay."

"I hope so, Aunt Jeannie. This is so hard. I don't understand why she hates me so much!"

"She doesn't hate you, Lisa, how could she? She doesn't even know you. Try to be patient, give them both time. At least Nicholas seems to want you in their life. I hope he is sincere. I worry about you."

"Oh I believe him, Aunt Jeannie. I am not sure why, but I just do," I replied to reassure myself more than her.

My Uncle J.T. also weighed in and told me right from the beginning, "Leave well enough alone. You don't need this man in your life." I brushed my uncle's reaction off as overprotection.

I wondered if anyone else in Nicholas's family knew Karen well. Maybe they could offer some insight about this situation. Nicholas rarely mentioned the rest of his family. He was close to his cousin, Julie, whom he had stayed with when he came to Detroit to visit me for the first time. I had spoken with her and she was kind and accepting of me. She had a warm, bubbly personality. I could see why they were so close.

Nicholas also had two sisters, Christine and Shirly Ann, and a brother, Michael. Each time I asked about them, he dismissed me. His only response was "Stay away from them. They are nothing like me. They are too full of that better-than-anyone-else, Christian attitude. They never understood me."

Around this time, Christine actually reached out to me. During the brief interaction she wrote to me in an email that "Nick was a liar, and I was lucky I dodged a bullet." I was not open at all to any criticism about my birth father. I took his word that she was the one who was lying and did not pursue any further contact with her, or any of his siblings.

I was instead looking for reassurance about my present situation with Karen and Nicholas. Most folks in my life, collectively, agreed how horrible it was that Karen reacted to my presence the way Nicholas said she did. His emails described the chaos going on in their home.

"Michelle, I am sorry I did not call tonight. Super blow-out night, but I never once lost my temper, I listened... very revealing on several levels, very; will fill you in tomorrow".

Then a few days later, another email describing the conflict:

"I went downstairs a second time last night to settle the air. She was still up. It went nowhere... I went to the front room, and sat on the sofa in the dark with another glass of wine. Moments later, she came out and joined me...

In the past, I have tried to placate. Last night, I did not engage, I asked questions; when I was asked a question, I answered without hesitation: I cannot give her up, my daughter... But she's making you miserable, was her reply. I see it in your face.I did not say, No, you are making me miserable.I held my tongue. I need rest; I'm tired... I have already passed the years of life expectancy for a white male".

I still didn't know why Nicholas felt the need to give me a play-by-play of how she was reacting. I told him over and over, "please don't tell me this stuff, it only hurts me to hear." It only added to the feeling of being someone's mistake that had to be taken care of.

He would typically reassure me he understood and that he would stop telling me the play-by-play.

"I understand Michelle. I will spare you any further description of my days with Karen. I don't understand her reaction... You came into my life and she turned into something alien, even frightening at times. You wonder how I can live with it. I'm not sure... I often look around the house, this room or that room; I catalog what is mine, what is important to me..."

But he continued to share the details that wounded my heart. And continued to make me feel insecure and afraid any day, he would proclaim it was too much. *I* was too much.

At one point, Nicholas shared with me that her words were, "What more does she want? She had wonderful parents, she was lucky."

This fed precisely into the narrative that so many adoptees struggle with. Yes, I was *lucky*. I was also *grateful and striving to be perfect*. This allowed no room for grief, no room for the longing to know my birth family. And most insidious, no room for Nicholas to become an integral part of my life. Karen did not seem to understand, as so many don't, that just because I had wonderful parents, did not mean that the void was filled. And if she did not understand that, then how would she ever let me into their lives? Bruce and anyone close to me, including Nicholas, often said, "Why do you care what she thinks?"

But as you will see, my friend, I did. I cared so much. Karen's rejection of me symbolized the rejection every adoptee fears. And this was not *perceived rejection*; this was flat out rejection in my face. It allowed *Michelle*, the little girl in me, to let her fear of rejection run wild. And even worse, if she did not want me around, would she eventually keep my birth father from me? Or would he wake up one day and think, "My daughter is not worth the trouble?"

chapter 28

COVID 19

As Nicholas claimed to continue to negotiate with Karen to calm the waters regarding my existence, a different kind of storm was brewing. It was March 2020, and people started getting sick. Everything changed in my professional world—in fact, everything changed for the *entire* world. My clinic was a screening clinic and not considered essential. Tell that to my breast cancer survivors who wait with their hands wringing, holding their breath, as I walk in the room to tell them their results. My heart broke for them.

My experience caring for breast cancer survivors is that any testing, even an annual screening mammogram, strikes fear of another breast cancer or a recurrence. Nonetheless, testing that was considered *screening* had to stop, at least for a period of time.

Most of my colleagues were furloughed, or transitioned to providing telehealth. Although I believe telehealth has its place in healthcare, I felt strongly that breast patients needed in-person care. Women with a new diagnosis of breast cancer, breast cancer survivors, and women with new breast concerns, need face-to-face human connection. They are frequently fearful and anxious— survivors have experienced trauma, and those discussing a new diagnosis of breast cancer are experiencing new trauma. Their care should be provided with this in mind. Trauma-informed care includes measures such as providing a safe environment that fosters trust as well as watching patient's body language to avoid retraumatizing the patient (Quaile, 2020). Not to mention, a physical exam, which can't happen via telehealth.

The environment at my institution changed from hope to impending doom. It was palpable, even in the way that we exchanged looks of concern above our surgical masks. I felt the urgency to help in any way I could during this crisis. I sent an email to leadership that my clinic would do whatever was necessary to help and offered to be displaced to where the care was needed. I communicated to leadership that I had experience working in an intensive care unit, albeit twenty-five years ago. I had no idea if this would be valuable or not. Two weeks into the national shutdown, my chief nursing officer called me at home and asked me if I would consider helping in our center's intensive care unit, which was adapting to becoming a COVID-19 unit. I did not have to think about it and I did not ask Bruce how he felt. I accepted immediately.

When I did tell him I accepted the request to help in the ICU, he was angry.

"You are going to kill us!" He bellowed at me. "Did you even think to talk to me about this?"

Bruce feared I would bring this dreadful new virus home. The truth was, talking to him never entered my mind. Eventually, Bruce calmed down and seemed to understand that I could not stay home. I had to go. Now he seems proud and brags to others that his "wife went to the front lines during COVID."

The following Monday, I reported to the ICU. It was one of the most terrifying experiences of my life.

Those of us recruited were much needed warm bodies and tasked with helping put orders in for the nurses. These nurses were some of the most committed, brilliant, compassionate professionals I have ever had the honor of working alongside. Meanwhile, I barely remembered how to be a nurse in the hospital, let alone assume the role of *intern* among the staff. I went from being an expert in my field to feeling I was in the way.

We provided coverage for sixteen hours a day from 7:00 am to 11:00 pm. During those afternoon shifts when I was the only provider in sight, I would count the hours praying I would not mess up or, worse yet, have to make a decision. It reminded me of my first job as a nurse practitioner, where I was asked to leave after only six weeks.

I would stare at the heart rhythm monitors and listen to the nurses who seemed able to intuitively predict what each patient would need, as well as their likely prognosis. I watched so many people lose their battle against this new devious, relentless virus. I have no illusions that I made much of an impact during my time in the ICU, but I was certain there was no way I was staying home,watching the destruction, without somehow contributing to relief efforts.

There were moments when I knew I was needed. It was early in the pandemic and there was a theory that putting patients in prone positions (on their stomachs) would improve their outcome. This was done while patients were on ventilators. It took nine staff members, including the intensivist and a respiratory therapist, to coordinate carefully and simultaneously flipping patients onto their stomachs. I helped perform this many times, but this technique was not fully supported by the literature, and unfortunately did not improve outcomes (Fayed, et al., 2023).

Another role I was more comfortable in was talking to the heartbroken families who could not come see their loved ones, even as they lost their battle against this virus. End of life conversations had become a little easier for me, by this point, as I had experience caring for the elderly in the nursing home. Still, it was challenging—I will never forget some of those conversations. The sheer injustice of not being able to say goodbye in person was staggering. My heart was so heavy most days during this time.

Bruce accepted that this was something I was doing for a period of time. I think he treasured the fact that he could rescue me for a few days by taking me to our farmhouse in the country to escape the reality of what was happening around us. It was a welcome, peaceful solace. He still talks about that time and our escape to the farm that spring.

My time in the ICU ended when the COVID-19 cases stabilized June 2020. I returned to my clinic to put the pieces back together and began seeing my own patients again.

I feel fortunate to have had that experience. As I have mentioned, caring for others is like breathing to me. And while I was busy being the perfect daughter to my birth father in the eye of the Nicholas and Karen storm, I remembered I was also a nurse. My patients ground me. And they remind me of the power of compassion.

chapter 29

Father's Day

Around the same time I was putting my breast clinic back together after my time in the ICU, I was getting concerned over the fact that I had never actually had a conversation with Karen. I heard everything second-hand from Nicholas. Despite asking him to stop telling me about her rejection of me, I did not enforce this boundary. I was too busy being the *perfect* daughter or sounding board, for him to vent to. Amidst the drama, a pattern was being established. Nicholas would call, upset over the latest *rant* or *meltdown* Karen was reportedly having about me. She would be upset over him talking to me too long on the phone, talking to me too many times a day, texting me goodnight, or talking about me too much in his home which reportedly prompted her to tell him to stop mentioning my name.

In the early days of his discovery of me, Nicholas relayed that Karen said she had heard enough about me and I was "ruining Christmas." He relayed that she would often greet him bleary-eyed first thing in the morning, and proclaim that she "could not sleep all night" because of me—although I was not quite sure why I was the reason she could not sleep.

In time, I figured out it was Nicholas's reaction to me that was actually causing her so much angst. We had become enamored with each other and were in contact regularly. I talked either to him or about him. And I suspect he was doing the same. Izzy had felt left out, and perhaps Karen was feeling the same way. Izzy and I had talked things out and now she understood how important fostering this relationship was to me. Perhaps Karen and Nicholas had never had a similar conversation. I could understand her feeling left out, but it was still so hard to not take all of this personally. Not only had I always felt I was a mistake, him finding me seemed to be viewed by Karen as a mistake.

Eventually the drama between them would come to a head. Nicholas would call and say, "That's it! I can't live like this! I want to be able to freely have my daughter in my life!" He would, then, ask me to find him an apartment close to Detroit. The next few days he would talk about his plans to move. My hopes would rise at the thought that my birth father was actually fighting to keep me in his life. I was worth it, I would think to myself. He would write requesting help to come up with a plan:

"Michelle, I have few possessions: objects of aesthetic value or things I have made over the years. I dislike owning stuff, but I do love my car... my only object of independence.

Help me, my girl. Offer suggestions, criticism... a plan in outline. Help me fill in the blanks... If I were to leave here, my annual income would reduce by 50 percent. Yes, I am debt-free, but would I dare split the girls up? They have been together since birth. Think of a plan, use magic".

Then, a few days later, he would call me and describe their reconciliation. He would consistently say:

"Michelle, it's not her fault. She is basically a good person. She is just so threatened by you. She does not know what it is like to have a child. She can't. And I can't bring myself to hurt her."

Each and every time he planned to leave, this would be the pattern. And each and every time, I would experience the deep disappointment of abandonment, over and over. The abandonment I felt was less about him not moving and much more about his justification of the hurtful things he told me Karen said. I did not want Nicholas to end his marriage or have to uproot his life. I knew it was actually ridiculous that he would even have to consider this just to be able to keep in touch with me. But his rationalization of such hateful words towards me made me feel as if I did not matter.

My heart was broken over and over, each time he described their fights and the detailed exchanges between them—all over my existence. I would ask him point blank, "What did I do to make her hate me so much?"

"Nothing, my love. You just exist."

At times after a blow out, Nicholas would be more distant, as if a void formed. I would immediately fear that he was done with me. He had enough and was leaving me for good…only for him to resurface.

It was six months of this drama and my self-esteem was in the toilet. I spent my days waiting for calls, texts good night, emails, and any shred of reassurance I could get. I began settling for less and less, and allowed myself to be the source of whatever problem of the day Nicholas was having. He was drinking more and more, especially when the tension between him and Karen mounted.

And suddenly, the most unexpected thing happened. Karen emailed me for the first time since I had been discovered by Nicholas and invited me to their home for Father's Day weekend.

"Lisa,

I am writing to invite you to come and visit us for Father's Day weekend. I thought it would be a good time for us to finally meet. You will be with your father for Father's Day. You can also meet your brother, Scott, for the first time. I am requesting that you come alone. That way you can focus on spending time with us as a family. Let me know when you decide.

-Karen"

The email shocked me. My stomach dropped, not in a good way. I read the email over and over. She requested I come alone. I felt I was being toyed with and had no other recourse than to be distant. I held off giving them my answer for a few days. I talked it over with Bruce and Izzy. Bruce was not crazy about the idea of me going alone. Izzy, of course, did not want to be left out. I didn't blame her. It had been six months since we had last seen Nicholas, and in the time since, there had been so much drama. But then again, the thought of celebrating Father's Day with my birth father for the first time was so tempting. I had previously offered to go to them with my family. When Nicholas shot that down due to the "tension in the house", I had invited him to visit us for Father's Day. But I also wanted to meet my brother for the first time. Eventually I caved and let them know I would come for Father's Day alone.

In the days that followed, something shifted in the emails Nicholas sent: he began to talk about Judi more and more. I had grown up with the notion that Judi had no other good choice, but to give me up for adoption. I had lived and breathed the narrative that she did the best she could and gave me up because she loved me so much.

Nicholas threw a wrench in this narrative when he began telling me that he felt his choice in the matter was taken away. He frequently wrote,

"If I had known, Michelle, I would have stepped in. I would have stopped her and said I will take her and raise her myself."

This was followed by colorful imaginings of our father-daughter adventures as I grew up. There was, of course, no mention of the phone call where he announced he was the father of Judi's baby and either he hung up or my Aunt Jeannie hung up. After all, I had brought the phone call up the first time we spoke on the phone. Did he know about me, or not? Did he call, or not? We will never know the truth of that call.

Then, he sent one particular email that was different from the rest. This email outlined that Judi had willingly *given me up*. There was blame and accusation contained between the lines of this email.

"Michelle,

When will you see the truth? Why do you hide from it? She GAVE YOU UP! Judi did not want you. Instead of giving me the choice, she gave you away. I would have gladly taken you and raised you as my own. But I was not given the choice! You must see the truth. The truth is all that matters.

I should have been forceful. I should have called their house again and again. I should have shown up at the hospital the day Judi gave birth. I try to forgive myself with the same

155

worn-out excuse: You were only twenty-three, Nick. You were still a child...But it does not assuage the guilt".

I was angry and I wrote back,

"How dare you talk about her like this! She did what she thought was best!"

"But she gave you up, Michelle. She did not care about you! I would have never given you up."

Anne Heffron (2022) describes in her book *Truth and Agency Writing Ideas for Adopted People* the point in which adoptees experience *the fog* lifting. I suddenly understood what Nicholas meant. I did not want to think of it any other way, but there was no denying the fact that Judi, no matter the reasons, had given me up. The overarching narrative is how fortunate we are to be *chosen*. But, as Anne Heffron so poignantly points out, we must first be *unchosen* (2022).

I went through a time when I was angry at Nicholas for making me see this. I was angry, now, at Judi. And I was angry at everyone else for shoving the *you are so lucky* narrative down my throat. I realized in that moment, as the fog cleared, that *that* was where grateful and striving to be perfect lived. I was *lucky*, I was *chosen*, therefore I must show my gratitude and always be perfect for everyone so they do not give me up. I was never allowed to be sad or mad, feel grief, be imperfect, make mistakes, appear not grateful, or not strive to be the best. And the most frustrating reality about this: I was now supposed to be angry because Nicholas wanted me to be.

He wanted me to villainize Judi along with him. He wanted to take me down the slimy road of bitterness, rejection, and remorse. But what I am still not clear about to this day is why. Was it to justify what appeared to be his anger, frustration, and guilt over not knowing me all these years? Or was it to pull me away from my birth mother whose ghost may have been in the room with him as he struggled to sleep and stop the eerie pangs of regret?

Eventually I felt the anger, the grief, the remorse I had never allowed in. But who was I feeling it for? Was it for me or was I once again doing what others thought I should so they would want me? At this point in my life, I was so ensnared on the web I would have damn-near sold my soul for Nicholas to promise never to give me up again.

Father's Day weekend finally arrived. I tried not to have expectations when Nicholas told me to text him when I landed and he would pick me up at the airport. I pulled my mask off as I deplaned and looked up to see his smiling face in the crowd. I was so surprised, and touched that he would meet me like this.

Why should I be so surprised? He said he was coming. I was, after all, coming from four states away, alone, to the *belly of the beast*, to meet the woman who had rejected me over and over. And yes, I was also meeting my brother. Nicholas should have met me; it should have been expected. But I had come to lower my expectations and take what I could from this situation, including accepting everything on their terms.

I was so thrilled to finally see this man. I am sure my gawking smile lit up the room. He grabbed me and held me and all the tensions of the months leading up to this faded. We were finally face to face again. We made our way to my hotel and I fully expected Nicholas to simply tell me he would pick me up the next day and take me to meet Karen. But instead, he stayed for a while. We sat and laughed as easily as we had in those first days and I wondered how I could have been so angry with him over the past months.

Nicholas had told me Karen was a gardener, so I had pre-ordered flowers to be delivered to my room to take to her. No matter how she had felt about me, I was going to put my best foot forward. I was desperate for her to accept me. How could she not? I was her husband's daughter. I had just come all this way, alone, as per her request. Surely once she met me, she would see that I was likable, sincere, and gracious; and not out to take Nicholas away from her.

I first saw Karen in the distance as we pulled up to Nicholas's home. She was in the backyard talking to the neighbor. With flowers in my arms, I walked up and hugged her. I was shaking. I had no idea what to expect.

Smiling, Karen took the flowers and seemed genuinely happy to meet me.

"Hi Lisa, it's good to finally meet you," she said as she hugged me back. It was an informal half-hug, as she held the flowers in the other arm. I was awkward, and stammered to find conversation as she showed me around her shaded gardens that Nicholas had built for her.

"Oh my, your gardens are beautiful! Nicholas was right, you are a talented gardener!" I hoped I sounded sincere through my nerves. I knew my voice was shaking.

Karen seemed relaxed. Looking at her for the first time, it was hard to believe she had said all the ugly things Nicholas had relayed. She was an attractive woman in her seventies. She had shoulder-length, thick black hair and a slender build. Her makeup was simple, but accentuated her features. Her voice was even, and her smile was friendly enough. She seemed confident as she led me around showing me their home.

Their home was actually her home. Nicholas had told me, in the heat of their fights, that she had never put his name on the house. "All the easier to walk away from," he had said.

The afternoon was slightly awkward. But I managed to keep things light. At one point, Nicholas went upstairs to take a nap. I was not crazy about being left alone with Karen. I had no idea what she was thinking. After fighting with Nicholas about me and being named "that fucking bitch" for months, I was hoping she now saw that I was a good person, caught in a crazy circumstance. I meant no harm. I just had wanted time with my birth father to catch up after fifty-some years.

It was during this time, alone with Karen, she started to ask me questions about Judi and what I had learned so far about my beginning. It was awkward for me. I struggled to tell her things while skimming the surface.

"So how old was your birth mom, Judi, when she had you?"

"She was only nineteen."

"Do you think that's why she gave you up?"

"Well, she lived in a Catholic, tight-knit community. I think she did not feel she had a choice but to give me up."

"What else do you know about her?"

"Not much, only what my birth aunts have told me. Janice and Jeannie are amazing. We talk all the time. They have been in my life since my mid thirties."

"So what are they like? Your birth aunts?"

"Oh Jeannie is funny, sweet. She used to live across the country. Now she lives here. Close to Janice. Janice is a gardener too, like you! They are twins, very close. Janice calls herself a *dirt lady*. She is so warm. They both are so important to me."

As I answered each question, I felt like I was being interviewed. Karen did not comment much, she just stared at me from where she sat with her legs causally swung across the arm of her chair. I sat stiff, not sure if I was giving the right answers or not. She offered very little as far as warmth or reassurance.

I was doing my best but the conversation made me uncomfortable. I wanted to avoid telling her what I had been told about my beginning.

Later, she would tell Nicholas that she thought I was being superficial and felt the conversation lacked authenticity. What did she expect? I was trying to be gracious knowing what she had said about me, and how much drama I had caused. I have often thought about that time and wondered, what did she want me to say? What would have felt *authentic* to her? Would it have been better for me to look her in the eye and say, "So Karen, do you think Nicholas raped my birth mother, or do you think it was just a story to fit the narrative of the times?"

Next up in the festivities of the weekend was meeting my brother— my silver lining. Nicholas drove me to Scott's home, which was about five minutes away. I envied Scott already. He was always in close proximity to his father—and he still had his father. I wondered if he knew how lucky he was.

I had exchanged pictures with Scott and we had talked on the phone and texted dozens of times. But meeting birth family, especially a sibling you always wanted, in person is something you never get used to. Scott came out of his house, grabbed me in a bear hug and started to cry. I melted right there.

Nicholas stood by beaming. I can't imagine what that was like for him staring at his two children, the daughter he never knew existed, but claimed to have always wanted, and his son. It reminded me of what it was like to watch my Aunt Janice meet my Dad Paul. Now Nicholas was sitting back, watching the daughter he never knew meet his son for the first time much like I watched my aunt I never knew meet my dad Paul for the first time.

We visited with Scott for a bit and I felt myself relaxing in his presence. That feeling of not wanting to touch or be touched was gone with him, too. Scott had a warmth about him that was sincere. He lived in a modest home surrounded by stray cats, and one of his own. We sat on his couch and just stared at each other.

"I can't believe you are my sister! You are so pretty in person!"

"Awe, Scott, thank you! You are a pretty handsome guy, too!" We both laughed and looked at Nicholas. Then said in unison, "Good genes!"

"Next time you come back you have to bring Bruce and Izzy. I want to meet them."

Scott and I had talked about it being a bit odd that Karen wanted me to come alone.

"Yes, I will bring them next time. You and Bruce would get along great. You seem similar, you're both easy going guys. And both like old rock and roll."

"Yeah, I think I would get along great with Bruce!"

Scott was funny and, like his father, laughed easily. Scott and I do not share much in common, yet it was easy to be around him. I felt accepted and loved. He had a genuineness about him that was infectious. It was a quick visit, Scott had to go to work. We eventually said our goodbyes and planned to meet the next day for Father's Day dinner.

The next day was dinner in the city, with all four of us. I kept thinking how surreal this must feel for Nicholas, Father's Day dinner with both of his children. Dinner was a bit stiff. Nicholas told me later that Karen said I had stared across the table and looked at her with an icy look in my eyes. I am certain I did not actually do that. Thinking about this now, I wonder did she actually say this? What was going through my mind, at that time, was much more timid and desperate. I wanted her to like me, to want me. She was after all not just my birth father's wife, she was a stepmother. *My stepmother.*

When dinner was over, we dropped Scott off. I sat in his living room for a minute, both of us marveling over the fact that we thought we were only children until recently. Then later, we dropped Karen off, so Nicholas and I could spend some more time together. As Karen stood in the driveway, she hugged me goodbye with tears in her eyes.

"I am so glad you came. And I am glad you came alone. You got to meet your brother, and spend time with all of us as a family. I hope I meet Bruce and Izzy someday."

I was conflicted by this display of emotion. How could someone who had said the hateful things Nicholas told me she said actually seem this sincere. Did this mean I actually broke through? Was she now going to accept me? I was hopeful, but still not sure if I could trust that things would now be okay.

On the way back to my hotel, Nicholas looked over at me with a bit of a sneer on his face as he drove away and said, "Oh you are *really* good!"

"What do you mean? I *am* good!" I felt my eyes narrow as I said, "This was not a show, I want her to like me. And I am a good person. I genuinely want her to accept me. I accept her!"

"Ok, I get it." he said, shrugging his shoulders. "I know you are a good person. I thought, maybe, you were just trying really hard."

It upset me that he thought I was putting on some kind of show all weekend. Looking back, I realize I was drained because I was trying to undo the damage done to me. I was the one who was supposedly rejected by Karen for six months before her Father's Day invite. I was the daughter who had done nothing but respond to her birth father's request to get to know her. I simply wanted him in my life. I was not trying to sweep Karen under the carpet. I was also trying to not be the one swept under the carpet.

That evening Nicholas, perhaps fueled by the underlying tension of the last six months and the emotion of me being in his home, drank way too much. The next day, he arrived to take me to the airport hungover and exhausted. We said our goodbyes and he promised to not let there be so much time in between visits.

The next time I saw him would be three months later.

chapter 30

Time for a Change

Sometime mid-summer of 2020, most providers at the hospital cancer center where I practiced were back to seeing patients. One of the most valuable and sacred roles I have is telling patient's their breast biopsy results. I know how important it is to be sensitive when telling a person life-altering news—that moment is something they will never forget. I felt strongly then, and still do, that results be given in person, after which patients are referred to a surgeon.

However, one particular surgeon was still mostly seeing patients via telehealth. When patients asked me about scheduling with a surgeon, we reviewed availability together, including who saw patients in person vs telehealth. The reality was, patients usually wanted to choose surgeons who were seeing patients in person. This surgeon realized I was not referring as many patients to her. This did not go over well, and I was the scapegoat. What ensued was an attempt to undermine my clinic and remove some of our responsibilities.

This surgeon went to my nursing leadership, and demanded my clinic stop seeing patients who may eventually be referred to a surgeon, such as patients with new breast lumps or breast biopsy results that resulted in surgical referrals. This was a direct attack on my position and my clinic. Instead of defending me, a meeting was organized with nursing and physician leadership to "discuss changes to my clinic being proposed." Leading up to this meeting, my leadership did little to assure me that my position was not in jeopardy. The communication between myself and nursing leadership was confusing—one minute they seemed to support me, the next they could not guarantee my clinic's responsibilities would not change.

In the background of this attack on my clinic was the continued drama in my personal life. Nicholas and I stayed in constant communication, but the magical connection that happened between Karen and I over Father's Day weekend seemed to wear off, for reasons I still do not understand.

During the meeting to discuss my clinic's responsibilities, the surgeon would not meet my eyes. Instead, she spoke only to physician leadership. Fortunately, her demands were not considered reasonable. My clinic's responsibilities—and my position—remained intact.

Afterward, as we were walking out of the meeting my Chief Nursing Officer looked at me and said, "That was painful. And it was personal." It, indeed, seemed personal. Especially after everyone in attendance disagreed with the surgeon.

Despite the outcome, the impact of what this surgeon had done damaged my confidence and shook my faith in this institution. I had volunteered in the ICU during the worst days of the pandemic, changed the face of my clinic, earned awards, and garnered the admiration of staff and patients; but the unknown outcome leading up to the meeting, my leadership's lack of support during this process, and the notion that this surgeon could yield her power in this way, caused me to once again fear being *let go*. I am certain that my insecurities were also fueled by what was happening in my personal life. Having my clinic's responsibilities threatened in the backdrop of being afraid of being given up again because of Karen's rejection, coupled with Nicholas's reaction to her rejection, were interwoven like fabric.

Nicholas wrote to me during this time his version of what was happening in my clinic:

"Michelle, I wish I lived closer to you, in the same town, to offer support. What you are going through at your clinic has unseen side effects; I'd like to be there to buffer them... take the edge off. Their remark, "we'll not refer patients to you", should never have been said; it's like a child sticking their tongue out at you".

I appreciated his support, even if he was likely biased. It was support, nonetheless.

It became evident soon after, that leadership was not planning on letting me go because of a surgeon having a tantrum. But regardless, I did not feel as supported as I should have, and began thinking about looking for a new position elsewhere.

Fortunately, one of my very good friends and colleagues, Sharon, a radiologist I had collaborated with on projects, told me about another opportunity opening up. She was developing a new breast center in a large OB-GYN practice. It was the chance to bring my practice model caring for breast patients to a new setting and build from the ground up. It was tempting and COVID-19 changed so much for me in my current setting; a fresh start felt like a great idea.

I talked it over with Bruce, Izzy, and Nicholas. It was still so unreal that I again had a "father" to discuss major life changes with. Bruce was supportive, but Izzy was upset. She also worked at this cancer center as a nurse's aide, while in nursing school. She wanted me to stay. She loved coming to the clinic and visiting me while she was working on one of the floors of the hospital. We were sometimes able to carpool on occasion. Some of my most cherished memories are Izzy driving me into work when I worked in the ICU. She was so proud of me and wanted to support me. I would hear her tell her friends she was "so proud her mom stepped up and went to the front lines during COVID."

But, in the end, Izzy understood I needed a change and I decided to make the move.

As my last day approached, I saw an email that went to 36 employees of the cancer center entitled, "Chism Departure." My resignation was displacing over 1,600 patients. I read this with tears in my eyes. I was so sad to leave them. I had made an impact that was important to these patients. Yet I didn't feel supported anymore by my institution, and needed to do what was right for me.

My last day, my CNO threw an elegant lunch in my honor. Leaving was hard. I thought I would stay forever. It was here I discovered my passion that changed the trajectory of my practice as a nurse practitioner. To this day I remain grateful to this center.

In my new position, I was able to once again work with my friend and colleague, Sharon. Within months we were practicing in a brand-new breast suite in a spa-like atmosphere with state of the art equipment. The staff felt like family. One of my requests in this new center was my own office that I would decorate based on my vision. I had always wanted to give patients breast biopsy results in a setting that made my patients feel safe. I chose the decor which included a pink, velour couch. I added soft lighting, a writer's desk, a coffee and tea bar, pictures with warm colors, and my multicolored, fur chair that I would pull up across from my patient so I could sit close as I slowly described life-altering information and offered the hope of treatment. I am so grateful to say that my vision was achieved and my office has a reputation for calming patients at a time when they need calm and reassurance the most.

My practice and my patients remind me everyday how valuable showing compassion to others is. Especially when I introduce myself to a patient who is meeting me for the first time and about to hear what may be the most difficult news they may ever hear.

Each patient is different in how they may react to the news they have breast cancer. But those few minutes, before I tell them, are similar each time. I knock on the clinic room door, introduce myself, shake their hand while looking them directly in their eyes, "Hi there, I'm Lisa Chism. Why don't you bring your things and come with me across the hall?" I then lead them and their friends and/or family to my pink couch and ask them if they would like something to drink. Once they settle in, I pull my chair up close, look into their eyes and gently say, "How much do you understand about the results of your breast biopsy?"

As I sit with my patient, I want them to feel safe with me. I want them to know they are not alone. I give my cell phone number to every patient with breast cancer to reinforce that I am here for them. I will help them understand the next steps.

Writing about this kind of trauma-informed care reinforces for me how my own trauma has impacted how I practice. My own trauma has molded me into someone who recognizes how much fear and uncertainty can leave you feeling vulnerable and alone.

chapter 31

The Ragdoll

Nicholas and I had stayed in touch over the summer in our usual pattern. He was planning to visit again in the summer, but each time he broached the subject with Karen, he claimed it turned into a *war*.

One day, after promising to return, he wrote and said he could not make it. I was devastated. It was more than simply canceling a visit. It symbolized to me that I was not worth the effort. I was not worth the *fury* he claimed to have to endure if he wanted to visit me. He wrote:

"Michelle, Canceling my trip was an act of desperation, looking blindly for a way to quell the incessant heartburn and diarrhea brought on by Karen's campaign to minimalize your existence".

The negative comments about me were supposedly back in full swing. Despite Karen's attitude toward me, the communication between Nicholas and I stayed consistent. One particular email contained a story, *The Ragdoll*, that at the time melted my heart:

Charles was frustrated. She was only five-years-old, for crying out loud; he was in charge, a single parent, he had to make decisions for them both.

"No," she said and stormed off to her room.

Charles followed. "Natasha, come out. Please. We can talk about it."

"No, I hate you." She pushed the door closed. He heard her throw toys against the wall. "I hate you!"

Earlier in the day, Charles and his daughter had been at the park in lower Manhattan. Natasha found a discarded ragdoll. The doll was covered with ants and melted chocolate.

"I don't think so, sweetheart. I'll get you a new one, okay?"

"I want that one!"

Charles looked at the doll a second time. In his mind's eye, he pictured cholera and septic fever crawling all over it.

"No." he said and picked Natasha up to carry her out of the park. Young mothers behind strollers looked askance at him and shook their heads. Men... they have no idea.

Later that night as Charles lay in bed, ready to turn out the light, he paused.

He'd better go check on her. Just then Natasha appeared in the doorway. A few pajama buttons were in the wrong buttonholes, and she carried her old ragdoll by one arm.

She stood in the doorway and said nothing.

"You got ready for bed yourself. Good job."

"My room is dark," she said.

"Want to sleep here?"

She nodded and came to the side of the bed. Charles helped her up, and then switched off the light.

"Tomorrow I'm going shopping," he said.

"..up town."

"Why?"

"To find a doll with two ponytails and bangs."

"Why?"

"So, I don't have to sleep alone in the dark."

"You have me. I have bangs..."

Charles turned on his side to face her. "Yes, I do, my love. I have you."

(Reprinted with permission by J. W. Nicholas)

Tears stung my eyes. I felt loss at not knowing him as a little girl. I felt empathy for his loss of not being able to raise me. I felt anger at Karen for not accepting me and making a situation that could have been beautiful, instead heart-wrenching. I also felt the little girl inside me wish more than anything for Nicholas's love. And fear that he would one day let me go. I'm not sure if the fear was because of Karen's wrath. Or because as vulnerable as I was with him, he could hurt me so deeply.

I loved that story as much as The Silver Dollar story he had written months before. But instead of this story being one that should always warm my heart, it turned into one that made me feel less like a full-grown, accomplished adult and more like a sullen child.

After he sent it to me, each time Nicholas and I would get into a fight over whatever Karen-inflicted insult he shared with me, he would use the term "don't throw your toys against the wall" to make me feel as if I was overreacting. What was once a beautiful story was becoming a way to invalidate whatever I was upset about. But nothing made me feel more invalidated and misunderstood than when I read Karen's use of the term "throw her toys against the wall."

Several months after Nicholas and I met for the first time, an email Karen had written to him arrived in my inbox. Nicholas had forwarded it to me so I "would see what he had to deal with." Thinking back, he had to have known it would hurt me.

"Nick,

This past year has been one of the most difficult times in both our personal lives and marriage. I want our old life back where there was no tension and we have a peace that made our home a true sanctuary. If we can agree on changes with Lisa, I do believe this could happen with some changes. We need to stand together in a firm and consistent manner so that she does not see that she can get her way by playing us against each other or breaking you down to get her way. This will be made more difficult with the fact she does not want to share you and is so jealous of me or any attention you give me. I have created a travel calendar from last year to remind us how stressful her visits here, and yours to Michigan, were. My stomach is already bothering me thinking about her ever coming back here. We need time to heal from the events of this past year and let this all settle in without her showing up every month or two. As we get older change becomes harder and disruption every month makes this all even harder to handle.

This home should be our sanctuary of peace. I know you love Lisa. I have accepted that. I have even gone so far as to invite her down here, make her feel like an important part of our family. I honestly feel I have done everything possible to make things easier for you and help her accept me. I sense at this point she is so obsessed with you, she just doesn't want me to exist in your life.

I pray you will find a way to save our marriage and not let Lisa destroy our health, our marriage, and all we have left to live for."

The email painted me as a demanding child and I realized that was truly Karen's view of me. The email also made me *feel* like a child instead of an adult woman, wife, and mother who found her life's purpose caring for others. The email was followed by a "Travel Calendar" that outlined some of the visits Nicholas and I had. It struck me how different her perception was from what Nicholas was telling me.

"Beginning in December 2019, Nick suggested meeting Lisa so they could get to know each other in March or April. Lisa demanded he come the first part of January. Nick was excited but stressed about this travel. He was thoroughly exhausted and stressed."

I had offered to meet Nicholas sooner than April and wanted him to know I was comfortable with meeting him. In my excitement, I suggested January. He, in fact, picked the date he would meet me himself.

"Then Lisa wanted Nick to come back up in February. He had barely recuperated from the previous trip and was reluctant to make reservations when he fell twice. At that time the trip was canceled."

Nicholas called me a few weeks after he returned home from meeting me in January and told me he was planning on returning in February. He then told me because he fell, he was holding off traveling. I had not asked him to come.

"She demanded he come up in March and then April. Due to COVID-19, March was again called off and he backed out on her in April."

I had not demanded he travel. He was disappointed he had to cancel in February, so he planned to come in March instead. We mutually canceled because of the national shutdown.

"In May she started demanding he come up for Father's Day. When he said no, she asked if she, Bruce and Isabel could come down. We graciously agreed and invited them down only to find out a couple days later that she had decided not to come. At this point she relentlessly demanded Nick come up to Michigan instead. Keep in mind she expected him to fly three and a half weeks before major surgery on his back, knowing he could fall. At this point, Nick was so stressed. I, again, invited her down here to spend Father's Day with Nick. She did accept, but I must add that this was again very stressful for both Nick and myself."

Nicholas and I had discussed Father's Day and how special it would be to visit for our *first* Father's Day together. He indicated he wanted to come to Michigan but Karen was "giving him a hard time." I then offered to go there with my family. I never knew that Karen had actually agreed to this. Nicholas continued to describe how difficult Karen was being about my visit, so I decided we would not go. Then I accepted Karen's invitation to go to Missouri for Father's Day alone.

"The first of August, two weeks after Nick's major surgery, she again was demanding that he travel to see her at the end of August. At that time he told her no. She, again, was so relentless that he accepted. This stressed Nick in ways that made him physically ill and he canceled on her.

She immediately started demanding he come up in September. He was not ready for this trip, but decided to go anyway. He was so stressed that he had nausea and diarrhea. The nausea, and exhaustion and sleep issues, continued all summer. This trip was agreed upon with no trips to Michigan or here until after the first of the year."

Nicholas frequently told me he wanted to come to Michigan in the summer. He had described memories of July and expressed wanting to attend a special 4th of July event at the Ford Mansion. He indicated to me that he had put his trip off because he could not "handle the tension" in his house whenever he brought up coming to visit. Eventually, he decided to come in September.

"I understand she invited us up for the first of December. Keep in mind three weeks later Lisa, Bruce and Isabel offered to come down here for New Year's."

I did, in fact, tell Nicholas we should try to spend Christmas together, as a family. I wanted to include Karen. I had talked about our families being so small and that holidays were about family. So far, Nicholas had been the one to decide he would come to Michigan alone.

"Nick has already said he would not be going back to Michigan without Karen and the girls! This is not negotiable and there will be no exceptions. And yes, Lisa, you can throw every toy you own against the wall and it will change nothing!"

Nothing in the email accurately described what I was experiencing in my communications with Nicholas. Karen had taken a beautiful story Nicholas had written and used it as a way to make me look like someone who demanded to get their way and act like a spoiled child when they did not. I was devastated. All this time, I had thought perhaps it was not as bad as Nicholas had portrayed. But these were Karen's words. It was the epitome of rejection. Worse yet, there was zero sensitivity for what this was like for me, an adoptee who had gone her whole life wanting to know where she came from, who her birth parents were. The email described how this was affecting Karen and Nicholas, and the "damage" I was causing. Karen's words came from someone who seemed deeply threatened. Looking back I recognize now how territorial the email was. Karen was defending how she felt in the only way she could—by personally attacking me.

It finally occurred to me to question what Nicholas was telling her. More importantly, what Nicholas was actually saying about me, and my feelings about what was going on. I wrote to him and tried to confront how contradictory her email was to what Nicholas was actually saying to me.

"Nicholas, So these words Karen wrote to you…you understand it leaves me to question what you have been saying to her all this time.

She paints a picture of a spoiled child who demands your attention. A depiction of someone who has no right to want to know you. Did you really read it carefully?

I ask you, Nicholas. If you were me, how would you feel? Have I been alone all this time? Is what we have all in my imagination? I am sitting here feeling completely isolated. Alone. And abandoned. Her version is of a daughter who has demanded things of you. While all along, I thought you were where you wanted to be. Now I sit and wonder where I stand. Who am I to you? What do you really want of me? In my heart, I want to only remember all the things you have said. The time we have shared. But if you were me, and read these words, how would you feel?"

His response did not answer my questions as to what he was telling Karen. In fact, his response was only four words:

"I have had enough!"

His response did nothing to reassure me. Instead, he seemed angry at me. I was confused and hurt. I was even more afraid of being abandoned. I had no idea what to do with this information. I was angry at them both. I started to wonder, what kind of web was I ensnared in?

chapter 32

The Cemetery

As Karen had correctly outlined in her "travel calendar", Nicholas did eventually return to Michigan September 2020–alone. According to him, he had told her he wanted to come alone. I will never know how this decision was made. But it was one of the most impactful visits we had. Prior to his visit, Nicholas told me his stomach was upset as his acid reflux was returning. He blamed Karen's reaction to him traveling to visit and added, "Karen was relentless and I could feel the burning return. Can you call the pharmacy and prescribe something to help when I get there?"

He stayed in an apartment in the heart of the city. It was a magical place along the Detroit River. It smelled of cedarwood, and had an elevator that only worked part-time. We climbed the stairs and marveled at the old wood and architecture. The building was full of history. The lighting was soft and the ceiling was huge with long windows stretching up to the top. The river was below and freighters made their way by.

When Izzy and I picked him up and drove him to the apartment, I said "Isn't it adorable?" We both stared at Nicholas expectantly as he responded, "it's more like horrible."

We were heartbroken. We had carefully selected places to rent in the city based on what he said he wanted. Nicholas had chosen this particular one himself.

Eventually, Nicholas fell in love with the place and returned there for another visit the following year. He even went on to write a story about that special place on the Detroit River. The story was entitled *The Gift*:

My few days at the Loft were as fleeting as life. I was there and then I'm gone. I should have left something behind, some kind of mark; nothing to deface, something of my existence. Or did I...

Months into the future, a couple are at the front entrance to the building. She looks at the key in her hand, turns it one way and then another... which way does it go in? There... the key slides in, and she opens the door to the lobby.

"What kind of elevator is that?" her boyfriend asks, walking toward it.

She says nothing and pushes the first button, and they hear the elevator starting down. It arrives at the first floor and she tries to open the heavy door. It won't move; she uses both hands... still nothing. She gives her boyfriend a glance as if to say, "Are you going to help?" He gets the hint and they manage to slide the door open.

They arrive at the fourth floor, and again struggle to get the elevator door open. They both have backpacks and she, a small case. They look for apartment 414, but one of the numbers is missing. She fits the key to the lock and the door opens.

"This place is spooky," her boyfriend says.

She walks farther into the room; she stands still, looks around.

"What is it?" he asks, "You have an odd look on your face."

"I've been here before," she says. "I can feel it."

"Please," he says, "don't give me that out of body crap."

She ignores him...

They have a light dinner; she has wine, he prefers beer. He wants to watch TV, and she asks could they please not.

"The crap on TV is what I want to escape." She can see in his eyes that he doesn't understand, but she lets it go. Silence is her victory.

Near midnight they go to bed. He wants to "fool around" as he calls it.

"I'm not rejecting you," she says with sympathy, "but I'm not there. Tomorrow?" She touches his face with her fingertips. "Okay?"

He pouts a moment, then turns over and is quickly asleep.

She awakens in the middle of the night. There's a light on in the front room. She doesn't remember having left it on. She hears voices, soft spoken. One voice is deep, the other throaty, tender. She thinks to herself, "I'm not dreaming... I know I'm not."

She swings her legs around to place her feet on the floor. Her movements are quiet. She steps into the front room. There's a couple sitting on the sofa, they're holding wine in plastic cups. There's faint music in the background. The couple look like twins, but not of the same generation.

"Flora," the woman says, "please join us." She pats the sofa with her hand.

"We live here," the man says. "We have for years."

Flora stares at him. His hair is silver, and even in the dim light, his eyes are blue.

The woman touches Flora's hand. "Please sit with us." The woman has silver bangs, silver temples; the same silver as the man.

"We were discussing the depth of the Universe," he said. "Not in any measurable way. Metaphysically."

The woman with silver bangs stands, pours a third glass of wine and hands it to Flora. "I have Chardonnay if you like. Father prefers Pinot Grigio."

"Relax, Flora," the man says. "Enjoy the hour. Worry about nothing."

"In the morning," the woman says, "you will remember none of this."

"So, speak freely," the man says. "It is our gift to you..."

(Reprinted with permission from J. W. Nicholas)

While Nicholas was in town, we visited the cemetery where Judi was buried. I did not know it at the time, but as Izzy stayed back, near the car on the side of the winding cemetery road, she took pictures as we walked hand in hand. Izzy always loves to capture special moments. The pictures show the back of my birth father and I walking with our similar slight builds, his silver hair, my long dark hair with silver streaks escaping. Even the way we walked, our stance, was similar. I have often looked at these pictures and reminisced over how surreal those moments were as we approached Judi's grave together for the first time.

We stood at Judi's grave and Nicholas put his arms around me. It was a perfect September day, the sun was shining, a light breeze pushed my bangs from my eyes. He leaned over and kissed my forehead. I cannot imagine what that would be like for Judi to know that there we were; her daughter and the man responsible for the existence of her Michelle Marie. The man whose identity was lost when she left this earth almost five decades earlier.

chapter 33

She's Never Coming Back to Missouri Again.

S oon after returning to Michigan, Nicholas asked me to come visit in October. I was eager to keep up the pace of the visits. It might have been because the more I heard about Karen's rejection of me, the more fear I felt that something would disrupt the rhythm of him folding me into his life. I rented a cottage near his home that allowed pets so he could bring his beloved Papillons over. Karen had decided she would go out of town with a girlfriend during my visit. It was hurtful that she refused to be in town when I was visiting. Nicholas later told me that she insisted I "not be allowed in her house."

Nicholas drank entirely too much that weekend. I did not discover how much until I emptied out the refrigerator as I was packing up to go home and the boxed wine he had brought was completely empty.

During this visit, I began to see who he was when he drank too much. Karen already knew who he became when he drank, which is likely one of the 101 reasons she did not want me around. One evening, I wanted to impress him with my cooking skills. He often embellished stories of his own cooking and baking skills. I thought this, too, was something we could share. I envisioned us preparing a meal together and fantasized about the chance to cook side by side with my birth father. The reality was not what I had hoped for. I cooked alone while he sat and drank wine. By the end of it, he had barely touched his dinner—even after I had shopped specially for the ingredients of the pasta dish I had carefully prepared. I threw most of the meal out the next day.

The next morning, while I cleaned the kitchen, Karen called Nicholas on her way home from her weekend away, and because my birth father had an archaic flip phone, I could hear every word. During the phone call I heard Karen say, "She knows she is never coming back to Missouri, right?" Her voice was cold, shrill and clear. It was as if this had already been discussed and she was doubling down on my exit from their lives.

I was devastated. I stood dumbfounded as my father stammered some incoherent reply. When he hung up, I said, "Take me to the airport, I am going home."

Nicholas looked at me, with his eyes dark and narrowed, and shouted, "Shut the fuck up!"

That response should have told me I was right: I needed to go to the airport, get on a plane, and never look back. Instead, I stood shocked as hot, sloppy tears made their way down my face. I had no idea what to do or what to say. I wish Lisa would have been in charge. But Michelle was in the room with her birth father and she was desperate to be wanted.

I don't remember what happened next or how I found the strength to stay where I was. I hoped and prayed the next thing out of his mouth was an apology. It wasn't. Nicholas, instead, went on again about how he was the victim of Karen's abuse and my lack of understanding about what this was like for him.

At this point, Nicholas and I had had several disagreements, almost always related to Karen's reaction to me. Each time this happened, I felt myself backing down to him easier and easier, always afraid that if I didn't, he would decide I was not worth the effort to keep in his life.

We met my brother, Scott, for lunch later that day. Nicholas was drunk and sat in the restaurant scowling and refusing to eat anything. Scott and I filled the space with our own conversation. I tried to ignore how awkward it felt. I texted my brother later to tell him what I had overheard and what Nicholas's reaction had been.

His response was "Aren't you sorry you came. What a terrible visit."

I did not have a response. I wished I could go back. I should have called an Uber and actually gone to the airport like I had threatened to. But instead, I was so desperate to stay in his life that I stayed and tried to salvage the weekend, even as my birth father looked at the world through the haze of wine.

I asked him over and over, "How could she be so cruel?"

Over and over his response was, "See what I have to deal with."

Nicholas was so hungover the day I left he could not drive me. I had hoped for a few more precious moments sitting next to each other on the couch before I had to leave for the airport. Instead I drove myself while he sat next to me with his eyes closed behind his sunglasses. He later told me that he had to park after I got out of the car and sleep a while before he could drive home.

On my way home I felt confused, hurt, with the feelings of abandonment seeping in. I had tried my best to do everything perfectly. I did not understand what had just happened. Once I was home, I realized he never confronted Karen about declaring I was never returning to their town. Instead he wrote to me about "what a darling Karen was being" since she had returned home and I had left. That alone hurt me more than when he told me to "shut the fuck up." The fact he was not confronting her was something I was struggling to wrap my mind around.

This solidified the notion in my mind that I was not worth standing up for. Lisa would never have stood for this, even if she was eternally grateful and striving to be perfect. But I was Michelle with Nicholas. Not just in what he called me, but in who I became—the little girl who was desperate for his love.

Instead I began therapy with Dr. Sarah. I hoped to learn how to cope with the rejection I was beginning to expect, rejection that continued to feel less like *perceived rejection* and more like actual rejection. Therapy was a great help for me—as research suggested it would be. Jones (1997) relates the importance of therapy specific to some of the issues adoptees may struggle with such as rejection and abandonment. Therapy for adoptees, like me, typically centers around the notion of loss and grief, even in the background of feeling grateful.

Once home, Dr. Sarah and I discussed this latest visit.

"I could not believe my ears, as I was hearing her say I was not welcome. Actually hearing it. And Nicholas did nothing. He just sat there. And now I have little faith he will fight for me at all. How can he think this is okay?"

"Well, Lisa, have you thought about what may be going on between them that he is not telling you?"

When Dr. Sarah asked me this, I did not want to admit that this had already crossed my mind. I knew how confused so many things were making me, but I could not put my finger on it. I did not yet understand the concept of *gaslighting*. Later, with Dr. Sarah's help, I started to put it together—but at this point, I was so wrapped up in wanting my birth father to keep me that I couldn't see the truth.

"I can only imagine how hurt you are, Lisa. How can you not be? You were abandoned at birth and now all you feel is rejection from Karen and not being cared for properly by your birth father. It must be really painful. Who is taking care of you in this situation?"

Much later, I eventually understood that Karen and Nicholas were not. I was too busy taking care of them. I tried constantly to make things better for Nicholas and I desperately wanted Karen to accept me. And neither one of them cared how this whole situation was impacting me.

Dr. Sarah was, and continues to be, someone who has helped me process rejection and loss, despite being grateful for my life, as an adult adoptee.

chapter 34

New Years

Sometime after that horrible weekend in Missouri, I became determined to make things better between Karen and me. I set my sights on the holidays. Nicholas had told me earlier that Karen said she "was tired of hearing my name in their home and I was ruining Christmas." I was careful not to interfere with that holiday. But New Years seemed to be more neutral territory. Karen had not yet met Bruce or Izzy. Perhaps, I thought, after she meets my family, I will not seem as much of a threat. She will see that I have a family and I am not trying to steal hers.

I broached the subject with Nicholas and even sent a bright, cheery email to Karen asking how they felt about getting together as a *family* for New Years Eve. I was not giving up or going away. Not yet anyway.

Karen responded that they had discussed it, and it seemed like a good idea. I was surprised, but I was also trying really hard. Maybe she was finally accepting me. I even added that I would consult with them (her) regarding the festivities. Karen reminded me that they "were older" and therefore needed consideration for the fact that they were in their seventies. She even added, at one point, in an email that it was unfortunate I had met my birth father as an old man, instead of earlier in his life.

Eventually, plans were secured and we rented an apartment near their home. My brother was ecstatic to meet Bruce. They had already bonded over the phone and seemed kindred spirits. Bruce is a "man's man" kind of guy and Scott seemed to admire that. Bruce, Izzy, and I flew to Missouri and I was hopeful this trip would build bridges and allow me to be folded more seamlessly into my birth father's life.

The weekend started out rocky. During one of the pre-holiday phone calls, Nicholas had said he would meet me at the airport, even though we were renting a car. He added he wanted as much time with his daughter as he could get and would drive me to the apartment. I walked off the plane and there was no Nicholas. We went to retrieve our bags, still no Nicholas. My daughter sensed my disappointment.

"Are you okay, Mom?" She asked, looking into my tear-filled eyes.

"I will never be good enough, Izzy, I just won't," I replied with a sigh and blinked away the tears.

I did not know why I had my hopes up so high. It was not really realistic to expect that he would greet me when we had to get a car anyway. But he said he would. And that was what stuck. After picking up the rental car, I checked my voicemail on the way to the grocery store only to find a message from Nicholas telling me that my visit "brought so much difficulty with it." I listened to the message and felt my heart sinking. I sucked in my breath slowly, swallowing tears as the lump in my throat made it hard to swallow.

"It's not your fault, my girl, we will see you soon," he added.

Then *who's fault* was it?

As we perused the groceries, I tried to wrap my head around what to buy for the entire weekend. I wanted to make things as easy as possible for Karen and Nicholas. I planned an awesome buffet and charcuterie for the next day, New Year's Eve. I picked out special cheese, a Merlot Cheddar and smoked Gouda. I added blue cheese-stuffed olives, mini dill pickles, smoked sausages, and an assortment of crackers.

My brother worked at the same grocery store and as we turned into the produce section, he met Bruce and Izzy for the first time. He was so happy, it filled my heart. As we stood talking, my phone rang. I did not have to check to know it was Nicholas. He sounded tired and a bit distant. I told him I could not believe he would disappoint me like that. He claimed to have no idea what I was talking about. I reminded him he had promised to meet me at the airport. He was defensive, and reminded me again of the difficulty he had when I was in town.

I had not made up that he was meeting me. I was sure of what he said. I was trying so hard to make things better. But every step I made was met with a reminder that my existence was wrought with difficulty and *stress*. We hung up with tension in the air.

That night, I received my customary text goodnight with the promise he would see me in the morning. I was expecting more disappointment, but instead he did indeed show up to my house that morning. I answered the door to his sheepish, lopsided grin that said, "I know you are upset, but I am doing the best I can."

I flung my arms around him and the tension faded. Izzy was still sleeping. and in true Nicholas fashion, he crawled in bed with her and told me to get on the other side to make an "Izzy sandwich." Izzy loved this and giggled with delight. We took a selfie and to this day, that picture makes me nostalgic. Despite the pain that came with this visit, I long for what felt like the promise of family.

Nicholas and I then went for a drive to have some time together and soak up some rare father-daughter face to face time. We sat in a church parking lot and marveled at the fact that my family and his were spending a holiday together. We stopped by his house to say hi to Karen. She was sitting in her robe by the fireplace. It was the first time I had seen her since the Father's Day weekend. So much had happened since. I was not sure how she would act.

I immediately went to her and flung my arms around her. "Hi there! It's so good to see you again!"

She leaned up and hugged me back. She stayed in her chair and commented "how tired she was and had not gotten dressed yet."

I wasn't sure if this was directed as a slight at me for being there and disrupting her sleep again, but I chose to ignore it. Instead I smiled and said, "I have lots of yummy treats for you guys. Izzy and I are famous for our charcuterie spreads!"

"Oh great, looking forward to it," she said as she smiled. Her smile did not quite meet her eyes, but I took it anyway and smiled back.

Afterwards, Nicholas dropped me off at the apartment we were renting and I prepared for the evening.

It was so important to me that Karen see I was a capable, adult woman who could care not only for my family, but for she and Nicholas as well. And also that we were a normal family that treasured our time together. I put on the best spread I could for them. Izzy helped arrange the charcuterie we carefully prepared. I wanted it to be convenient and easy to spend time with us. Later, I pulled gifts out I had meticulously wrapped and brought with me. Two of the gifts were purely sentimental and my way of solidifying the father-daughter bond. I gave Nicholas my baby book and an old photo album filled with pictures of me as a baby. My parents were in the pictures as well, and I realized this may have been difficult for him to see. But it was my history, my childhood. It was important to me to give him a part of my life he missed out on.

When they arrived, we sat briefly and flipped through the pages of my baby book. Karen looked on, smiling gently, as if she understood the importance of this. Nicholas looked sad, but also smiled as he looked through the pictures. He would look at a picture, then back to me, and slowly shake his head as if he was sorry he had missed these years with me. As he came to a picture of my parents, he looked at me and said, "I could kiss their feet for taking such good care of my girl."

It was bittersweet, but these were the moments I lived for during this time. It showed he truly claimed me as his own, but also respected that I had parents who I cared for deeply.

The evening ended early, as I had planned, because they "were older," as Karen had put it. I refrained from telling her that when Nicholas was in Detroit, we often sat up until 2:00 am talking. The rest of the evening was for Scott. He was coming over after work to ring in the new year with us.

The minute Scott arrived, he and Bruce embraced.

"Hey buddy, it's so good to hang out with you!" Bruce said, smiling widely, and he hugged him.

"Wow, you are a big guy! How tall are you?" Scott asked as he was enveloped in Bruce's hug. "I can't believe I have a new brother!" Scott said and I saw the tears in his eyes. It reminded me of when I had met Scott. He was so warm and genuine. He and Bruce became fast friends in person, and the four of us rang in the New Year together. All in all, it had been a good day.

The next day we planned to all go out to dinner. In the restaurant, Scott continued to chat it up with Bruce. It was so fun to watch my actual brother and my husband form a friendship. My heart was happy. Izzy sat next to Nicholas and the two of them giggled and cracked jokes. Izzy, always wanting to capture the moments, grabbed her phone and took a video of their antics.

I sat and smiled and could not have been happier that she and Nicholas also had some much needed time together.

Karen sat across from them and watched on. She seemed to not be able to take her eyes off of the two of them giggling and carrying on. I tried to take advantage of the time to chat more with her. I wanted her to feel included and also take what seemed awkward attention off of Izzy and Nicholas.

"So Karen, have you been home to see your family in Wisconsin lately?"

"No, I have not been home in a few years. There has been so much going on with Nick lately. His surgeries, recovering…" Karen let her voice trail off when she said this.

"Do you have a big family? Did you used to spend the holidays together?"

"Well my mom died when I was young, a teenager. And my brother was mentally disabled. That made things difficult. But I have another brother I am close to."

This made me sad and for one of the first times, I saw Karen's vulnerability. She did not have much family; Nick *was* her family. I knew how hard it was to lose my mom at thirty-two. I could not imagine how hard it would be to lose her in my teens.

"Oh, that had to be painful, I am so sorry," I said as I looked directly into her eyes. I know I saw a flicker of connection at that moment. "I don't know if Nicholas told you, my mom, Judy, died when I was thirty-two. I understand how hard losing a parent is."

Later, as we sat talking, Karen's nose started bleeding. I jumped up, took her by the arm and led her into the bathroom.

"Come on with me," I said as I walked with her. In the bathroom, I grabbed hand towels and pinched her nose.

"Lean your head back, I know it's hard, but it will help."

Karen nodded and did what I said. Eventually the bleeding stopped. Karen leaned her head back up and said, "This has been happening a lot lately. I have developed high blood pressure."

I knew this already, as Nicholas had told me.

A few months back, Nicholas had said, "Now, Karen claims she has high blood pressure. Apparently this is your fault, Michelle." I had apparently caused so much stress in their lives that her health was affected. No matter what Karen thought of me, the last thing I would ever do is cause harm. It went against my very nature. As a nurse *and* a caring human being.

Karen recovered but this seemed to end the evening. Izzy and I went home with them and Bruce went with Scott to his home; The two of them were going to spend more time being *bros*. As Izzy and I dropped Karen and Nicholas off at their home, Nicholas insisted we come in for a while. I could feel Karen's displeasure but pushed it away as if it was my imagination. She told us she had a headache and went to bed. Nicholas was giddy as the three of us giggled and told stories. Every now and then, Nicholas would get up and go into his bedroom. The door was shut. At one point I told Izzy we should go, it was getting awkward. Nicholas finally emerged and pointed at his bedroom door and rolled his eyes. We finally said our goodbyes and planned for the next day.

Our final day in Missouri, we took the leftover charcuterie to Nicholas and Karen's home to share. At one point, Karen and I were alone. She looked directly at me and said, "Those baby books are really hard for Nick to look at."

I looked at her as I popped a piece of cheese in my mouth. I did not know what to say to her. Was I supposed to not share this part of my past? And what about me? Did she think it was easy for me? This is messy stuff, but it is my life.

I wanted to say, "Yeah I know, Karen, it's a blast for me too."

But instead, I silently met her icy stare. The moment was thankfully interrupted when I heard my father's voice, "Michelle, come sit with me." Karen continued to stare at me as I walked into their living room to find Nicholas looking through my baby books. He was smiling and flipping through the pages.

"Look at you! You were such a beautiful baby!" he said and put his arm around me to pull me closer to him. We flipped through the pictures together again. This remains one of the best memories I have of this time in my life. The tensions of the conflict my presence seemed to create faded and we were simply father and daughter, reunited after fifty years.

Later, as I hung onto the final moments with my birth father, Karen gathered our coats. The message was clear; time to go, she had had enough. She added a dramatic yawn and expressed how *exhausted* she was. We said our goodbyes and as we did, I came up with an idea.

I looked at Karen and said, "Why don't Izzy and I come visit in March? Your birthday is only three days after mine, right? We will celebrate our birthdays and spend some time together."

She narrowed her eyes and said nothing. No nod either way, no mention of how she felt about this. Just a deadpan stare. Her face was void of any warmth. She simply stared at me, then looked at Nicholas, as if daring him to agree to my plan.

I was hopeful Nicholas would chime in and agree, but he just smiled at me. It struck me later that I was literally begging to spend time with them.

chapter 35

The 21st Birthday

few weeks later, I saw an email in my inbox from Karen and held my breath. My stomach dropped as I knew it could not be good. Nicholas never warned me that this email was coming, despite usually giving me a play-by-play of Karen's ranting about not wanting us there. I had faith he would intervene about my proposed March visit and insist that his daughter and granddaughter were always welcome. But this email let me know something different.

"Lisa,
You have known for most of your life that you were adopted and at least eight months before your father and I that your birth father was within your grasp. You also had this time to process these thoughts and emotions."

The phrase "in your grasp" was unsettling and conveyed an ugliness to me knowing Nicholas existed. It portrayed me as someone who was trying to snatch him out of his life. The reality had been quite the opposite. I had known and did not make contact out of respect for him and his family. I did not want to be what I was constantly accused of being—a stressful disruption.

"As I have said before, Nick is a loner and I am very shy and reserved. Neither of us like conflict or confrontation. Our home has always been a peaceful and quiet sanctuary. We have developed our relationship, lifestyle and homelife based on these qualities. As you can only imagine, how surprising, stressful and disruptive finding out Nick has a daughter was for both of us, being in our seventies."

Here in black and white were her words "stressful disruption." The description of their peaceful home, now filled with conflict and confrontation implied that I was the cause of the conflict and confrontation. The reality was I never confronted Karen. I only heard from Nicholas how much she hated me and wished I did not exist. According to him, each time he said my name, mentioned wanting to visit me or that I go visit them was met with an onslaught of attacks against me.

"I know this is very difficult for you to understand, but at our age change and stress is hard to process and handle. This has caused some health issues both Nick and I are working on to get our life back to a new normal that includes our daughter, Lisa Chism. I want to reassure you that we love you to pieces, and I do mean that from the bottom of my heart."

I did not nor have I ever felt Karen "loved me to pieces". In fact, I felt the opposite. I had done nothing but fight for her acceptance and love only to continue to hear about how much she did not accept me or want me around. Referring to me as "Lisa Chism" made her reference to me as "our daughter" feel forced and completely insincere. The email continued:

"After a year of disruption and stress, it has become apparent that some changes need to be made to address our health issues and find what will work best for all people involved. As a professional in the medical field, I'm sure you understand how damaging stress can be. Nick and I need some time for all this to settle in. Nick has always been more comfortable visiting you in Detroit and that is why last year he suggested all visits should be up there. Therefore, all visits in the foreseeable future will be in Detroit."

I had no idea Nicholas had agreed to only coming to Detroit to visit us.

"Nick has just informed me that you plan to come the first of March. Nick and I both request that you cancel your March trip."

I had asked each of them, together, when we were leaving their house over New Year's weekend, if Izzy and I could come in March and we could celebrate mine and Karen's birthday together. Nicholas later expressed excitement about my idea to visit and celebrate our birthdays together. He often added, "You are my daughter. You are always welcome."

"This trip has already caused stress and anxiety that we need to avoid. Visits between you and Nick have always been stressful."

Nicholas had always told me that the stress around our visits was due to Karen's resistance and "tantrums" that she had each time he suggested spending time with me or my family. In fact, when Nicholas and I were together, we laughed, marveled at the miracle that we knew each other, and truly enjoyed each other's company. Until he started drinking more and more.

"In September before he came to visit, he was so stressed that he had diarrhea, vomiting, severe acid reflux, and night sweats. You had to prescribe nausea medicine while he was there. He felt so bad, both Scott and I encouraged him to cancel this trip."

I later asked Scott about this. He told me that he never told his father not to visit me. And when Nicholas arrived in Detroit last September, he indeed asked me to prescribe something for his stomach and added that his symptoms were due to Karen's "relentless campaign" against me.

"As for your visit in October, he was so sick the morning you left, you had to drive to the airport. After he saw you off, he had to rest in the car before he could drive back here."

The day I went home from that trip, Nicholas was too sick to drive and "had to rest" because he was hungover. He had drunk wine the entire time I was there. He could barely hold his head up and had to keep his sunglasses on. Karen then mentioned the New Year's trip:

"Your trip here over New Year's was very stressful for both of us. Nick has tried to hide this from you, but the symptoms should have been obvious."

Nicholas had told me that the trip was wonderful and the only stress was Karen's constant negative comments and snide remarks about me.

"In the future we respectfully request that you do not invite yourself, make reservations, and then tell us you are coming. We can't continue to live this way. He said he has a trip planned for May to Detroit. I beg of you to try and understand how hard this is for us to work through and will need your help, understanding, and patience."

I was so confused by these statements. Each and every trip had been mutually planned and each time Nicholas adjusted trips he claimed it was because Karen was against him visiting me. I discussed plans with Nicholas each time. The reservations were not made without him being aware of plans that we had discussed. In fact, he gave me his American Express card to book his flights and reservations for him. If I believed Nicholas's version of what happened when he suggested visiting with me, the stress seemed to be coming from Karen's reaction to Nicholas's reaction to me being in his life. Karen's last remarks remained inconsistent with what she was actually conveying:

"I am a very sensitive and caring person, and it is as hard for me to send this email as it will be for you to receive it. I am also a believer that families should be open and honest with each other and work through personal issues together. I truly understand it's not the best timing for you and Nick to discover each other at this time in your lives, and living four states apart doesn't help."

I wish I could have asked her, "When exactly is a good time to finally meet your birth father that you never imagined you would meet?"

191

"The blessing is that you now have each other. It is also important for you to have a relationship that meets both of your needs. Please try to always keep in mind that Nick is seventy-six.

I honestly love you and want you to be a part of our lives.

Karen"

The last line was so inconsistent that if I had not been in tears, I would have laughed out loud. Who did she think she was trying to convince that she loved me and wanted me to be part of their lives? Me or her?

As I read it, the tears streamed down my cheeks. Bruce looked over worried, "What's wrong?"

"She wrote to me and told me to cancel our visit."

"What do you mean? Why?"

"Apparently my presence in their lives is too stressful and disruptive. And she claims Nicholas just told her that Izzy and I are coming to visit. She is basically telling me to stay away. I make my birth father sick."

"That's it! Get them on the phone! I have had enough of this bullshit. Let's get all the players in the room and find out what the hell is going on! Someone is lying, either Nick or Karen. Let's just sort this out right now!"

"No! I can't do that! I am so afraid, what if he gets mad and I never hear from him again?"

"I have had enough of this shit, Lisa! You don't deserve this! You are being *played!*"

Bruce finally backed down and agreed not to call anyone.

I was so heartbroken I never got off that couch the rest of the day. Later, my phone rang and it was Nicholas.

Bruce grabbed the phone and hung up. "Turn that goddamn thing off!" He shouted, "Enough is enough, Lisa!"

I let him take my phone. I was too dumbfounded to react. Bruce was angry. It was the beginning of him ending the "Team Nick" attitude he had had up to this point.

I learned some weeks later that Nicholas knew about the email and her plans to tell me not to come. It was, then, that my heart broke further into little pieces. My birth father was, once again, not standing for me. He was not choosing *me*. I was, once again, *unchosen*. I was more and more confused.

The damage that email did to my self-esteem would take years to undo. At the time, I held in there and tried to salvage the relationship with Nicholas and invited him to visit us for Izzy's twenty-first birthday. I was desperate to continue to fold him into our lives and be in his. I was still emailing and talking to Nicholas on a regular basis. He was still drinking and, as the drama between him and Karen intensified, he seemed to be drinking more and more.

For Izzy's twenty-first birthday, we had an extravaganza planned in our backyard, themed around the Netflix show *Bridgerton*. I bought decorations, arranged for a caterer—there was so much anticipation around it. Nicholas was even planning on coming into town. I had rented the same flat in Detroit per Nicholas's request. Nicholas had said he wanted to be there but it was going to be *hell* getting Karen to understand.

Then he called me in the afternoon on Mother's Day, just a few weeks before her party, and said, "I can't take it anymore. I want my life back. I want my art back. I am canceling my trip!" I had no idea what he meant by "my art back." But at the time, it was the least of my concerns.

Panic gripped me; the cold ice of his words creeped into my bones. The first thing out of my mouth was "I don't understand, Daddy! What have I done? Why would you cancel?"

And with that Nicholas hung up.

I had begun calling Nicholas "Daddy" in an effort to further solidify a bond between us, as a reminder that he was indeed my birth father and it was normal for me to want him to fight to keep me. I would do anything to ensure he would not give me up, but it was an exhausting, daily quest to be good enough to keep.

He called back later that night and told me he was, in fact, coming. Bruce and Izzy were angry he had ruined my Mother's Day, but I moved on and tried to be grateful that despite "all he had to deal with," he was coming to see us.

I threw Izzy the best twenty-first birthday shindig I could dream up with the help of a party planner and a checkbook. My backyard was transformed into an 1800s oasis with florals and pastels. I had raised Izzy to know that she was special to us, and that big milestones should be celebrated. I found out later that Nicholas and Karen had both commented on how *spoiled* Izzy was.

The day after the party my house was upside down. Nicholas sat in my family room and napped while I cleaned up, and at one point, I looked over at him and saw him watching me. The look of love on his face was enough to energize me, despite my fatigue. He later told me that it annoyed him that I buzzed around while everyone else let me wait on them. It sounded so paternal and protective. My anger and hurt would melt away during times like this and I would be even more committed to making this relationship work.

A few days later, on her actual birthday, Izzy made plans with her friends and her boyfriend to go to a bar and order her first drink as a legitimate twenty-one year old. She wanted me and Bruce there. She also wanted Nicholas there, but the reality was that Nicholas would likely not be able to endure a late night at a bar in the city. And I knew that spending a long time in a bar was not the best idea for him. We took a separate car to the bar, so we could leave early.

When Nicholas and I walked in, a young woman walked up to us and leaned over to me and said with a raised eyebrow, "Sugar daddy?"

I laughed out loud and said, "No!"

I told him what she had said and he laughed, "No! Genetic Daddy!"

The pride showed through in his eyes as he beamed. She looked at us embarrassed for her mistake and said, "Oh I can't come back from this!"

We laughed about this for months. It was another one of those moments that caused me to cling to the notion that we had a bond worth fighting for.

I stayed celebrating with Izzy until about 10:00 pm. I could tell Nicholas had had enough of the music and reverie. So we said our goodbyes.

I'll never forget the sad look in Izzy's eyes when I told her I was taking him home. I had once again chosen my birth father over her. I could feel her disappointment. At the time, I couldn't help it. The power he had over me was so strong.

Bruce stayed and I heard the stories about how they celebrated until 2:00 am. The realization hit me later: I can't ever get that time back. My daughter will never, again, turn twenty-one years old. I should have been at that bar with everyone celebrating. I have added this event to my list of things I wish I could do differently.

chapter 36

Rehab

I t had been months since I had last seen Nicholas and several things were alarming me. One, he was drinking more and more. Two, he was suffering from excruciating back pain and considering surgery. He told me the biggest reason he wanted to have surgery was he knew he could not drink and be on pain medication at the same time. He would be forced to quit drinking. I was alarmed he was considering back surgery as a means to stop drinking. Then one day, he called me with a different decision: he was going to rehab in California. I was not sure why California, but it seemed important to him to go to this particular place nestled in the Hollywood Hills.

The first time he went across the country, he stayed in rehab for about a week. The rule had been no phones. Nicholas refused to comply—he insisted on being able to use his phone and maintain contact with me—and went home. Any further talk of back surgery was on hold. His back pain seemed to have dissipated.

The next time he went back to the same rehab, he struck a deal with one of the employees. He would stay, if he could keep his phone. So he stayed a whole month. While he was there, he called every day and we would talk. He sounded free. He told me he did not want to go home. He fantasized about staying in California and starting a new life…or so he told me. When his stay was nearing an end, he told me he wanted to come stay with me for a while. I was ecstatic. He was choosing to visit me. I had waited so long to hear this. To feel *wanted*. He expressed how much easier it would be this time because he would not have to deal with constant resistance from Karen.

Mid-December, he asked me to book his flight. Izzy and I were so excited to spend part of the Christmas holiday with him. It spoke so much to the little girl inside of me that he wanted to come to me. Previous visits had been wrought with apprehension, waiting for him to cancel "due to the pressure he was enduring."

The joy I was feeling soon dissipated into thin air as he called me from his seat on the plane and asked, "Do you have wine?"

I did not respond and instead chose to ignore the question hoping that this was a brief relapse after a month of rehab. But it was not. Nicholas proceeded to drink the entire time he was at my house—ten days straight.

Initially, he was still composed. One evening, Nicholas asked to go to my hair salon with me. After my appointment, as we sat in the car to go home, he turned the volume up on my car radio, got out of the car, and asked me to come over and join him. We danced to the music right there in the parking lot. It reminded me of better, more whimsical days.

But as the days went on, the situation became more and more tenuous. The drinking became more of an issue, and I was uncomfortable around him. Nicholas was again spiraling. My birth father was asking for more and more wine and I felt powerless against his requests. I was vulnerable and desperate. I was put in the position a daughter would never want to be put in. Worse yet, Izzy was put into situations she never should have been put in.

At one point while he and Izzy went on a drive, Nicholas talked Izzy into stopping at a liquor store. Nicholas bought a bottle of wine and as they drove home, Izzy pleaded, "Please Grandpa, don't drink all of that. I want to hang out with you. Maybe we can watch a movie."

Nicholas's response was to open the door and attempt to get out of the car while it was moving down the road.

Izzy screamed, "No! Please, Grandpa, don't get out!" He slowed down only to wait until she approached our subdivision at which time he got out of the car, and walked to our home. Izzy was beside herself and called me to tell me.

"Mom, it was horrible! He almost got out of the car as I was driving down the road! I was so scared! And now he's in the house and didn't even apologize. It's like he's mad at me!"

Izzy was beside herself. I felt helpless. My heart sank both because of what she was going through and because of the sheer disappointment I was feeling. *What was I going to do?* I felt trapped and desperate.

"It's okay, Izzy, I am so sorry. It's not your fault. You did nothing wrong. I'll be home soon." I tried to reassure her, but I don't know who I was reassuring—me or her. As her mother, I once again ignored the urge to protect her and chose to cater to Nicholas's requests.

Until, toward the end of this visit, Lisa finally stepped in. And she had had enough.

Ten days after he had arrived, Nicholas was scheduled to fly home. Bruce was taking him to the airport. He had been drinking all night. Yes, there was alcohol in my home—alcohol that he had purchased. He had also told me not to hide alcohol before he came because he "would know that I had it." The whole trip, he had helped himself to whatever I had.

I spent the whole ten days trying to keep him happy, talk him into not drinking, and deal with the countless episodes that occurred, including him falling and bruising his lower lip in my kitchen. He showed up drunk at my practice after taking an Uber to my office. One of the medical assistants helped him out of the Uber and brought him to my office. He proceeded to dance in the hallway just outside my clinic rooms. I frantically shushed him and locked him in my office to keep him from disrupting patients. I care for women who are sometimes hearing the most difficult news they will ever hear—I couldn't have a drunk man dancing in the halls. He eventually fell asleep on my pink couch in my office reserved for my patients who need to be in a calm environment. At this point, *I* needed to be on that couch!

I was ready for him to leave, but I was not equipped to deal with this. I had so much anticipation and was now left with disappointment and heartbreak. Again.

I cried all the way to work the morning he was supposed to go home. I was exhausted and felt broken in ways I could not understand or describe. When Bruce called me later and told me he could not take Nicholas to the airport because he was too drunk to leave, something inside of me broke even further. I was in a haze and felt trapped. *How did this happen? Why did this happen?* It was not until Izzy called me sobbing that I snapped out of my haze.

Izzy had heard a conversation between Karen and Nicholas that morning. He still had the archaic flip phone, so she could hear both sides of the conversation clearly. Through her tears, Izzy described Karen's words:

"I am trying to help you Nick, they won't let me. Her home is unhealthy for you! It's her fault you drank, and now you can't get home!"

Karen carried on while tears streamed down Izzy's face. Nicholas listened, nodding and never stopped Karen from blaming me.

I drove home with a fury still that burns through me today. My daughter's sobbing had triggered Lisa to wake up and take over for Michelle. I was in full protective mode, and I was angry.

I arrived home to find Nicholas sitting on the couch. He innocently looked at me with raised eyebrows and said, "Is something wrong?"

"Yes. And it's time for you to go!" I grabbed my laptop, sat next to him, and pulled up the airline website, "Pick your flight, you are either going to L.A.—back to rehab—or home. But you are not staying here. You and Karen have hurt me and my daughter enough!"

As I sat next to Nicholas and told him to decide where he was going, he called Karen.

"I am coming home. My daughter doesn't want me."

I promptly and loud enough for Karen to hear me replied, "No, it is not that I don't want you! It's that I am done being hurt by you and Karen!"

Karen's reply through the phone rang out, "I am done with you hurting us, Lisa!"

I have often thought back to this exchange and thought, what exactly did I do to hurt you Karen? I never rejected you. I did not nickname you "that fucking bitch." I did not make my birth father choose between me and you.

But the reality is, considering how much Nicholas told me about the horrific play-by-play between he and Karen regarding my existence, I will never really know what he was telling Karen about me. He could have been pitting us against each other for reasons unknown.

Eventually later that night, we took Nicholas to the airport. I recruited a kind airport employee to help him to his gate. Izzy said goodbye first. I then hugged him goodbye, but my sincerity was hollow. As I looked in his eyes, I saw emptiness reflected back at me. I felt lost and defeated. Where was the man who reached out to me on the AncestryDNA app? Was *this* the real Nicholas? I had tried so hard to be the perfect daughter. I was not sure whether the emptiness in his eyes was because of his intoxication, or because he knew I was kicking him out and sending him home. I had no idea what would happen when he got home or whether I would hear from him again. And at this point, I honestly did not care. I wanted to protect my daughter and myself from the continued pain.

When I went home, I collapsed on my couch, and sat staring. I was drained. My emotions were in a tailspin. I felt as if someone had wrenched out my soul, stepped on it, and left it lying on the ground as scraps for vultures. The energy in my house was so negative it took days for me to shake it.

My cat, Tiffany, who was always in the same room as us, had retreated upstairs a day after Nicholas's arrival. She finally made her way downstairs a few hours after Nicholas was gone. I am certain she could sense the toxic energy in the house and finally felt safe to come out of hiding again.

I had no idea when that would happen for me.

chapter 37

Beverly Hills

For several days after Nicholas went home, I did not hear from him. This had become the pattern whenever things escalated to the breaking point. I tried to heal and took the lack of communication as a gift. I figured Karen went into savior mode to nurse Nicholas back to health after his narrow escape at the clutches of his evil daughter.

Scott, much like Nicholas, sometimes told me details that I could live the rest of my life not knowing. The latest included a slew of untruths that Nicholas told Karen, including that I had open bottles of wine all over the house and I left him laying dehydrated and drunk on the kitchen floor after he fell. Apparently Scott and Karen actually got into a fight over this as she poked him in his chest with her finger and said, "What kind of a person does that?" Scott confronted her, but she continued to imply that Nicholas's drinking was entirely because of me.

The weeks passed into months with intermittent contact between Nicholas and I. Eventually he let me know he was going back to California again and this time was potentially *permanent*. Nicholas often added to his proposed plans that he fantasized about moving away permanently,

200

reminiscent of the days when he asked me to find an apartment in Detroit for him to move to.

He was in rehab again for about four weeks and once there, he began calling me again regularly. During one of our conversations I randomly said, "What if Izzy and I came there to see you?"

Izzy and I were always up for a mother-daughter trip and it seemed a safe atmosphere. He wouldn't be drinking. I wanted a redo after what had happened in December at my house. I was always mindful of the time we had left and the time we had lost. I thought if we went there, we could reconnect and things could be better again. I was always hoping to restore the magic of our earlier visits. I was tragically still holding on to hope.

Izzy also expressed wanting another chance to have a meaningful visit with her grandfather. I often did not acknowledge at the time how painful this experience was for her. More regrets, my friend. Giving her a *redo* wrapped up in a trip to California seemed a way to acknowledge her loss.

Nicholas and I did not speak about his last trip to Michigan, and I did not question him in regards to what he was telling Karen about his time in my home. I was once again, avoiding confrontation, afraid that if I did confront him, I would not hear from him again. When I did ask him if he wanted us to come he exclaimed "Yes! I would love it if you came here!" This made my heart soar. It was all I ever wanted. *To be wanted.*

Izzy and I arrived in LA and had dinner with my Aunt Wendi, J.T.'s wife (my birth uncle who had passed away). We missed Wendi and reconnecting with her was like wrapping ourselves up in a warm blanket before we braced ourselves for the weekend visiting Nicholas.

Izzy was excited to see Nicholas, but we both had been through so much and had become accustomed to things going backward. We were both anxious but hopeful. After all, at least he could not drink while he was physically under the watchful eyes of the rehab employees.

After dinner, my Aunt Wendi dropped us off at the home in the Hollywood Hills that served as a rehab facility. Nicholas was riding an exercise bike in the garage when we pulled up. He jumped off and embraced us both. He looked wonderful, face full, color restored, and more youthful than he had months before. And once again, all was forgotten for a while.

Izzy and I brought a speaker to play music off of our phones as we sat and visited with Nicholas. We sat outside, under the bright sunshine next to a pool in the courtyard. These moments were special as we sat and talked, listening to music. At one point, Nicholas came over to me and reached out his hand to ask me to dance with him. Izzy took pictures of us. I was so happy at that moment.

As we danced, he leaned over and said in my ear, "Oh Michelle, if I am ever forced to choose between you and Karen, I choose you."

I was touched and looked at him as he pulled me into a hug. My only response was to hug him back.

This struck me on so many levels. Although I wanted to be wanted, I did not understand why he should *have* to choose. And why was it always about the choice between Karen and I? Why couldn't it be both of us? Was it Karen or was it Nicholas who felt there had to be a choice?

We visited with Nicholas throughout the weekend, including taking him to lunch on Rodeo Drive. The owner of the rehab knew we were coming and because of the uniqueness of our story and Nicholas's progress, had granted him a day pass. As we strolled along the beautiful shops, I showed him a Chanel belt I put on layaway at a consignment shop. Nicholas pulled out his credit card and said, "How much do you need? I will pay it off." I accepted his offer. I had not ever asked anything of him. And it was clear I did not want or need anything material from him, but I knew this would be a momento from the trip. And it made me feel special that he offered.

I still wonder if this was his attempt to be paternal—or was Nicholas trying to be someone he wasn't? Was it his way to try to compete with my adoptive parents who had clearly shown me safety and security, sometimes in the form of *spoiling* me?

The weekend hinted at the magic of earlier times. Unfortunately, Karen's opinion of me crept up again. Nicholas took a phone call from her one evening we were there and came out of his bedroom shaking his head. He told me Karen was upset we were there and added that her words were, "It's that bitch's fault you are in there."

When I turned my eyes downward and sighed, his response to me was, "Don't do that." Apparently I was not supposed to show how defeated and painful it was to always be the reason for the upheaval in their lives, including Nicholas's drinking.

I had become so accustomed to not speaking up, for fear that I would upset him. Or worse, he would not want me in his life. And I did what a dutiful, grateful and striving to be perfect daughter would do—I obeyed my birth father.

chapter 38

The Red Eye Rescue

When Nicholas was in rehab, he was free to call me whenever he wanted. There were no time limits on our phone calls and no play-by-play of the tirades that apparently took place whenever the subject of me came up. Nicholas often shared how much easier life was when he was in California, in his oasis. Nicholas tried to stay longer in the oasis of rehab but eventually had to go home.

He started drinking a few weeks later and made plans to return to rehab again. I knew he was leaving one Saturday afternoon and was waiting for his call.

But instead of a phone call from Nicholas came a phone call from Karen. I was grocery shopping and looking forward to a relaxing evening at home. I saw her name and panicked.

I answered, "Karen, what's wrong?" I knew there had to be something bad for her to call me.

"Lisa, I need help. I can't get Nick on the plane. They told him he was too drunk to board. Can you come here and help get him to LA?"

Scott lived nearby, but Nicholas apparently asked for me, specifically. And that was all I needed to know. I was the daughter. I was the nurse. I was the fixer.

My mind was reeling, but not because I was questioning whether or not I would do this. I knew I would do this—what I was worried about was how I was going to tell Bruce I was flying to Missouri only to get on another plane the next day to fly Nicholas to LA. I would have to take a red-eye home to get back in time and not miss my clinic. I had a full schedule of patients that Monday and I did not want to cancel their appointments.

I told Karen to give me a few minutes to talk to Bruce and figure it out. I texted Joseph, one of the employees of the rehab facility. He and I had become friends over the last few months and even met in person when we visited. I told Joseph I was trying to work it out and help Nicholas get back to LA.

When I walked in the door from grocery shopping, I broke the news to Bruce. To say he was not happy was an understatement.

"Are you crazy Lisa! Why would you do this? This is ridiculous!"

"I know; but I have to Bruce, you don't understand, they need me," I pleaded with him.

"They are just going to abuse you more, don't you get that?! That's all these people have ever done to you. Your father abuses you! Karen is such a bitch to you! They are both crazy! You don't need this, Lisa! You have been through enough! And what about Scott? Why don't they just ask Scott to help—or wait for Nick to sober up? This is ridiculous!"

I knew he was right. But I had to go. I had to show them I could be counted on when they needed me. I was going to show Nicholas and Karen once and for all that I was a *good daughter* and a *good person*. I was going to be there for them. As a caretaker, it was my nature. Despite all that had happened, I would not let them down.

Bruce was not happy, but eventually let it go. He knew he could not change my mind. Nothing could back then. I had tunnel vision aimed at earning their love and acceptance.

I tried to call Karen to tell her my flight itinerary and I kept getting bumped to voicemail. Then it hit me; I was blocked. Joseph had to text her and tell her to unblock me. I was actually not surprised she had blocked me. Nicholas had told me she always threatened to do so. But I was surprised I was blocked now, when she had reached out for my help.

Nicholas and Karen picked me up at the airport, four hours after she had called me. Karen was, of course, driving as Nicholas sat with sunglasses on.

"Hi, Lisa," she said, "thank you so much for coming. We really do appreciate it."

"You're welcome," I responded as I basked in being their savior. It had also occurred to me that if Karen blamed me for Nicholas's drinking, she likely felt justified asking for my help. I wondered if this was *proving grounds* for me.

"Yes, thank you, sweetheart, for coming," Nicholas added quietly.

He was more subdued than I expected.

"Karen, can we stop for wine?" he asked.

"We have wine at the house, Nick. We will get some when we get home."

As I sat in the backseat and listened to this exchange, I thought how ironic it was that Karen was now in the difficult position of placating a grown man who should clearly not be drinking; especially because she blamed his current state entirely on me.

Once back at their house, it was already late and I was exhausted. I spent the night in their guest room. The next morning, Nicholas laid down next to me and put his arms around me. "I can't believe you came to help me, Michelle. Thank you."

At that moment, I realized I would have done anything just to hear him say this. The pain and disappointments washed away. In that moment, I was allowed to shine as the *perfect* daughter. Surely, they would both now see that me being in their lives was not a bad thing. I just wanted to be loved. I wanted to be wanted.

Joseph met us at the LA airport. By this time, Nicholas was drunk. I did not know how to stop my father from drinking. Especially in public and while on the plane. I don't think he ate anything that day, despite Karen and I trying to get him to have some dinner. And the wine went immediately to his head.

Joseph sailed down the LA freeway on the way to the rehab facility, with me in the front seat and Nicholas in the back. Nicholas asked him to stop and get more wine. When Joseph said no, Nicholas rolled down the backseat window and tried to climb out of the car, just as he had done with Izzy.

I started screaming, "Daddy, no stop!"

Joseph was thankfully a muscular guy; he quickly pulled over and stopped Nicholas from getting out of the car. It was terrifying. We got Nicholas back to rehab, but I was exhausted—and still had another flight ahead of me.

On the red-eye flight home, I tried to sleep but the stress of the last twenty-four hours was catching up. I was too tired to sleep. I thought about what I had just done and hoped it would make an impression on Karen and that things would finally be different. I called her after I got back to the airport to let her know that Nicholas was safely delivered to Joseph. She seemed grateful.

"Thank you, Lisa, I really appreciate you coming and helping. Maybe now Nick will finally get more help and understand he can't keep doing this."

And for a while, I basked in her approval.

chapter 39

The Intervention

Nicholas stayed in rehab two weeks this time. Once he arrived home, he quickly resumed drinking. Karen called me once again and asked me to help with an idea she had. She asked if I would come again for the weekend for an *intervention* of sorts. Despite the fact that I had just shown my commitment to helping them by getting Nicholas on the plane weeks before, I was surprised by this. It was still so foreign to me to be accepted by Karen as an integral part of their family. I was, of course, going to jump at this. I am a caregiver. And I had only ever wanted to be part of their lives. It did not matter how rocky the last few years had been, I was still desperate to be included.

Karen told me that she was hoping that if Nicholas saw how much his drinking was hurting everyone, maybe he would see the light and turn things around. I agreed immediately. I was once again being called to save my birth father and further solidify my worthiness of being kept.

Bruce was, once again, not happy. But he knew at this point there was no talking me out of it.

Karen and Nicholas picked me up at the airport. Karen had told Nicholas I was "just coming to visit."

Scott was happy I was in town but surprised at my constant steadfast commitment to Nicholas's sobriety. He felt, much like Bruce, that I had been abused enough by Karen, Nicholas, and the entire situation. This much is true, but I was not giving up.

Yet.

The goal for the weekend, per Karen's request, was that at some point, I appeal to Nicholas's sense of family and request that *for us*, he stop drinking. Scott would be there as well, sharing the sentiment. I made up my mind I was up for the challenge. I would make a difference. After all, I was accustomed to helping people.

The moment of truth came the next afternoon. We were gathered around Nicholas and looking at old photos. When the moment seemed right, I looked up at Nicholas and said, "Daddy, you know how much we love you. We want us to all be together, as a family. But if you keep drinking, you are going to shorten that time. You need to do something to stop. I care about you. We all do. Please do something. Please go back to rehab and take it seriously this time. You can't just keep coming home and start drinking again." My voice was pleading and I started to choke up.

At this point, I could tell Nicholas sensed the motive behind my *visit*. I watched as the switch went off and his eyes turned cold. I had seen this switch first at my house months before. I recognized what was about to happen. He looked away as if to dismiss me and end the conversation.

"Now, Michelle, that's enough." That was it. No earth shattering revelation that he understood and knew how important this was—just a quick shutdown. I had failed my mission. No one threw me a life raft; Scott and Karen both looked down, somewhat defeated, but said nothing. I alone had broached the subject and I alone had been shut down.

Later that night, Nicholas had been drinking all day and was starting to get to that point where his personality shifted into someone I did not recognize. Someone terrifying. In an effort to keep him calm, Karen offered to take him and me for a ride. She knew he was escalating.

As we were driving down the road, Nicholas—in the passenger seat—asked to stop and get wine and Karen said "no, Nick, you have had enough. "

That set him off, and as Karen drove, I watched from the backseat as Nicholas once again opened the door and tried to get out. Karen yelled, "Nick, stop!" and attempted to grab the back of his shirt as he tried to get out of the moving car. As Karen continued to scream with fear laced in her voice, I snapped out of my exhausted trance.

In my anger and frustration I yelled, "Stop! What is wrong with you?"

Karen pulled off to the side of the road—I jumped out of the car and ran to the passenger side door, wrestling him back in. Despite Nicholas being slight in build, he was strong and he pushed back at me. I eventually got him back into his seat, shut the passenger door, then climbed back in the backseat.

As the night went on, things progressively got worse. I was exhausted and Nicholas once again went out to the garage to get more of the wine he had stashed in the trunk of his car. I don't recall exactly what precipitated the next series of events, but at one point, while he was ranting about wine and cursing at me and Karen, I pulled out my phone and started recording him.

When he saw what I was doing, he became someone I did not want to ever see again. His eyes went black and his face was red and squinched up. Through snarling teeth he sneered "You son of a bitch!"

He repeated this over and over and tried to pry the phone from my hands. I pulled away and ran up the stairs. There was more commotion—I shut the guest room door. I no longer felt safe and wanted to bury myself in the blankets. I cried myself to sleep that night.

The next day, I went downstairs to find Karen sitting in the living room. She looked tired, with bags under her eyes. Despite being fatigued, she had gone to Dunkin Donuts and brought me back my favorite coffee and bagel bites. I sat down in the seat next to her and said, "Oh my, I needed this, thank you so much."

As I sipped on my coffee I asked, "Do you want to see the video?"

She sighed and said, "Yes, show me."

We sat together and watched Nicholas's drunken rant. I started to cry and Karen put her arm around me.

"I am so sorry he hurt you like this. This is not Nick. I feel bad you are seeing him like this." She went on to say, "Lisa, I now see a different side to you I never saw before."

I wondered if she had not *wanted* to see a different side to me before now. But she seemed sincere, and for a moment, we bonded over our love for Nicholas and our despair at what he was doing to his family and to himself. We both cared deeply for this man, that was clear.

Nicholas came strolling into the room we were sitting in and asked in an innocent, absent-minded sort of way, "Am I in trouble?"

I recalled later that this was a similar pattern. When his behavior was so hurtful, so despicable, it was hard to comprehend, he often claimed to not remember what had happened. I, of course, took the opportunity to enlighten him. I was angry—Lisa was taking over. I showed him the video of the night before.

As Nicholas watched himself curse his daughter, and become someone I am certain he was not proud of, his expression changed. It was not one of remorse, but instead one of defiance.

He looked at me and said, "The fact that you took that video and showed it to me is all I need to know."

As he said this I felt the drop in the pit of my stomach. This was not the reaction I was hoping for. I had hoped for an "Oh Michelle, I am so sorry I said those awful things to you!"

But instead he was calculated and callous. His eyes were cold when he looked at me and turned and left the room. I realized at this moment that I had not ever witnessed Nicholas take responsibility for hurting people. Especially when he was drunk. And thinking back, I wonder even more if he contributed to how Karen felt about me early on in our relationship. He simply makes excuses and blames other people for his own situations. It was triangulation, right before my eyes.

I looked at Karen and she looked away and I swear I saw a hint of relief that she had not been the one to take the video. She said nothing to come to my rescue. I was alone in my confrontation of my birth father's behavior.

I felt my world collapsing around me. I sat and wept in the chair next to Karen and she put her arms around me.

"Oh Lisa, I am so sorry. I know you are hurting. We all are."

I had no words. I was in disbelief that this was happening. She held me until I stopped sobbing.

At that moment, I believed her and I still believe her now. The pain in that room that she and I shared was raw and it was real. It was probably the most authentic time she and I ever spent together.

Nicholas walked back in a few minutes later and announced he was going for a ride. He found the keys, looked in my direction and said, "Lisa, are you taking an Uber to the airport?"

If I thought the world as I knew it had just ended, this sent it into orbit. For the first time ever since I had known him, he called me by my *real* name.

And I could not find enough air in the room. My chest felt like it was caving in. He was cutting this connection off. And worse of all, I knew he knew it.

Karen drove me to the airport a bit later. She said she needed the break and the drive to clear her head. She dropped me off and got out of the car.

As she approached me, she leaned over and hugged and said, "I love you. I am so sorry about all this."

"I love you too, I really wish I could have helped more. I might have made things worse, taking that video."

"No, you did not make things worse. You tried your best to help, I know that."

All this time, all I had wanted was her love and acceptance. I finally had it, but I had to be put through hell to get it.

I sat in the airport bar at 11:00 am and called Bruce while I sipped a Chardonnay as fast as I could reasonably get it down without drawing attention to myself. As I described what had happened, tears streamed down my face. I could barely talk to him for fear the deep, guttural wailing would ensue. Bruce later told me that in the thirty-some years he has known me, he has never heard me sound like that. I have lost both my parents, experienced my share of various disappointments and heartbreak, and I have to agree, I have never felt that kind of pain before.

chapter 40

Halloween

S everal weeks went by. Nicholas went to rehab again, a different rehab—and by the time he got there, he was in bad shape. So much so that the facility called Karen and told her they could not handle his level of care and he needed a nursing facility.

Karen reached out to me and asked "given my connections in the health field, could he come to Detroit and get help?"

I was petrified at this point to be around him at all, never mind when he's been drinking. I had had enough pain to last a lifetime and I felt an obligation to protect my family, especially my daughter. I had put Izzy through enough. I knew Bruce would never agree. He no longer gave Nicholas the benefit of the doubt and was not convinced things would ever be different.

I told Karen no, I was sorry but I could not help. I am sure she was not happy and I fell down a rung or two on the ladder of her good graces, but that couldn't take priority over my family, and my family and I had been through enough.

Nicholas came home and, according to Karen, was indeed not the same man who had left days before. He was unable to walk on his own and was confused. He was diagnosed with Korsakoff syndrome due to alcohol abuse, which means he had cognitive changes related to his drinking.

As the weeks went by, he remained sober and eventually started doing better. He was able to walk unassisted again and was much more coherent. He was in touch with me more and more, and things seemed okay—but then, one day, out of the blue, I picked up his call for him to sneer through the phone, "Karen said that she asked if I could come to Detroit and you said no."

So, she'd told him what I'd said. The familiar pit in my stomach seized up and I said, "yes, but let me explain—"

I never got to explain. Nicholas hung up. Shocking, I know. I later sent him an email detailing everything he had done to hurt me over and over, including coming to my office drunk and dancing in my hallway. He barely acknowledged the email.

Months went by, and near the end of summer he, once again, contacted me. My email was not mentioned, but he did tell me that he had not been drinking for several months. He was healing and seemed like himself. He asked if he could come visit. I was surprised—I had doubted he would ever come back to Michigan. I told him yes, but he would need to bring Karen. I did not trust him to not try and drink, and I was not going to be put in a dangerous position again without Karen around to help. They settled on Halloween and Izzy and I, with a renewed sense of hope, made plans to host them for our favorite holiday. Bruce went along with our plans. He was reserved when it came to Nicholas. I think he just wanted me to be happy and understood I was still trying to salvage something out of this relationship.

Izzy and I love Halloween. We have hosted witch-themed parties, have made several trips to Salem, Massachusetts in October, and always decorated our house with a plethora of Halloween-themed decor. Izzy and I were excited to show them our home in full Halloween mode. We made plans for their visit including handing out Halloween candy, a pastime Nicholas had told me he loved. We rented an apartment near our home for them and planned a menu to make their visit pleasant and easy. When they arrived I had a Crockpot of broccoli cheddar soup waiting for them.

Their visit was uneventful with Nicholas under Karen's watchful eye, especially compared to previous visits. Nicholas still talked about drinking all the time, but remained sober. Including at a special event we took them to The Whitney. The restored home-turned-restaurant was putting on a special

Halloween brunch. We all dressed up—I bought Karen a witch hat to match Izzy and me. Nicholas was quiet at the restaurant and asked for wine each time the server came by. Karen spoke up and said "No, Nick; no wine."

Izzy and I once again tried our hardest to create special memories but it felt that our efforts fell flat. As we sat at the Whitney, Nicholas hardly spoke. He did not eat, and complained of feeling *spacey* the whole time. I have no idea if this was his way of pouting because he did not get any wine, or if he indeed did not feel good. Each time we tried to engage with him, he barely spoke and just looked at us with a blank stare.

There were a few good moments. Karen went to bed early and Izzy lay her head in my lap as Nicholas and I listened to music and talked until two in the morning. During those hours, my hope to hold on to my fantasies of my birth father loving me, folding me into his life, were rekindled. It felt as if the earlier magic was just within reach…only to slip through my fingers like water. Overall, there were no hurtful things said, no significant drama of the past visits and we took it as a win. It was the best we could hope for.

chapter 41

Out in the Cold

Nicholas seemed to have a renewed sense of urgency regarding time. As Christmas came near, he seemed a bit nostalgic and wanted me to visit. Karen wanted to go home to her family in Wisconsin, and asked if I would come and stay with Nicholas. Izzy and I made plans to visit for his birthday on January twentieth.

Somewhere along the way, Nicholas started drinking again. Scott called me a few days before our trip to Missouri and said, "Are you sure you want to come here? He's bad again."

Scott then told me about an episode that happened earlier in the week. Nick was at his house, drunk, and had swung at him to hit him. Scott had to hold him back. Scott had no idea why he was so angry. But thought it had something to do with not wanting to give Nick alcohol. Scott was still so upset by the exchange between them. He was barely speaking to Nicholas.

"I already told Karen I would be there." I said.

"Does Bruce know Nick's drinking again?"

"Yes, but not all the details of what happened between you two."

I had not told Bruce about Nicholas swinging at Scott. I know I should have, but I was on autopilot, trying so hard to once again overlook the bad

215

and step up as a dutiful daughter and caregiver. I knew Karen needed me to come so she could go home to Wisconsin. Her step mother was declining in a nursing home and she needed to see her brother. She was wary of leaving Nicholas home alone since he had started drinking again.

She in fact requested over text that we come for a longer visit. "Lisa, can you come Monday and stay for six days?"

I thought about this. I had been through so much. And if he was drinking again, I had no intention of being there that long. I only had so much time off from my practice. I wanted to help Karen and I wanted to spend time with Nicholas. But I was not up for that long of a visit. I had been through enough.

"No Karen, but I will come right after work on Thursday. Izzy and I will fly out that evening."

I had hoped that was enough time for her. I sensed a bit of irritation but you never know when you are texting. Maybe I was reading into it.

I don't know what the catalyst to Nicholas drinking again truly was, or if there was one. He always seemed to blame it on Karen's reaction to me. This time when he tried that excuse, I was confused. I was under the impression things were finally better and I told him so. His response was, "No Michelle, she is threatened by you and always will be."

In my head, I questioned whether this was true or not. Was he seeking an excuse to drink? Or were things with Karen changing again behind the scenes? The only thing I knew for sure was that we were indeed welcome this time.

Izzy and I arrived the day before his birthday at 11:00 pm to find him sleeping in his office chair. I could tell by the voicemails he had left while I was in flight that he had been drinking all evening. We woke him up and sleepily, he acted shocked to see us as if we had broken in.

One particular comment Nicholas made to my daughter that night still haunts me to this day. Initially, I tried to brush it off as just a drunken comment, but now the comment sickens me. Izzy had on a red sweater pant set that complimented her figure. Nicholas looked her up and down and said, "Wow, look at you! Have you ever been raped?"

Izzy looked at me, eyes wide, startled by this comment. I looked back at her with my mouth open. I was speechless for a moment.

But when I found my voice, I looked at Nicholas and said, "You know, Dad, rape is an act of violence."

He looked at me and seemed shocked I actually spoke up to him this way. "Well, yes, I know that! I was just kidding."

That comment should have sent me home at that moment. I regret so much not doing more for Izzy when he said that.

But while I didn't do enough in that moment, something inside me shifted because of that comment. It had never occurred to me earlier to recognize that the story of my beginning was being weaved by an expert storyteller.

It was years later when my therapist Dr. Sarah pointed out to me, "Lisa, you are a certified sexual health counselor. You really believe that there was no penetration?"

When she said it like that, the truth seemed obvious. But wanting to believe something is very powerful. So powerful that I did, in fact, believe his story. Until now. Now that he treated rape—the rape of my daughter, no less—like a joke, I was starting to question everything he had ever told me.

Looking back, I tried to overlook the sense of dread I was beginning to feel. Despite our fears for what may lie ahead in the next few days, we tried to be hopeful and the next day, Nicholas's birthday, we gave him gifts we had carefully picked out for him. We went to breakfast and my main objective became to keep him fed to avoid him becoming so intoxicated that he reached that point where his eyes turned dark and he became someone I feared.

The day after his birthday, sometime in the afternoon, I began to sense the change. I was desperately trying to get him to eat. I don't know the exact time I saw the shift start to happen, but I could feel the icy panic in my chest as I realized we may be at the point of no return. While I rushed to put together dinner, Nicholas was preoccupied with a sliver that was stuck in his arm and became determined to cut it out with a razor blade. He picked this particular moment to enlist my help. As a nurse, I know *bathroom surgery* is never a good idea.

I told him. "No, not now; not with the razor blade."

He looked at me with those dark eyes and sneered, "Oh okay, Dr. Chism, then I will do it myself."

He continued to mutter under his breath and make snide comments about me not willing to help him. I blocked out much of what he said. Izzy was standing in the doorway of the bathroom and I could sense she was getting angry listening to how he was treating me. Her eyes narrowed and lips were pursed as if she were resisting telling him to stop.

217

In the meantime, he sliced his arm open with the razor blade and success-fully removed the sliver.

"There, see, I don't need your help." He was defiant and stormed off, dripping blood along the way. I chased after him to try to stop the bleeding, but he was storming around too much to catch up with him. Blood was dripping all over the floor as he stormed from room to room. The grisly scene seemed to symbolize what was to come.

I sensed trouble and told Izzy to go upstairs. Izzy did as I asked. She was getting a migraine and I offered to go get her some ibuprofen. At this point, I was trying anything I could to keep things calm. Nicholas went upstairs and asked Izzy where I had gone. "She went to get me some ibuprofen."

Nicholas looked at Izzy and sneered, "You have two legs! Get up off your ass and get it yourself!"

To which Izzy responded in true Izzy form laced with sarcasm, "Oh, are you gonna be a dick to me, too?"

Nicholas responded to Izzy by screaming at her, "Fuck you, you spoiled little bitch!"

"Oh here we go, now you *are* going to be a dick!" Izzy said back to him.

"You have had everything handed to you your whole life! You are beyond spoiled!" he said through gritted teeth.

I heard an exchange from downstairs and I flew up the stairs. I, then, said in a calm yet loud voice, "Do not talk to my daughter that way."

I looked at Izzy and said, "Get your study materials and go to the guest room." She looked at me as if to say "are you going to just take this?" but I looked her in the eyes and said with a pleading tone to my voice, "Izzy, I said get out of here now, it's gonna get worse, please go in the other room!"

He then turned toward me and proceeded to scream at me, too.

"She has the brain the size of a pea! Her and her piece of shit father!"

Izzy then turned and screamed through her angry tears, "My piece of shit father? You have not been in her life for fifty years and you are calling *my dad* a piece of shit?"

Nicholas's eyes were black and spit flew out of his mouth as he looked at me and said, "I fucking hate her! She's an alien! I am done hiding it!" His face was red and he was banging his hand so hard on the wall the nurse in me thought for a second, "he's going to break his hand."

I do remember something inside of me splitting in two. As if the weight of all the pain, all the drama of the last three years was too much anymore. I slumped on the floor and crumbled at his feet and crawled away. I yelled for Izzy who had run into the guest room and shut the door.

"Izzy, stay there, I am coming!"

I finally stood up and busted into the room to find her sobbing and shaking. My heart broke into even finer shreds at this point.

"Please," I pleaded with her, "stay here and keep the door shut! Do not come out or let him in!"

I then heard shouting, banging and the garage door opening from downstairs. I was terrified he was going to drive and kill himself, or someone else. I ran back down stairs and opened up the door to the garage and yelled, "Don't leave! You can't drive like this!"

I chased him around his car to try to get his keys. That's when I noticed Izzy had followed me. She then did what I had done months before and started to video him. I knew this was not a good idea. But you tell that to a young twenty-something girl as her mother is being screamed at by her birth father.

Nicholas saw her and lunged at her, trying to pry her phone away from her. Izzy is stronger than me and pushed him off of her.

Screaming, I told him, "Get your hands off my daughter!"

Nicholas looked at me with vacant, dark eyes and yelled in a deep growl I can still hear, "You! You ruined my life! I never want to see you again! No emails, no phone calls, nothing! I never loved you, I just pretended to love you! Get out of my house!"

In that moment, I truly understood what it meant to feel broken. Then Michelle moved aside, and Lisa took over.

I looked my birth father in the eyes and said slowly in a quiet, methodical tone, "You're right, we are done."

I told Izzy to pack her things which at this point was almost impossible for her. Her hot angry tears turned into sobs and she could not seem to get herself together enough to pack. I packed for us both as Nicholas stammered around the house demanding, "what the hell is taking us so long?" I tried to call Karen at several points as things were imploding in their house, but she did not answer.

At one point, Nicholas was throwing hundred dollar bills at us. Why, I still have no idea. Dr. Sarah shed some insight on this during one of our sessions later and speculated that he was trying to pay us off. Maybe through the intoxicated haze, Nicholas was displaying the guilt he felt in not being around when I grew up.

At one point during the chaos, he approached me and said, "Michelle, can I talk to you alone?"

But Michelle had left the building and Lisa would not even look him in the eye.

Eventually we were packed and dragged our suitcases downstairs. I texted my brother and told him what was going on and asked if we could go to his house to figure out where to go next. I was holding it together until I could get an Uber, but none were available.

As I tried over and over to get a ride to my brother's house, the resolve I had pulled from somewhere deep inside me started to falter. I began hyperventilating in my sheer panic that I was trapped in the house with a cold, calculating, drunk, mad man that had just terrorized my daughter and I. Worse, I had failed to protect my daughter *again*.

I had put my own needs to be loved and accepted by this man over her. I had to know this was going to be a bad situation, didn't I? Scott had warned me not to come. And although Bruce did not know how bad things were before I came, he was not happy about us going given what had happened before. But I did not listen and came anyway. With my daughter, no less.

My daughter was now worried about me as I struggled to gain control over my breathing. This made me feel worse, if that was even possible. Finally, an Uber came. Izzy and I dragged our suitcases as fast as we could out the front door as Nicholas watched and continued to tell us to "get the fuck out of his house."

My daughter had to have the last word, which usually frustrates me, but not this time. This time I was proud as she looked at him and with hate in her eyes said, "You're an asshole!"

Once in the Uber on our way to my brother's house, I let myself breathe slow deep breaths. Relief started to seep in that I would never have to be in that situation again. I still felt outside of myself, but also felt assured that at some point, I would return to myself and when I did, I would be fueled with the knowledge that my birth father had told me I had ruined his life. He had kicked his daughter and granddaughter out of his house, in the cold, at night, in a town that was not theirs.

chapter 42

No Contact

Izzy and I regrouped at my brother's house and booked a hotel near the airport for the night. My brother's house was small and he had a roommate. Neither Izzy or I were comfortable sleeping on his couch. We tried to recount the events of the night to Scott who sat and listened. He felt for us but as he said, he had warned me not to come.

Karen finally called. I sat quietly sobbing, describing what had just happened. She seemed empathetic and in a resolved, calm voice said, "I am not changing my plans. I will be home Monday."

It was Saturday night. Nicholas would likely drink the rest of the weekend. There was no telling what kind of shape he would be in when she finally got home.

I found myself apologizing for leaving him alone and pleading with Karen to understand that I truly had no choice. I feared for mine and my daughter's safety. Karen said she understood but I wondered if she really did, or if she still blamed me. It was clear Nicholas had been drinking the days prior to our visit, but I was conditioned at this point to feel utterly responsible for each and every stressful, disruptive event that occurred in their lives. After all, she had written to me the year before that my presence in their lives was "stressful and disruptive."

Izzy and I made it to the hotel and it felt like an oasis in a brutal desert. We started to come down from the adrenaline storm that had surged through us. The next day, we went out to lunch as an effort to recover. We stopped to see Scott before the ride to the airport. I knew in my heart I may never see him again. It made me sad. I asked myself for the thousandth time, why can't things be different? Why couldn't Karen have accepted me as a step-daughter right away? Why did Nicholas have to deal with his demons the way he did and let them destroy everyone else in his path?

Once we were home, Bruce thankfully saved the *I told you so* lecture, and instead wrapped his arms around me. We agreed not to rehash the last few days until I was ready. I texted Dr. Sarah and gave her a heads up about what had happened. She indicated she would be there that week for our session.

I blocked Nicholas on my phone when we were in the back of the Uber as we pulled away from his house. Over the next twenty-four hours, he left twelve voicemails asking me, through slurred speech, where we had gone. I have no idea if he realized what happened or if this was the absent-minded professor act. It did not matter. I was done. I was finally going *no contact*.

And I did. For eight months.

part three
Compassion

Where Hope Lives

I searched inside
And went within
To find the strength
And let it in
What had I lost?
Was it meant for me?
Did I need their love?
For me to be me?
For me to be whole
And one who gives
Perhaps letting go
Is where hope lives

chapter 43

Pretending to Forgive

O ver eight months of no contact, I could still receive emails and voicemails, but after that first twenty-four hours, no further messages came.

I stayed in touch with Karen for a few days after being kicked out of their house.

She texted me "Nick is in bad shape. He went without food or liquids for forty-eight hours."

Something in the tone of the texts felt as if she was holding me accountable. *Again.*

I finally mustered up the nerve to cut her off as well. I sent her a text that said I was ending contact with them both. I had done all I could, but I could not be part of this abusive relationship. But then, I told her to contact me if they ever needed anything health-related. I can not shut off the nurse part of who I am.

Karen never responded. I swallowed the guilt by thinking about what my daughter and I had just been through. My birthday came around and I heard nothing from Nick. Nicholas, who had become *Daddy* in my effort to appeal to his sense of paternal instincts, was now Nick. He had lost the privilege of being called *Dad* or *Daddy*, and he certainly was no longer "Nicholas" as I had called him in the formative days of our relationship. Now he was someone else. Someone I was disconnecting from. Changing his name helped. To me, he was Nick. To him, I told myself I was just someone he used to know. The notion that he could see me as his daughter, and still treat me the way he did was something my fragile self could not process.

Izzy treated me to a birthday away in the city and I immersed myself in the moment. I began to realize that I was not tied to my phone, waiting for a call. I was not in the vulnerable position of receiving a phone call accompanied by the rant of the day, the play-by-play of how "disruptive and stressful" my existence was, or an abrupt hang up if the mood struck Nick. I was feeling free.

I wrote emails to him I never sent. It was cathartic to describe what he had done along with the realization that what had happened over the past three years was not my fault. I did not know if I would ever have the courage to send these emails, but I hoped one day I would.

The months went on. I reached out to Nick's sister, Christine, who had attempted to connect with me a few years ago. At first, I was not ready to face anyone on his side of the family. But months after I went no contact with Nick, I was ready. I was desperate to salvage a connection to this side of my family, and to hear her side of things. There had to be more than the pain and rejection I had experienced thus far.

I spoke to my Aunt Christine on the phone and appreciated her willingness to connect with me. I had experienced so much rejection for so long and was timid in trusting anyone from my birth father's family, but I agreed to attend their family reunion, since Nick and Karen would not be there. Christine made it clear that she had also cut contact with them.

That summer, my family and I met Christine's family. It was a sharp contrast to how I had been treated by Karen and Nick. They were warm, kind, and inviting. It was a positive experience.

At the reunion, Christine shared with me how abusive her father and grandfather were. Especially to Nick. She had even published a book about growing up in the setting of abuse (Perchacek, 2013).

I decided to read my aunt's book about her home life growing up. She described in detail episodes of Nick's father beating him. One episode, in particular, she described hiding from her father and being worried about

"Nicky" as she heard her father relentlessly beat him off in the distance. She approached Nick after and whispered, "Nicky, are you okay?"

"Yes, I am okay," he whispered back. Both were apparently afraid of upsetting their father any further which would result in more beatings. Her mother, my grandmother, apparently was afraid of their father, as well, but never confronted him. Eventually Nick and Christine's parents divorced when Nick's mom discovered he was having an affair with the next door neighbor. From this vantage point, I was beginning to see things differently.

Nick had only told me how much his father loved him, over and over; abused children often excuse their parents for the abuse they faced (Bonds, 2011). I had indeed done exactly the same thing with Nick's abuse—for too long. I now looked at him as someone who had experienced trauma. It did not excuse what he had done to me and Izzy, but I understood he was a man in pain.

A few months later, I asked my brother to help me get back the baby book and photo album I had given Nick. These books contained precious memories of my early life. As long as they were in Nick and Karen's house, it felt as if a piece of me was still trapped in a tower of pain. I did not want them to have any part of me.

Scott was eager to help. He began asking Nick for my baby book and album each time he saw him. Nick apparently said, "Ok, I will send them to her." After a few months, Scott texted me and said, "Nick does not remember what happened in January. He wants you to call him."

I did not know if this was true or not but it didn't matter. Too many times, I had witnessed the innocent, absent-minded professor persona that Nick employed after an episode of binge drinking and inflicting pain. What happened had happened. I felt no different. Except I was more detached. Lisa had taken up residence while Michelle was inside, protected.

As if on cue, almost eight months to the day from when I'd cut off contact, the email I had somehow expected came. Nick wrote,

"I understand you want your albums back. I will ensure that they get sent to you this week. I don't remember what happened when you were here. Blame it on alcohol. We can beat it with a stick together. Your forever father, my blood runs through your veins."

227

I was fuming. I immediately responded as Lisa, not Michelle and wrote back,

"Alcohol is not an adequate excuse for what you did to me and my daughter. Write to me when you have an apology worth reading."

It was not lost on me that he had referred to *blood*. It was Nick's go-to when he wanted to emphasize that we were related; hence, I was supposed to forgive and forget.

I received the baby book and album in the mail. Soon after, I received another email, a simple, somewhat more contrite response,

"I'm sorry for what I did."

The email that I had been writing and revising as a form of catharsis was in its latest version and detailed the journey of exhilaration and pain that I had succumbed to over the last three years. Just like that, I had the courage to finally send it. I had no idea how he would respond. I did not care. The damage Nick had done fueled my resolve to say my peace, and I pressed send:

"Nick,

I received my album and baby book. Thank you for sending. I have been writing a letter to you for close to eight months. This letter is hard for me to send. I am still healing from your rejection. But time has given me the courage to stand up for myself and for my daughter.

I heard from you recently for the first time since January; several months after I was there with my daughter. I waited and waited for you to reach out, to tell me you did not mean what you said to me, to take it all back. But as time went on, I began to believe you were speaking your truth. Otherwise, how could you hurt us the way you did, and not try to reach me?

You wrote to me that you do not remember what happened in your home on January 21. Maybe you don't. But I do. And I think it is time we shared the memory. You offered an apology. But you have no idea what you are apologizing for. How do you apologize for something when you have no idea the impact?

You have said to me in the past "put yourself in my shoes." Now I will tell you what it has been like to be in my shoes. I spent decades wondering what it would be like to meet my birth parents. It played over and over in my head. When I

learned Judi was gone, my heart broke. And I thought any chance of knowing my birth father died along with her.

On December 14, 2019, you reached out to me. I had known of your existence for nine months. Out of fear of rejection, I did not contact you. I was afraid I would be a burden, an inconvenience.

Then one day, you contacted me. You appeared as a fantasy. You pulled me in. You took me over. I would have done anything for you. And in the process, I lost myself. Lisa was replaced by Michelle. I read the emails I sent you and saw a desperate girl who was begging to be loved. I have so much compassion for her now. The little girl inside me craved your love; Needed you to want *me. And in exchange, I did whatever you asked me to. Your power over me was palpable. All in the name of your love—no matter what it cost me.*

On January 21, in your garage, when my daughter and I were last in your house, you screamed at me "You ruined my life! I never loved you! I faked it the whole time! I want you out of my life!" When I heard those words, something inside of me broke.

You then made fun of Izzy; called her horrible names, said things that are still with her. She was shaking and sobbing; my heart broke for her. She is your granddaughter and my daughter. And as we wept from the sheer cruelty of your words, you stood in the hall and mocked us.

These were powerful words from my birth father; the ultimate rejection I had always feared. In the cruelest way possible. You then physically kicked me and my daughter out of your home. We were left in the cold, at night, with nowhere to go, in a town we did not belong. I called Karen over and over. When she finally contacted me, I was at Scott's house trying to calm down. I told her everything that happened. I was worried about leaving you alone even after how you treated us. She then said, "I am not changing my plans." I feared she would blame me as she always had and, in the end, I could tell she did. It was not my fault. It never was.

You may not remember these events. You may deny that this happened. Whatever your reaction, it will not change what is true. I have no reason to lie. In fact, I wish it was not true. But it is the truth.

I wanted to be the daughter you said you "always wanted." I gave you my love, time, devotion, laughter, tears, acceptance, patience, and a sense of kindred spirit that is rare and hard to find. I trusted you with my fragile heart.

I met my aunts and my uncle—your siblings— recently. I anticipated your siblings' indifference to me. I feared they too would make me feel as if my existence was a burden, an inconvenience, a "stressful disruption" that they "had to heal from" as Karen had expressed over and over. I read emails she sent me with disbelief that anyone could be so cold. Her words were cruel and ironic; I am the one who needs to heal. I was so conditioned to believe that my presence in your lives was not welcome that I was prepared for the worst.

But instead, your family, my family, welcomed me. What touched me the most was their sense of family and how they care for one another. Which is why it is even harder to understand what you did to me.

I learned more about your parents and grandparents. I learned more about what life was like for all of you. I learned of the abuse that occurred through generations. It was deeply impactful.

I do not pretend to understand you or what you went through. And it does not excuse how you have treated me or how you discarded me. But as time goes by, I do see things from a different perspective. I know that what you did to me is more about you than me. I am not responsible for your behavior or choices. I was a victim. Now I am a survivor.

I wonder if after you read this, will you stay silent? Or will you be honest with me? Do you think I ruined your life? You often tell me, "Wine is truth." Maybe how you have treated me is your truth after all. I can accept the truth. It is all I ever wanted from you.

I guess time will be my answer.

Despite my pain, I have empathy for you, and I will always care for you. I see your face each time I look in the mirror.

Your Daughter"

Sending this email was me finally standing up for my daughter and myself—something I had wished he could do for me all those months.

His response was more contrite. He acknowledged what he had done and wrote,

"After all you have been through, I treated you so awful. I am sorry."

I was glad he finally took some ownership over what he had done. But it was brief and did not fully express the remorse I was hoping for. I wondered if he was even capable of that level of remorse.

Nick also called Izzy and formally apologized to her, but not until I told him to. Izzy knew he only called because I had asked him to. She was hurt still and the hollowness of his apology only worsened the pain. Needless to say, the apology did little to change how she felt. I admire this about Izzy. She is stronger than me. But then again, this was a grandfather to her, not a father—never mind a birth father of someone who had gone her whole life wanting to know who she came from, wanting love from a birth parent.

Alcoholics relapse. And so did I. Despite my efforts to stay aloof and distant, my fortress cracked the minute he began contact with me again. It took so little to rekindle the hope that I held that things would be different. Nick was starting to text me again and call when he could. Michelle was starting to peek out from inside Lisa's protective shield.

Emotionally, the familiar need to be wanted by him was easing its way back into my heart. I told him I forgave him but I am not sure I actually had. I was, once again, starving for a new start that was healthier and free from the abuse or the constant feeling that I was a "disruptive stressor."

Then Nick started drinking again.

Nick had supposedly not drunk alcohol the entire time we were not in contact. The fact that he began drinking after we began talking again, I am certain, gave Karen all the justification she needed. Apparently, Karen had recently told Nick she did not want him to have any contact with me at all.

"She wants me to end all contact with you, Michelle. I will never do that."

As I heard once again that Karen wanted me out of their lives, I tried to salvage the relationship I had with her. I emailed Karen and explained why I had initially ended contact with her as well. I told her Nick had apologized, and I told Karen I forgave her too—though I really hadn't forgiven either of them. Saying that I forgave them, putting the intention out into the universe, seemed more a wish than truth. As Dr. Sarah so poignantly expressed, "You do not have to forgive to heal."

It was clear Karen did not want me in their lives. She never responded to my email. And her responses to my texts attempting to be friendly were curt. Nick told me she said, "I am going to block her if she keeps texting me. I want nothing from her."

I stopped trying and reserved any contact with Karen to well wishes on holidays and her birthday. Nick continued to drink; there were times when he stopped, only to start again.

The binges continued until one day, Karen had apparently had enough. My brother messaged me after I had not heard from Nick for several days and told me that Karen had found Nick an apartment. He was out, unless he never drank again. It was clear to me that her ultimatum likely included stopping any contact with me since I was viewed as the reason why Nick drinks.

I was hurt but the pain was all too familiar. This time, Lisa was standing beside Michelle. I realized that despite being grateful and perfect for Nick, nothing was ever going to change—he was never going to stop drinking, and he was never going to stop hurting me. As I held Michelle's hand by my side, we both began to understand that this was not about us. The damage was not because of us, *but despite us.* We could not fix it and it was not our responsibility.

That is when I realized that healing was possible. I began to feel hope; not hope that things with Nick and Karen would be different. Hope that I would heal.

chapter 44

Healing

Healing is a continuum. We don't always heal moving forward; sometimes, we heal by moving back and going in a circle. Healing looks different every day. Healing for me means making my way towards understanding that what happened to me was not my fault. The way I reacted was also not my fault. This understanding leads to compassion.

What I realize now, looking back, the beginning of my relationship with Nick—between the multiple emails, texts, and phone calls—was when the love bombing began. I mistook obsessive attention as an expression of love. According to Psychology Today (2024), love bombing refers to a pattern of overly showing affection, compliments, and attention. In general, love bombing is an attempt to gain control over someone and is generally considered manipulative. Peer-reviewed literature regarding *love bombing* is limited. But nonetheless, this concept has made its way into modern psychology for this type of behavior. I had no idea that this was happening and truly thought this was Nicholas showing me he loved me and wanted me in his life. It made me want to fold this man who claimed to love me so much into my life. And also pushed the questions about how I came to be further to the back of my mind. I didn't realize it, but thinking back, I was more vulnerable than I had ever been in my life.

Years later, with help from Dr. Sarah, I came to better understand what was happening. I was in the middle of being triangulated between Nicholas and Karen. Triangulation refers to a form of communication pattern that involves one person (the victim), using a third party (the rescuer), as an intermediary instead of communicating directly with the person they have the conflict with (persecutor) (Frothingham, 2023). Triangulation creates misunderstandings and serves as a way for someone to gain power and control in relationships. The letter Karen sent me asking me to cancel our visit in March was a perfect example of me being pulled into a triangle of lies between Nicholas and Karen. Had I let Bruce make that call to both of them at the time, instead of fearing I would be let go, this pattern of behavior may have been more clear to me. But I was so afraid of rejection and abandonment.

Thinking back, I also realize most of my confusion around how I was being treated by both Nicholas and Karen was because of the constant gaslighting. *Gaslighting* refers to a form of manipulation that involves deliberately feeding others false information that leads them to question what they know to be true, often about themselves causing one to doubt their memory and perception of the events (Psychology Today, 2024). I think back to how confusing and inaccurate Karen's painful emails were. Or why I expected Nicholas to pick me up from the airport New Year's weekend only to have him tell me he never said he would. I also think about Karen's relentless litany regarding how stressful and disruptive my presence in their lives was. Or her claim that I constantly forced Nick to visit me. I will never know what Nick was telling Karen about me. And I will never understand why she did not try to understand my perspective and instead chose to attack me over and over. No matter who was gaslighting who, I was finally beginning to understand that I was ensnared in a web of lies and manipulation.

It also felt familiar. It reminded me of how Jim had treated me. I recognized abuse, then. And I was beginning to recognize it now.

The fact that I so often felt trapped in this web of abuse is a perfect example of trauma bonding. *Trauma bonding* involves developing a bond with someone who abuses you through threats of harm, manipulation, or gaslighting alternating with times of calm and reassurance (Psychology Today, 2024). The pattern of high and lows in the relationship maintains the attachment. I was trauma-bonded over and over with Nick. I can recall many times I wish I would have stood up to him. Some of his abuse was insidious and not as obvious at the time, while some events remain seared in my memory.

I wish I would have had the courage to confront Nick and Karen. While it was easier in the moment, I know even as an adult, it affected me negatively to continue avoiding confrontation. The literature discusses conflict resolution and as a nurse, I should have known better. A paper by Bruce and colleagues (2022) discussed the harm done when conflict is avoided. It was found that conflict resolution actually reduced stress, whereas conflict avoidance induced stress (Bruce et al, 2022). But I was fearful of rejection and fighting desperately to remain in Nick's life at any cost, even that of my own well-being.

I also have begun to realize the journey I have been on was somehow necessary for me to finally understand myself and my responses to grief and trauma. I often tell my patients, "This journey will change you. You will be different. But you will heal. You will find your strength and you will know yourself better." Being told you have a life-threatening health condition may be the most difficult news someone can hear. Trauma is defined by The Substance Abuse and Mental Health Services Administration as any experience that causes an intense psychological or physical stress reaction (SAMHSA, 2014a; SAMHSA, 2014b). Trauma is trauma. And healing is healing.

As I look in my patients' eyes, I see the familiar pain that reminds me of the desperate hope I had each time Nick broke my heart. Or I was afraid of rejection. Or I was not wanted. Or I would be let go, by Nick, by my parents, by everyone. Their journey will change them, just as this journey has changed me. I am different. I found my strength. I know myself better.

I have also finally allowed myself to grieve. I never grieved Judi. I never grieved my mom or my dad. I pushed myself to move on without ever really allowing for the pain to move in. I was numb to loss. But it had caught up with me. Understanding that I would never be wanted enough, never have the relationship with Nick I had hoped for, and never heal the abandonment wound snowballed.

Kris Carr (2023) relates in her book, *I Am Not a Mourning Person,* that grief never happens in isolation. Instead, one loss leads to past losses. She also points out that grief is not just about death. We mourn all kinds of losses— for example, I had to mourn the fantasy that I would be wanted by my birth parents. Judi was gone. And Nick was simply not capable of showing me the love I craved.

I also need to continue to accept that I cannot do this alone. I need my family, my friends and all those around me who have sat back patiently and watched me as I strived to be *perfect,* only to be hurt over and over.

I cannot stress enough how important therapy has been in my journey toward healing. Therapy can be helpful for any kind of grief or trauma. My sessions with Dr. Sarah have been an integral part of my road to healing, and I encourage others to reach out when they need help. Especially if you feel like hurting yourself or someone else. As a nurse, and a healthcare provider, I know how important it is to recognize when you need help. I have included an appendix at the back of the book with resources.

In addition to therapy and support from my family and friends, I have learned other ways to help me on my journey towards healing. When I finally worked up the courage to send Nick that email after what he did to me and Izzy, I realized that journaling helps so much. There is a sense of release as you write the words down that express your pain. Even if no one ever sees them. Smyth and colleagues (2018) found that journaling reduced mental stress and improved overall mood when used as a coping skill. I have since used this technique to express my emotions and release some of the pain I have experienced.

I also find that guided imagery has helped when feeling anxious or feeling the sadness creeping in. *Guided imagery* is a relaxation technique that is based on the interactions of the brain, mind, body, and behavior. In it, all senses are activated through the imagination of pleasing objects, places, or events that produce pleasant feelings and relaxation. Guided imagery can be self directed or assisted by someone else (Fitzgerald & Langevin, 2014). Guided imagery has been found to reduce anxiety and improve quality of life when used as a technique in dealing with stress and anxiety (Kumari & Jaideep, 2023). I picture trips I have been on with Izzy and Bruce, or I remember how much I may have helped a patient in my practice. I put myself back in these settings in my mind and imagine all the positive feelings I experienced at the time, and this helps me find the peace I need.

I have found through my experience caring for patients, and personally, that spirituality can be a source of strength and coping with anxiety and stress. Spiritual care was even the focus of my doctoral work under the guidance of my mentor, Dr. Morris Magnan. The literature supports my belief that spirituality can be a source of coping in times of stress (Chism & Magnan, 2009; Boscaglia, Clarke, Jobling, & Quinn, 2003; Hayden, Bosworth, Park, McQuoid, Hays, & Steffens, 2003; Baetz & Toews, 2009). As I have shared, my spirituality is complex and evolving. Connecting with nature, spending time in prayer, honoring a higher power, and recognizing my own inner voice are ways in which I connect with my spirituality as a source of strength to help not only myself, but others as well.

Mindfulness is another meditation technique that has been found to help reduce stress and anxiety (Niazi & Niazi, 2011). Mindfulness meditation involves the non-judgmental acceptance of how you are feeling in the moment, including how your body feels, what is going on in your mind, your thoughts, emotions, memories or impulses (Kabat-Zinn, 2013). I have found mindfulness to be particularly helpful in allowing myself permission to feel how I am feeling. This was especially helpful when I was grappling with my emotions around how I had allowed myself and my daughter to be put in dangerous positions over and over. Mindfulness also allows me to let go of the judgments about how I see myself as an adopted person, grateful and striving to be perfect to ensure I am not *let go*. As I release judgment, compassion has space to take over.

Healing expands through compassion. It is easy for me to have compassion for my patients; it is as natural as breathing. But compassion for those who have hurt me or rejected me is a whole new level of compassion that has taken my heart for a ride. This ride is leading me to the most important destination on this journey: compassion for myself. Instead of looking back and thinking, "How could I let someone treat me that way," I need to hold Michelle in my heart and have compassion for her. I have to understand how bad I wanted to be *wanted*. I also need to accept that I am not perfect, but I *am* worthy of love and acceptance. I am not a mistake. I am wanted. And those who do not want me, do not deserve me. I am a work in progress and this will be the Mount Everest of my climb to healing.

chapter 45

Space for Pain

The well of pain can sometimes be so deep it feels endless. With this kind of pain comes the absence of hope. Pain can sometimes be so traumatizing that it can't be spoken about out loud. For those who understand this kind of trauma, this kind of pain, I give you permission to not describe your pain out loud...but I do believe that pain this traumatic deserves the space to be held and acknowledged. I believe that when we acknowledge the pain and make it real, we give ourselves permission to feel and we can find our way to hope. Where there is hope, there is healing.

Some aspects of what I have been through in this journey are so painful, I am not able to say them out loud or write the words on the pages. Instead, I give the pain the space it deserves on these blank pages. I invite you, my friend, to do the same if you have felt pain that is so deep, so visceral, that you cannot speak of it out loud or write the words to describe it. I dedicate these next few pages to pain. We will acknowledge it and hold space for it together. I am here, my friend. You are not alone.

the adopted nurse

239

Lisa Astalos Chism DNP, RN

chapter 46

Finding Compassion

My compassion for Nick was initially in response to his endless diatribes about Karen's lack of understanding that he loved me or wanted me in his life. He cast himself as the eternal victim for so many months.

Nick's victimhood overshadowed any room for who was the real victim. I understand that now. I learned over time from pieces I put together that Nick's early life was filled with trauma. His father was abusive, especially towards him. Similar to my own journey, I think Nick always strived to be *good enough,* but never felt he was. When I think back to the details about his life he shared with me early on, I see the pattern. He joined the Marines because his father was in the Air Force. He became a pilot because his father flew planes. He often told me he wanted his father to be proud of him, but instead he expressed that his father made fun of him. I don't know if Nick ever felt his father's pride. He lost his mom and dad young, and seemed to run from that pain his whole life. I believe his trauma wounds are deep, flooded by substance abuse, or any other means to not feel pain. And as reflected in the literature, the abused sometimes turn into abusers (Bonds, 2011).

I also now reflect back to what it must have been like when Nick learned he had a daughter. I recognize now, I was hyper-focused on my own reaction to this news. Nick learned one day, out of the blue in his mid-seventies, that he had a daughter. For the first time, he couldn't run from his past—his past stared him straight in the face. I cannot imagine the shock he felt when he looked at the AncestryDNA match and saw me looking back at him. I am certain he looked me up and when he saw a physical carbon copy of himself, he was overwhelmed. Early on, I often felt Nick focused on my accolades or accomplishments as if I were a shiny new toy that reflected positively back on himself. I understand now he was looking at me with the eyes of someone who never felt quite whole. Seeing his past stare back at him brought up the ghosts of his own trauma and regret that he had never properly dealt with before.

And the elephant in the room—did he rape my birth mom? Was I a constant reminder of something he did that he actually associated with shame and regret?

Once upon a time, I owned Nick's pain. I wore it like armor as if it was mine to carry, and did all I could to try to heal it. Now, I understand that I do not own Nick's pain. I am not responsible for his trauma. It is not my fault he drank. It was not my fault he was abusive. In the end, I believe it was easier for Nick to unload his pain onto me, instead of looking inside.

As I heal, I find myself beginning to understand Karen better, too. She lost her mom early in life. I understand this trauma. She and Nick met later in life. She was established on her own. Nick is a very charming, handsome man and I am sure she fell hard for him. Nick had never been married, nor had she. It seemed he fit into the mold of her life she had envisioned. They seemed to be good companions and did everything together. They both had very little contact with their extended family and instead seemed to isolate themselves from the rest of the world.

Karen had never had children or pets, but despite this, I think Karen has maternal instincts. I have seen them with those Nick has brought into her life. I think fondly of the time I came to her aid to help Nick get back to rehab and I woke up to my favorite Dunkin Donuts coffee waiting for me. Karen can be very loving, and she made it her mission to care for and protect Nick. But then, after twenty comfortable years with a man she adores and has made a home with, the adult daughter entered the scene. The daughter who looks like her husband. The daughter who shares so many uncanny attributes with her husband. The daughter who in her overwhelming need to be wanted, craved her birth father's attention. The daughter who also did not feel safe enough to integrate Karen into her life.

I can only imagine how scary and threatening this must have felt for Karen. Nick and I were in the honeymoon phase of finding each other. Karen had not had children and although she had a caring nature, this was new territory and there was no room for her. There was, in fact, no room for anyone but Nick and myself.

Even now, as Karen keeps Nick from having contact with me, I have empathy for her. She is doing what she feels she has to do to protect Nick— not really from me, but from himself. I can understand this even if I don't agree with it. Her motivation is to take care of her family, and Nick is her family.

Finding forgiveness is complex. Finding compassion for both Nick and Karen is more profound than forgiveness. It means I have come to a place of understanding why they did what they did, and doing so sets me free. Feeling free from the burden of believing I am the cause of what is wrong in their world allows me to look at the situation through the eyes of someone who recognizes trauma. Knowing they, too, have experienced trauma opens the door to compassion.

chapter 47

Where Hope Lives

Throughout my life, the lens I view my adoption through has influenced how I have reacted to every situation or circumstance. Nancy Verrier discussed in her book *The Primal Wound* that adoptees may rebel and exhibit behaviors that sabotage their situation, good or bad. Or they may take on the identity of the forever grateful child. Every decision they make, every action, every behavior is done to pay others back for the gifts they have been given. And to take this a step further, adoptees may also strive to be grateful and perfect to ensure they are never *given up again*—by anyone.

I have lived my life through the eyes of the latter, in a constant state of gratefulness and striving toward perfection out of a sense of abandonment, or being someone's mistake that had to be taken care of. But now, finally, I am beginning to heal.

As promised, my friend, I have unpacked my journey and shared my story with you. As you've seen, for some, being grateful and striving to be perfect is a choice—but for me, it was never a choice. It was a state of being that resulted from being given up and feeling that my beginning was a mistake, and, therefore, if someone was willing to *fix* this mistake by giving me a home, then I must be grateful and perfect. Some would argue that the choice to be someone else, someone who did not feel this sense of gratefulness or perfection, was taken from me. Had I been born into my birth family, without feeling I was someone's mistake to take care of, someone given up, who would I have been? Had I not felt the ever-present sense of gratefulness and perfection, would I have made the life choices I made? Would I be who I am?

Despite not having a choice in feeling grateful, it was and is how I feel to my core. Not only am I grateful for the life my parents gave me, the love they showed me, and who I turned out to be, I am grateful that my beginning led me to this state of being. Because without my beginning being what it was, without this innate sense of gratitude, then who would I have turned out to be? With this also comes the understanding that if I could live my life any other way, I would choose to live with a grateful heart and the ability to show and feel compassion.

I also no longer question the nature vs nurture debate. I am indeed a product of both. In her book *Coming Home to Self*, Nancy Verrier related that we come into the world with a genetic code, but our environment shapes how we use the gifts we're born with.

In my environment growing up, my parents showed me so much love and care, that I understood at an early age how important caring for others is. I have spent my life caring for others, whether they were my own family, or my patients. It felt *normal,* like breathing; and my environment helped me turn this gift into my life's purpose. And because of my parents' love and caring, my own trauma informs how I care for others experiencing trauma.

Genetically, Nick gave me a flair for the eccentric and being different. I express my art through my appearance. I wear the silver streaks in my hair proudly. As an adult, I celebrate my *differentness*. Nick gave me the gift of words and the ability to tell a story. I used that gift here, in this book, to share my story with you.

I am a product of nature and nurture. And despite the pain experienced on this journey, I am glad I went through it—because now, I know more completely who I am.

Only now, in the last third of my life, am I beginning to understand the complexity of adoption trauma. When I was growing up, no one talked about adoption and trauma in the same sentence. The mantra that echoed around me was that my birth mother "loved me so much she chose to give me a better life." Maybe that is the truth. Or maybe Judi felt so much shame as a member of a Catholic family in the 60s, that she found herself feeling she had no other choice. Maybe she was raped, or maybe that story helped ease the brunt of my birth grandparents' wrath. I will never really know the truth.

Adoptees are given a narrative and are never given the space to consider anything else. Typically, so little information is given about the birth family that fantasies replace reality—like my fantasy that every year on my birthday, my birth mother was thinking about me, only to learn later she had died by my sixth birthday.

Believing I am not responsible for all the wrongs in the world has been my first step toward compassion for myself. I am not responsible for my birth mother's trauma. Yet I feel compassion for her. Compassion leads to questioning: Why wasn't she supported more? Was she really raped? Why did she end up alone, in a home for unwed mothers, as she carried me? How did she let me go once she heard me cry? I wonder at times, how much did her own trauma contribute to her death at such an early age? These questions will never be answered, but nonetheless deserve to be acknowledged. Acknowledging unanswered questions like these takes courage, and courage leads to compassion.

Growing up grateful and striving to be perfect has led to many accomplishments with no space for failure. Failure has always meant being given up again. I have worked so hard in my life to be *good enough* to keep. I was afraid, for so long, to tell my parents I was molested. I never shared with my parents how much I wondered about where I came from. I married the first man who seemed to want me enough, only to experience control and abuse. I experienced trauma in my workplace, too, and instead of receiving support and encouragement, I was let go. I was afraid to upset my next employer, even when he was blatantly inappropriate. Then, later, I was used as a scapegoat when someone else's ego was bruised. I came to expect failure in each position I held, despite giving my patients the best care I knew how to give. And when my birth father found me, I gave him my heart and soul hoping he would not walk away again. But no matter how perfect I tried to be for him, I was abandoned over and over.

The realization washes over me when I allow it: I was always good enough for everyone else, just not good enough for myself. That, my friend, is where adoption trauma lives for me. As I continue to find where hope lives, compassion for myself finds me.

Compassion, too, for Michelle, the little girl inside me, seeps in. Michelle was there all along, begging for love. Striving to be good enough to keep. Until one day, Michelle came bubbling out when she looked into the eyes of her birth father. Then she could not contain her overwhelming need for him to love her. She sacrificed her self-worth; and over and over tried to be good enough, until Lisa stepped in and showed Michelle the compassion she needed. Lisa understands that everything Michelle did, she did because she wanted to heal her wounds of abandonment that had hovered below the surface for so long. Understanding Michelle leads to compassion.

I am not alone. Many have walked in these shoes and continue to struggle with the trauma of abandonment and feeling not good enough. Many have known their birth family, only to be retraumatized through a renewed sense of abandonment. My empathy for those who know this trauma flows deeply.

I hold empathy too for birth mothers, birth fathers, and adoptive parents, and this empathy extends through the lens of an adoptee who understands the trauma and pain that is sometimes too surreal to explain. My prayer is that all adoptees, birth parents and adoptive parents who are hurting in some way find where hope lives. We all need to acknowledge the grief that may come with the adoption experience for anyone in the adoption triad and allow compassion for each other and ourselves to flow.

Today, I find compassion for myself in simple ways. I wrap my arms around Michelle and tell her, "You are good enough. You are not broken. It is not your fault you want love."

Each time I remember a position I lost, I remind myself of the love and compassion reflected back to me each time I help my patients heal. My patients likely have no idea how much they heal me. There is a beautiful connection there that feeds my soul.

Each time I wonder if I am a good enough wife or mother or friend, I look into the eyes of those who love me and allow myself to feel their love reflected back to me. That, too, is where hope lives.

As I look into the eyes of someone who is looking to me for hope and compassion, I am reminded of how fragile we all are. Imagine what I feel as I sit with a patient and look into her eyes, only to see pain and fear. As you imagine looking into her eyes, imagine you are really looking into your own eyes, into the eyes of anyone experiencing pain—and let compassion flow.

We all have the capacity to be a vessel of understanding, a vessel of healing, and a vessel of compassion. For this is where hope lives.

A Standing Ovation

I would like to extend a standing ovation to those who have traveled along with me on this adventure called life. You have all touched my heart and given me hope.

To my mom Judy and my dad Paul; you taught me what it is to truly love and care for others.

To my daughter Izzy and my husband Bruce; you are what family means to me.

To my girl tribe; Jill, Tonya, Beth, Suz, Nora, and Angie; you are always there, even when I am not perfect.

To my mentor Morris; I feel you are guiding my writing from the heavens. And laughing with me at dirty jokes.

To my menopause sister Diane; for your mentorship, wisdom, and friendship.

To Barb; for caring how I am and truly understanding the journey toward healing.

To Sharon; for being my soul sister.

To the Aunties Janice, Jeannie, and Wendi; Judi is with me through your love. Thank you for showing me how birth families can love and heal.

To my "other daughter" Jeannie; for your empathic heart and wisdom beyond your years.

To my beauty tribe Jessica, Shannon, Amanda, and Stephanie; because you listened and cared. And not just because you had to.

To Dr. Sarah; because you gave Michelle a voice.

To Mia; for your invaluable talent and inspiration to help my cover photo ideas come to life.

To the one and only Nickolas Hawthorne; because of your invaluable insight. And for being a bestie.

To Anne Heffron; because you helped me "to be real".

To Christina Bagni for her wonderful editorial guidance; everyone needs that editor who pushes you and stays with you until you get it right.

To Taylor; because you reminded this "over 50 Swiftie" that it's okay to write about hard shit.

To Adoptees everywhere; because I believe in you.

Appendix

Crisis Resources

National Suicide Prevention Lifeline – 1-800-273-8255 OR Dial or Text 988
If you or someone you know is struggling or in crisis, help is available. Call
    or text 988 or chat 988lifeline.org. You'll be able to speak with a trained
    crisis counselor any time of day or night.
Resources for Sexual Abuse Survivors
RAINN National Hotline for Sexual Abuse Survivors 1-800-656-4673;
    online.rainn.org
National Sexual Violence Resource Center https://www.nsvrc.org/survivors
American Association of Sexuality Educators, and Counselors (AASECT)
https://www.aasect.org/referral-directory

Resources for Addiction Affected Families

Substance Abuse and Mental Health Services Administration Hotline
    1-800-487-4889
Confidential Treatment Referral Service Via Text Message (text 5 digit zip
    code to 435748)

Resources for Adoptees

NationalCouncil for Adoption https://adoptioncouncil.org/education/adopted-individuals/

Adoptees Connect https://adopteesconnect.com/adoptee-recommended-resources/

Adoptee Rights Law https://adopteerightslaw.com

Adoptees with Disabilities https://intercountryadopteevoices.com/2022/12/15/navigating-disability-and-rare-medical-conditions-as-an-intercountry-adoptee/

Global Adoption News https://adoptionland.org

Intercountry Adoptee Voices (ICAV) https://intercountryadopteevoices.com

International Directory of Adoption-Informed Therapists https //intercountry adopteevoices.com/post-adoption-support/

National Center on Adoption & Permanency https://www.nationalcenteron adoptionandpermanency.net/

U.S. National Directory of Adoptee-Therapists https://growbeyondwords. com/adoptee-therapist-directory/

Adoptees' Voices and Adoption Connection

Instagram @evolvingadoptees

Instagram @adopteehealingcollective

Instagram @unravelingadoption and unravelingadoption.com

Instagram @anne_heffron and anneheffron.com

Instagram @adoptedvoices

Instagram @adopteeson and www.adopteeson.com

Instagram @adoptionknowledgeaffiliates

Instagram @adoptee_thoughts

Instagram @AdopteesDishPodcast

The Lost Daughters: http://www.thelostdaughters.com

Thriving Adoptees https://www.thrivingadoptees.com

Only Black Girl: https://www.onlyblackgirl.com/

References

Baetz & Toews, (2009). Clinical Implications of Research on Religion, Spirituality, and Mental Health, The Canadian Journal of Psychiatry, 54(5) accessed from https://journals.sagepub.com/doi/abs/10.1177/070674370905400503.

Branagh, K. (2015). *Cinderella*. Walt Disney Studios Motion Pictures.

Bonds, S. R. (2011). Toxic Parents: Hurt People Hurt National Crisis of Epidemic Proportion. Accessed from https://www.allaboutloveinc.org/toxic-parents-hurt-people-hurt-national-crisis-of-epidemic-proportion.

Boscaglia N, Clarke DM, Jobling TW, Quinn MA. (2005). The contribution of spirituality and spiritual coping to anxiety and depression in women with a recent diagnosis of gynecological cancer. International Journal of Gynecological Care, 12, accessed from https://onlinelibrary.wiley.com/doi/full/10.1111/j.1525-1438.2005.00248.x.

Bruce, M., Chang, A.,Evans, L., Streb, M., Dehon, J., & Handal, P. (2022). Relationship of Conflict Avoidance, and Conflict Resolution to Psychological Adjustment, Psychological Reports, 0(0), p. 1-10.

Carr, K. (2023) I am not a Mourning Person. Hay House, NY.

Chism, L. & Magnan, M. (2009). The relationship of nursing students' spiritual care perspectives to their expressions of spiritual empathy. Journal of Nursing Education, Nov;48(11):597-605.

Chism, L. A. (2024). The Doctor of Nursing Practice: A Guidebook for Role Development and Professional Issues. Jones and Bartlett, Boston, MA.

Fayed, M., Maroun, W., Elnahla, A., Yeldo, N., Was, J., & Penning, D. (2023). Prone vs Supine Ventilation in Intubated COVID 19 Patients: A Systematic Review and Meta Analysis. Cureus, 15(5).

Feeney, J. (2004). Adult Attachment and Relationship Functioning Under Stressful Conditions: Understanding Partners' Responses to Conflict and Challenge. In J. A. Simpson & W. S. Roles (Eds.), Adult Attachment: New Directions and Emerging Issues (pp. 339-364). New York: Guilford.

Feeney, J. (2005). Attachment and Perceived Rejection: Findings From Studies of Hurt Feelings and the Adoption Experience. E-Journal of Applied Psychology: Social Section, 1(1), 41-49.

Gegios, A., Peterson, M., & Fowler, A. (2023). Breast Cancer Screening and Diagnosis: Recent Advances in Imaging and Current Limitations. PET Clin (18), p. 459-471

Fitzgerald M, Langevin M. Imagery. In: Lindquist R, Snyder M, Tracy MF, editors. Complementary and Alternative Therapies in Nursing. Part II: Mind-Body-Spirit-Therapies. 7th ed. New York: Springer Publishing; 2014. p. 73–98

Frothingham, M. (2023). Triangulation in Psychology: Impact on Relationships and How to Respond accessed from https://www.simply-psychology.org/what-is-triangulation-in-psychology.html.

Hayden, Bosworth, Park, McQuoid, Hays, & Steffens, (2003). The impact of religious practice and religious coping on geriatric depression accessed from https://onlinelibrary.wiley.com/doi/10.1002/gps.945.

Heffron, A. (2016). You Don't Look Adopted. Anne Heffron.

Heffron, A. (2019). Truth and Agency for Adoptees Writing

Hoffman, A. (1995). Practical Magic. Scribner, UK.

Institute of Medicine. (1999). To Err is Human:Building a Safer Health System.

Jones, A. (1997). Issues Relevant to Therapy with Adoptees. Psychotherapy, 34(1). P. 64-68.

Kabat-Zinn J (2013). Full Catastrophe Living: Using the Wisdom of Your Body and Mind to Face Stress, Pain, and Illness. New York: Bantam Dell.

Kaplan, M. (2010). SPIKES: A Framework for Breaking Bad News to Patients with Cancer. Clinical Journal of Nursing Oncology, 14(4), p. 514-518.

Kumari, D. & Jaideep, P. (2023). Guided imagery for anxiety disorder: Therapeutic efficacy and changes in quality of life. *Industrial Psychiatry Journal* 32(Suppl 1):p S191-S195, November 2023 accessed from https://journals.lww.com/inpj/fulltext/2023/32001/guided_imagery_for_anxiety_disorder__therapeutic.33.aspx.

Niazi, A. K & Niazi, S. K. (2011). Mindfulness-based stress reduction: a non-pharmacological approach for chronic illnesses. N Am J Med Sci. 2011 Jan; 3(1): 20–23 accessed from https://www.ncbi.nlm.nih.gov/pmc/articles/PMC3336928/.

Perchacek, C (2013). If I wanted a Trip to Hell I Would Have Bought My Own Ticket. C. Perchasek

Psychology Today (2024). Love Bombing accessed from https://www.psychologytoday.com/us/basics/love-bombing.

Psychology Today (2024). Gaslighting accessed from https://www.psychologytoday.com/us/basics/gaslighting.

Psychology Today (2024). Trauma Bonding accessed from https://www.psychologytoday.com/us/basics/trauma-bonding.

Quaile, H. (2020). Trauma informed care for the primary care provider. Women's Healthcare accessed from https://www.npwomenshealthcare.com/trauma-informed-care-for-the-primary-care-provider/

Substance Abuse and Mental Health Services Administration. TIP 57: Trauma-Informed Care in Behavioral Health Services. Rockville, MD: SAMHSA; 2014.

Substance Abuse and Mental Health Services Administration. SAMHSA's Concept of Trauma and Guidance for a Trauma Informed Approach. SAMHSA's Trauma and Justice Strategic Initiative. Rockville, MD: SAMHSA; 2014.

Substance Abuse and Mental Health Services Administration Concept of Trauma and Guidance for a Trauma-Informed Approach Prepared by SAMHSA's Trauma and Justice Strategic Initiative July 2014 https://ncsacw.acf.hhs.gov/userfiles/files/SAMHSA_Trauma.pdf

Smyth, J., Johnson, J., Auer, B., Lehman, E., Talamo, G., & Sciamanna. (2018). Online Positive Affect Journaling in the Improvement of Mental Distress and Well-Being in General Medical Patients With Elevated Anxiety Symptoms: A Preliminary Randomized Controlled Trial. JMRI Mental Health, 5(4) accessed from https://www.ncbi.nlm.nih.gov/pmc/articles/PMC6305886/.

Verrier, N. (2003). Coming Home to Self. Gateway Press, Baltimore, MD.
Verrier, N. (1993). The Primal Wound. Gateway Press, Baltimore, MD.

Printed in Great Britain
by Amazon

51317701R00149